FUNDAMENTALS OF
MS OFFICE 2007

REVISED EDITION

MARK CONNELL • GRETCHEN DOUGLAS

FUNDAMENTALS OF
MS OFFICE 2007
REVISED EDITION

MARK CONNELL • GRETCHEN DOUGLAS

Custom Publishing

New York   Boston   San Francisco
London   Toronto   Sydney   Tokyo   Singapore   Madrid
Mexico City   Munich   Paris   Cape Town   Hong Kong   Montreal

Printed in the United States of America

10 9 8 7 6 5 4 3 2 1

2009200139

LR/RH

Pearson
Custom Publishing
is a division of

www.pearsonhighered.com

ISBN 10: 0-558-37985-0
ISBN 13: 978-0-558-37985-8

Contents

Fundamentals of Microsoft Office 2007

The primary objective of this book is to teach SUNY Cortland students and staff about the potential of Office 2007 (Word, Excel, PowerPoint and Access). This introduction contains information specifically for those students enrolled in Cortland's CAP 100 course. The four application components (tutorials) can be used by anyone with the correct software and set of data files.

CAP 100 students need to obtain a list of class assignments from their individual instructors. These assignments are based upon the completion of the corresponding tutorials and are available to others upon request.

This manual was compiled, formatted, edited, and co-authored by:

Mark Connell and Gretchen Douglas -Computer Applications Program (CAP) at SUNY Cortland
PCM Courseware –Jefferson, Maryland
Revised: Summer 2009

1 COURSE PREREQUISITES

1.1 Hardware/Software

To complete the four tutorials you will need to have **access to a computer with** MS Office 2007 properly installed.

SUNY Cortland students with a valid student ID have access to a number of labs on campus with a sufficient setup. Most of the computers in the labs do not have floppy diskette drives. Suitable alternatives to store the course data files are necessary. It is recommended that any user of a College computer lab obtain a USB flash memory devices for storage of personal or course-related files. CD-RW's and DVD-RW's could also be used for this course.

1.2 It is assumed that you have:

- A knowledge of personal computer fundamentals.
- Experience in working in the Microsoft Windows environment.
- A reasonable degree of keyboard proficiency.
- Experience in using a mouse.

1.3 You should know how to do the following in Windows

- Log on to the network.
- Use the Start menu.
- Log off of Windows XP.
- Select commands in a Windows XP application.
- Create a new folder.
- Copy and move a file.
- Rename a file or folder.
- Delete a file or folder.
- Search for a file or folder.
- Change the screen display.
- Use Windows XP accessories (Paint and Calculator).
- Use Microsoft Internet Explorer.
- Display Help information.

CAP 100 students can use their MyITLab accounts to do the Windows XP training component.

1.4 You need to know how to do the following in MS Word

- Start and Quit Word
- Open a document
- Enter text into a document
- Check Spelling as you type
- Save a document
- Undo and redo commands
- Print a document

CAP 100 students can use their MyITLab accounts to do the Word- training components

1.5 You need to know how to do the following in MS PowerPoint

- Start and quit PowerPoint
- Open a presentation
- Use the PowerPoint help system
- Create a Title slide
- Create a slide with bulleted lists
- Change the font size and the font style
- Save a presentation
- Decide which view (slide show, outline, slide sorter or normal) is appropriate for the task at hand.

CAP 100 students can use their MyITLab accounts to do the introductory PowerPoint training components.

1.6 You need to know how to do the following in MS Excel

- Start and Quit Excel
- Enter text and numbers into cells

CAP 100 students can seek help from their lab teaching assistants.

1.7　Course documents

- **For CAP 100 students:** Files needed to complete the tutorials are available on the CAP department's server (Capserve). These can be easily downloaded in the CAP Lab (B-117, Memorial Library). Copy the folder named Course Docs from the server to your memory device. Keep all the course files **in your copy of this folder** throughout the duration of the course.

- **For other users,** files are available upon demand.

You will often be asked to open files in order to complete the assigned exercises. All of these files have extensions in their names (such as: **.doc**, **.xlsx**, **.pptx**, **.accdb**). If you cannot see the extensions then **show them** by doing the following.

- In the window for My Documents, choose Folder Options.

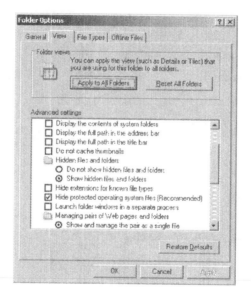

- Click on the View tab.
- **Uncheck** the 'Hide extensions for known file types' option.
- Click on the OK button.

This manual is composed of four tutorials (Word, Excel, PowerPoint, Access). Each tutorial consists of multiple lessons and a written quiz. Each lesson is subdivided into multiple sections. Each section covers a particular skill or concept related to the main lesson topic. In each section you will find a brief introduction to the section topic. Most sections have a hands-on exercise which students are required to complete. All required exercises are preceded by a blue checkmark. Some sections are strictly informative and contain no student exercises.

Course Agreement for
SUNY Cortland Students
Enrolled in CAP 100

With your signature below, you agree:

1. To be responsible for all assignments given during class or lab times.
2. To do all graded assignments on your own.
3. To attend all labs, unless formally excused.
4. To read and understand the syllabus.
5. To communicate regularly with your Lab Teaching Assistant.

Name (please print) _____

Signature _____

Lab Section _____

Date _____

Fundamentals of MS Office 2007

An Introduction to Word 2007

Table of Contents

Lesson 1 - Word Basics

1.1 The Word Environment

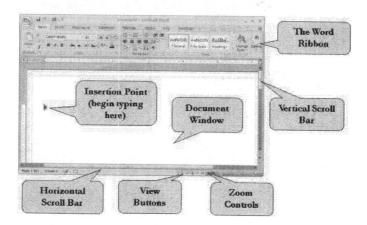

When you first start Microsoft Word, the application opens to a blank document along with the parts of the Microsoft Word screen shown in the screen shot above. If you have worked with previous versions of Word, you will immediately notice that the user interface has been completely redesigned. The menu and toolbar system have been replaced by the **Ribbon**. The Ribbon is designed to help you quickly find the commands you need to complete a task. On the Ribbon, the menu bar has been replaced by **Command Tabs** that relate to the tasks you wish to accomplish. The default Command Tabs in Word are: **Home, Insert, Page Layout, References, Mailings, Review** and **View**.

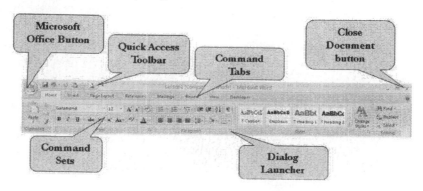

Different command icons, called **Command Sets** appear under each Command Tab. Each command set is grouped by its function. For example, the Insert tab contains commands to add pages, tables, headers, footers, symbols and text objects to your document.

On the bottom of many of the Command Sets is a **Dialog Launcher** that, when clicked, will launch a dialog box for that set of commands.

To the right of the **Microsoft Office icon**, is the **Quick Access Toolbar**. This toolbar contains, by default, the Save, Undo, and Redo commands. In addition, clicking the drop-down arrow to the right allows you to customize the Quick Access Toolbar by adding other tools that you use regularly. You can choose tools from the list to display on the Quick Access Toolbar or select **More Commands** to add commands to the list.

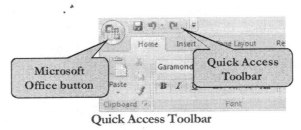

Quick Access Toolbar

You will be working with the various Word tabs and commands in subsequent lessons.

1.2   Opening an Existing Document

If you have worked with previous versions of Word, you will notice that the **File >
Open** command on the menu is no longer available. Instead of the word "File", the
Microsoft Office Button indicates where the file menu commands are now
located. To open an existing document, click the Microsoft Office button and then
click the **Open** icon to display the Open dialog box. From there, navigate to the folder
that contains that Word document you wish to open. If you have recently opened a
document, it may be listed in the right pane. Click on the document name in the recent
files list to quickly open it.

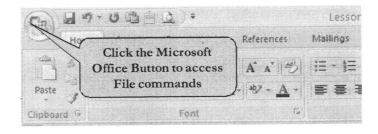

As you will quickly discover, there are several ways to accomplish the same task. Many commands under the File Options menu have an equivalent keyboard command that will accomplish the same thing. For instance, to open an existing document in Microsoft Word, you can also use the keystroke combination **Ctrl + O** which will bypass the File Options menu and directly display the Open dialog box. To display the File Options menu, you can press the **Alt + F** keystroke combination rather than clicking the Microsoft Office button.

✓ Open an Existing Document

1. Click the **Microsoft Office Button** on the top left of your screen to display the **File Options** menu.
2. Click **Open** in the left pane to display the Open dialog box.
3. **Open** your copy of the **Course Docs** folder.
4. Double Click the **Word Tutorials** folder to open it
5. Click on the file named **Lesson1a** to select it
6. Click the **Open** button.

1.3 Entering Text into a Document

When you create a new blank document, the **insertion point (the location where you begin entering text)** automatically begins at the top left of the document. As you type, the text will automatically wrap to the next line. To insert a new blank line, press the **Enter** key.

To add text to an existing document, move your mouse cursor to the location where you wish to begin typing and click your left mouse button. This will move the insertion point to the new location.

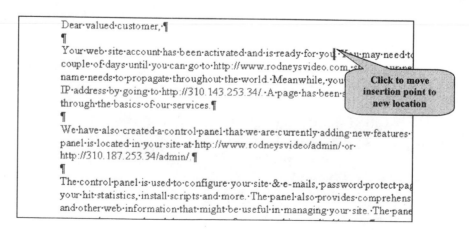

✓ Enter Text in your Document

1. Make sure **Lesson1a** is open. Move your mouse pointer before the period of the first sentence, after the words: **for you** and Click your left mouse button. This sets the insertion point.
2. Press the **spacebar** and type the words: **to use**
3. Move your cursor to the end of the last sentence in the last paragraph, after the words: **PCM Hosting.** and click with your left mouse button.
4. Press **Enter** twice. This inserts a new paragraph, with a blank line between the last paragraph and the new paragraph.
5. Type the words: **We wish you the best of luck with your new site and lots of success on the web!.**

Text for new paragraph

1.4 Correcting Mistakes

As you type, you may discover that you need to make a change in a document – perhaps correct a misspelled word or remove words from a sentence. You can delete text by using either the **Backspace** key or the **Delete** key. Pressing the Backspace key will delete text to the left of the insertion point whereas pressing the Delete key will delete text to the right of the insertion point.

✓ Delete Text in a Document

1. Make sure **Lesson1a.doc** is open. Move your mouse cursor after the **comma** in the greeting: **Dear valued customer,** .

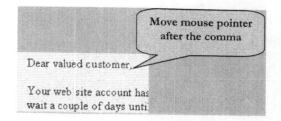

2. Click with your left mouse button to set the insertion point.
3. Press the **Backspace** key. This deletes the comma from the sentence.
4. Hold down the **Shift** key and press the **Colon** (:) key. This inserts a colon after the salutation.
5. Move your mouse cursor in front of the **ampersand (&)** in the last line of the third paragraph, after the word: **username** and click with your left mouse button.
6. Press the **Delete** key to delete the ampersand.
7. Type the word: **and** .

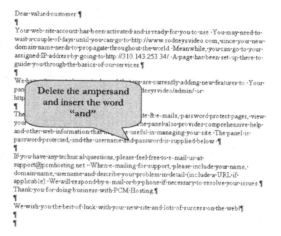

1.5 Navigating a Document

You have already learned how to move the insertion point from one location to another in a document. However, moving around in a document becomes more challenging as your document becomes longer. Luckily, Microsoft Word contains many ways to navigate a document.

- **Scroll Bars** – Scroll bars allow you to move quickly from one area or page of your document to another. Word contains both **horizontal and vertical scroll bars**. Clicking and dragging the scroll bar moves you to the position or page in the document where you release the scroll bar. As you scroll through a document, the page number appears in a small display box. .

- **Scroll Buttons** – Clicking on the **scroll up** and **scroll down** buttons allow you to move upwards or downwards your document one line at a time. Clicking on the page up scroll button or the page down scroll button moves you backward or forward by one page.

- **Keyboard Shortcuts** – You can also use keyboard shortcuts (pressing one or more keys on your keyboard) to move around in your document. Here are some common keyboard navigation shortcuts.

Keyboard Navigation Shortcuts

Method	Action
Move Left one Character at a Time	Left Arrow Key
Move Right one Character at a Time	Right Arrow Key
Move Down one Line at a Time	Down Arrow Key
Move Up one Line at a Time	Up Arrow Key
Move to Beginning of Document	Ctrl + Home keys
Move to End of Document	Ctrl + End keys

1.6   Setting Word Options

In previous versions of Word, you could set preferences for specific program settings from the Options dialog box. The Options command has been moved to the **Word Options** button on the File Options menu which displays when you click the **Microsoft Office Button**.

From the Word Options dialog box, you can specify such options as setting the color scheme for the Word application, specifying a default location to save files, setting the default file format, and much more.

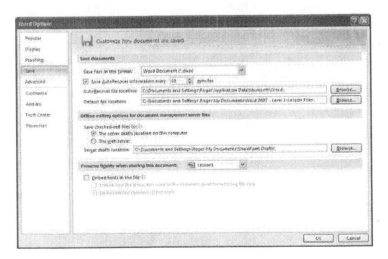

✓ Set the Save Options

1. Make sure **Lesson1a.doc** is open. Display the **File Options** menu.
2. Click the **Word Options** button to display the Word Options dialog box.

3. Click the **Save** category in the left pane.
4. Click the **Browse** button to the right of the **Default File Location** box to display the Browse window.

5. Locate your copy of the Course Docs folder
6. **Double-click** on the **Course Docs** folder.
7. Click **OK** to close the Browse window.
8. Click **OK** to close the Word Options window and apply the changes.

1.7 Changing Document Views

Views control how your document appears on the screen. You can quickly switch views by clicking on one of the **View Buttons** located on the lower right hand corner of the document window. You can also switch between views by clicking the **View** tab and then clicking the desired View command button on the Ribbon.

The available views are:

- **Print Layout** — Used for entering, editing and formatting text. In Print Layout view, a small gray gap is displayed between each page.

- **Full Screen Reading** — Displays the document in full screen and hides the scroll bars and the Ribbon.

- **Web Layout** — Allows you to see how your document would display in a Web browser.

- **Outline** — Displays your document in outline format with headings and subheadings.

- **Draft** — Displays your document without any gaps between pages.

 Switch between Views

1. Click the appropriate View button on the lower-right corner of your screen **Or** Click the **View** tab and then click the desired View command button on the Ribbon.

1.8 Using Help

The **Help system** is designed to provide **assistance** to users whether you are online or offline. To access the Help system, press **F1** or click the **Help icon** on the upper right-hand corner of the Word window. The Help system toolbar includes the familiar Back, Forward and Stop commands. Additionally, you will find the new **Refresh** tool, which allows you to update the content of the Help window. The **Application Home** tool brings you to the Word starting point, where you can browse through information related to the Microsoft Word application. The **TOC** tool displays a listing of available help topics through which you can browse. If you wish to increase or decrease the text size in the Help window, click the **Text Size** tool. Another nice feature on the Help toolbar is the **Keep on Top** tool, which allows you to keep the current Help page open while you work.

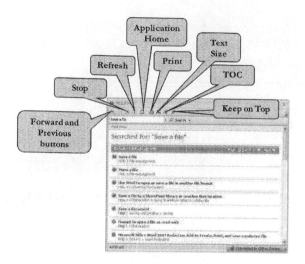

✓ Use the Help System

1. Make sure **Lesson1a** is open. Click the **Microsoft Office Word Help icon** on the upper right-hand corner of the screen as shown. This Displays the Word Help System window.

2. In the **Search box**, type: **Save a file**.

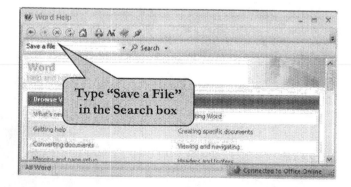

3. Press **Enter**. The results are displayed in the Search Results pane.
4. Click the **Save a file** link in the Search Results pane.

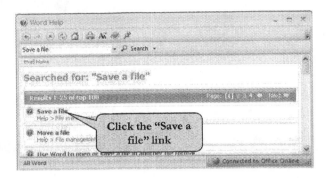

Click the "Save a file" link

5. Click the **Table of Contents** button on the toolbar. This displays a listing of Microsoft Word help topics.

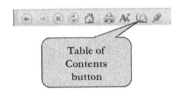

Table of Contents button

6. Click the **Table of Contents** button again to hide the Table of Contents.
7. Click the Word Help **Close button** on the upper right-hand corner of the screen.

Lesson 2 - Editing Text

2.1 Selecting Text

In the last chapter, you saw how to delete one character at a time from a document. However, often you will want to delete, copy, move or apply formatting changes to an entire word, sentence or paragraph. In order to do this, you must first **select** the text you wish to delete.

Once the text is selected, you can replace the selected text by simply typing in new text. This action overwrites the highlighted text with what you have typed.

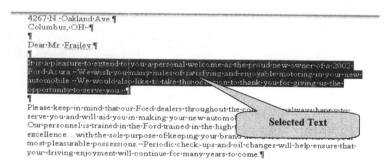

There are many other ways to select blocks of text. For instance, you can select a word by **double-clicking** on it. The table below outlines several techniques you can use to select text in a document.

To Select This:	Do This:
A word	Double-click on the word.
A line of text	Click to the left of the line in the margin.
Several lines of text	Click to the left of a line in the margin and drag upwards or downwards.
A sentence	Hold down the **Ctrl** key and click anywhere in the sentence.
A paragraph	Double-click to the left of the paragraph in the margin or **triple-click** anywhere within

To Select This:	Do This:
	the paragraph.
A block of text	Place the insertion point at the beginning of the block to be selected. Hold down the **Shift** key and click at the end of the block you wish to select.
Non-adjacent blocks of text	Hold down the **Ctrl** key and select the desired non-adjacent blocks of text.
The entire document	Press the **Ctrl + A** keystroke combination or click the **Select** button on the Home Ribbon and choose **Select All** from the list.
To the end of a document	Ctrl+Shift+End
To the beginning of a document	Ctrl+Shift+Home

Note: You can also select text with your keyboard. Hold down the **Shift** key and press the arrow keys to select the desired text.

 ## Select Text With Your Mouse:

1. Click the **Microsoft Office button** and then click **Open** on the menu.
2. Open the **Lesson2a.doc** file found in your copy of the Course Docs folder
3. Place the insertion point before the word **"warm"** in the first sentence of the first paragraph.
4. Select the word "warm" as shown.

> extend·to·you·a·warm·welcome·as·t
> you·many·miles·of·satisfying·and·e1
> would·also·like·to·take·this·occasion

5. Type: **personal.** This replaces the selected text "warm" with the word "personal"
6. In the fifth line of the second paragraph, **double-click** the word: **pleasurable,** to select the entire word.
7. Type: **satisfying.**
8. Move your mouse pointer to the left of the words **Yours Truly** in the margin until the pointer transforms into an arrow. **Click** with your left mouse button to select the entire line of text.
9. Type: **Sincerely,**
10. Hold down your **Ctrl** key and then click anywhere in the last sentence of the second paragraph (Periodic check-ups…). This selects the entire sentence.
11. Press the **Delete** key to delete the selected sentence.

12. **Double-click** to the left of the second paragraph in the margin to select it as shown. This selects the entire second paragraph.

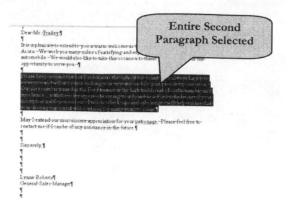

13. **Save** the active document.

2.2 Copying and Pasting Text

Y ou can copy any selected text to another location in your document, to another document or even to a document in another application by using the **Copy** and **Paste** commands. When you copy a selection, it is placed on the **Windows Clipboard**, a temporary holding area in memory for your data. You can then insert the selection in another location by using the **Paste** command.

✓ Copy and Paste Data

1. Make sure the **Lesson2a.doc** file is active. Place the insertion point before the **first word** (It) in the **first paragraph.**
2. Click and drag downwards until the entire document is selected.

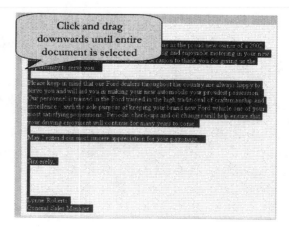

---

3. Click the **Copy icon** in the Clipboard group on the Home Ribbon.
4. Click the **Microsoft Office button** and then click **Open** on the menu.
5. **Open** the **Lesson2b.doc** file found in your copy of the Course Docs folder
6. Place the insertion point after the **colon** in the greeting **Dear Ms. Wolfe:**
7. Insert two blank lines.

8. Click the **Paste icon** on the Home Ribbon. This inserts the copied text in the Lesson2b document.
9. Click the **Microsoft Office button** and then click **Close** on the menu. Click **Yes** when asked if you wish to save changes. This closes the **Lesson2b.doc** document and saves the changes.

> **Tip:** You can also **right-click** on selected text and then choose Copy from the menu. Right-click and choose Paste after you have set the insertion point where you want to insert the copied text.

2.3   Cutting and Pasting Text

Cutting and pasting text is similar to the copy and paste text commands that you worked with in the last section, except that rather than making a duplicate of text, the cut and paste command physically removes (deletes) the selected text from its original location and moves it to a new location. Using the **Cut and Paste commands** allows you to rearrange sentences and paragraphs with ease.

✓ Cut and Paste Data

1. Make sure the **Lesson2a file** is active. Click anywhere in your document.
2. Hold down the **Ctrl** key and click anywhere in **the second sentence of the first paragraph** (We wish you…) to select the entire sentence.
3. Hold down the **Ctrl** key and then press the **X** key (Ctrl + X). This removes the sentence from its original location and places the selection on the Clipboard.
4. Place the insertion point at the end of the third paragraph.
5. Insert two blank lines by pressing the Enter key twice.
6. Hold down the **Ctrl** key and then press the **V** key (Ctrl + V). This inserts the sentence that you removed at the insertion point.
7. Press the **Ctrl + O** keyboard shortcut. Click on the **Lesson2b** file and click **Open**.

8. Place the insertion point at the end of the third paragraph.
9. Press the **Enter** key twice to insert two blank lines
10. Insert the sentence that you removed from the Lesson2a document into the Lesson2b document. Notice that the selection you cut remained in the Clipboard. You can continue pasting the text until you either copy another selection or close the Microsoft Word application.

2.4   Using Drag-and-Drop

I f you want to copy or move text only a short distance, such as from one location to another in the same document, the **drag-and-drop** method is another option. You can also drag-and-drop text from one open document to another.

Dragging-and-dropping consists of selecting the text that you wish to move or copy, clicking and holding down the mouse button, and then dragging the text to the desired location. If you wish to copy the text rather then move it, hold down the **Ctrl** key before dragging.

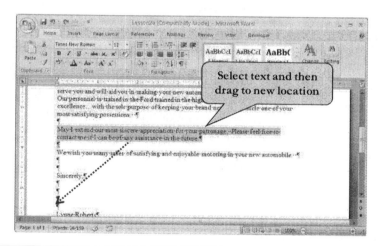

✓ Copy or Move Text with Drag-and-Drop

1. Make sure the **Lesson2a file** is active. Place the insertion point at the end of the third paragraph, after the word **"future."**
2. Insert two blank spaces after the word "future".
3. Select the last sentence of the second paragraph, beginning with the words **"Our personnel"**.

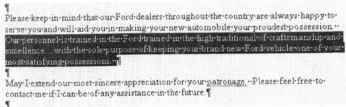

4. Click on the selected sentence and keep the mouse button held down. You are now ready to drag the selected sentence to its new location.

5. To select the destination area for your text, drag the selected sentence until the small gray bar is in front of the paragraph marker after the word **"future"** at the end of the 3rd paragraph and release the mouse button

Drag text to front of paragraph marker

6. Click the **Microsoft Office** button and click **Close**. Click **Yes** when asked if you wish to save your changes.

2.5   Using the Office Clipboard

The **Office Clipboard** allows you to gather data from several locations in the same document or from different Office documents, and then paste the items into any Microsoft Office document. Unlike the Windows clipboard which holds only one item, the Office Clipboard can store up to 24 items that you have cut or copied.

To use the Office Clipboard feature, ensure that the Clipboard Task Pane is visible by clicking the **Clipboard Dialog Launcher** on the bottom right corner of the Clipboard command group. Then, use the standard copy or cut commands. Each item, up to 24, that you copy or cut will be individually placed in the Clipboard for your later use.

Clipboard Dialog Launcher

Once you exit Word, all items from the Office Clipboard are removed.

✓ Use the Office Clipboard

1.   Open the **Lesson2c.doc document** located in your copy of the Course Docs folder.

2.   On the **Home** tab in the **Clipboard** command group, click the **Clipboard Dialog Box Launcher**.

3.   Click the **Clear All** button. This removes any existing items from the clipboard.

4.   Select all items under the **Breakfast 2** category as shown. (Click before the word Blueberry and drag downward until all items under Breakfast 2 are selected). Do not select the title.

5.   Press **Ctrl + C** to place the selected text on the Office Clipboard.

6.   Select all items under the **Breakfast 4** category.

7.   Press **Ctrl + C**. This places the selected text as the 2nd item on the Office Clipboard.

8.   Click the **Microsoft Office button** and then click **Open** from the menu.

9.   Open the **Lesson2d.doc** document located in your copy of the Course Docs folder

10. If the Clipboard Task Pane is not visible, click the **Clipboard Dialog Box Launcher** on the Clipboard command group.

11. Place the insertion point on the first blank line under **Item 1** as shown.

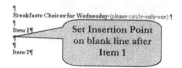

12. Click on the **second item** in the **Clipboard List** (Blueberry Pancakes, Sausage Links, …)

13. Place the insertion point after the word **Item 2**.
14. Press the **Enter** key to insert a new blank line.
15. Click on the **first item** in the **Clipboard List**.
16. Save the active document.
17. Remove all items from the Office Clipboard.
18　Click the **Close button** (x) on the Clipboard task pane.

2.6　Finding and Replacing Text

The **Find** feature allows you to quickly locate text in your document and replace it with other text. You can set various preferences for your search such as all caps, lower case, or matches of the entire word.

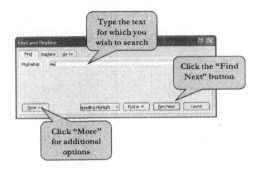

A new addition to the Find and Replace dialog box is the **Reading Highlight** command. It highlights every occurrence of the search item on the screen, helping you to quickly find the text. Click the Reading Highlight button and select Highlight All. To turn off this feature, select Clear All from the Reading Highlight drop-down list.

You also have the ability to search for **wildcards**. To see a list of available Wildcard characters, search for Find and Replace in the Microsoft Word Help system.

✔ Use Find and Replace

1. Open the **Lesson2c.doc file** in your copy of the Course Docs folder. Hold down the **Ctrl** key then press the **Home** key (Ctrl + Home). Word moves to the beginning of the document.
2. Press the **Ctrl + F** keyboard shortcut to display the **Find and Replace** dialog box.
3. In the **Find what:** text box, type: **me**.

4. Click the **More** button to display additional search options.

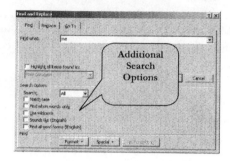

5. Click the check box next to: **Find whole words only** to search only for entire words matching text.
6. Click the **Find Next** button. This searches for the first instance of the text.
7. Click **Find Next** again. This searches for the next instance of the text. Since there was only once instance of the text, the message "Word has finished searching the document" was displayed.
8. Click **OK** to closes the message box.
9. In the **Find what:** text box, type: **blueberry**.
10. Click the **Reading Highlight** button and select **Highlight All** from the menu.
11. Click **Close**. Notice the search term is still highlighted.
12. Open the **Find and Replace** dialog box.
13. Click the **Reading Highlight** button and select **Clear Highlighting**
14. Switch to Find and Replace options.
15. In the **Find what:** text box, type: **Sausage Links**
16. In the **Replace with:** text box, type: **Bacon**.

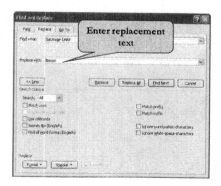

17. **Find** the first instance of the text.
18. Click **Replace**. This replaces the found text then automatically jumps to the next instance of the search text.
19. **Replace** the next instance of the text.
20. Click **OK.** This closes the message box and informs you that Word has finished searching the document.
21. **Close** the Find and Replace dialog box.
22. **Save** any changes to the active document.
23. **Close** the **Lesson 2c.doc** document.

> **Tip:** You can also click the **Replace** button on the Home Ribbon to directly jump to the Replace tab of the Find and Replace dialog box.

2.7 Checking Spelling and Grammar

Microsoft Word has a built-in **spelling and grammar checker** that allows you to automatically check for errors as you type. You can also check an entire document for spelling and grammatical errors by clicking the **Spelling and Grammar** button on the **Review tab**. Microsoft Word will use its built-in dictionary to offer suggestions for any errors it finds. You can then choose the correct spelling of the word from the Suggestions list or add the word to the dictionary so that Microsoft Word will not flag the word in the future.

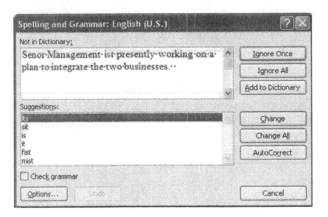

When Word finds a questionable spelling error, a dialog box displays, prompting for a suggested action:

- **Change** – Change this instance of the spelling error to the selected suggestion.
- **Change All** – Change all instances of the spelling error in the document to the selected suggestion.

- **Ignore Once** – Ignores this instance of the spelling error and continues to check the rest of the document.
- **Ignore All** – Ignores all instances of the spelling error and continues to check the rest of the document.
- **Add to Dictionary** – Adds the word in question to the built-in dictionary so that it will not be flagged in the future.

When Word finds a questionable grammar error, you can choose to ignore the grammar rule for one instance or for the entire document.

Word will also check spelling and grammar as you type, and highlight misspelled works by underlining them with red and grammatical errors by underlining them in green. You can then right-click the highlighted word and use one of Word's suggestions from the pop-up list. To display the Spelling and Grammar window, select **Spelling** or **Grammar** from the pop-up shortcut menu.

If you would prefer that Word not display underlining while you are working, display the **Word Options dialog box,** click the **Proofing** category, and uncheck the '**Mark Grammar Errors as you type**' and/or the '**Check Spelling as you type**' checkboxes.

✔ Check Spelling and Grammar

1. Display the Open dialog box.
2. **Open** the **Lesson2e.doc** file in your copy of the Course Docs folder.
3. Move to the beginning of the document.
4. Click the **Review** tab.

5. Click the **Spelling and Grammar** button on the Proofing command set. If an error is found, the Spelling and Grammar dialog box will open with the error highlighted in red.

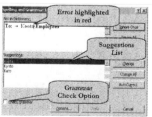

6. If it is checked, click in the check box next to **Check grammar.** This deselects the check grammar option. You only want to check spelling in this document.
7. Click the **Add to Dictionary** button as shown. Word cannot find "Keoto" in the dictionary. Since this is the name of the company, add it to the built-in

---

dictionary so that Word will not consider it an error in the future. Word continues checking the document.

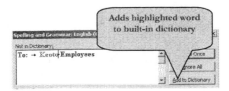

8. Click on the word **is** in the **Suggestions** list. This selects the correct spelling for the word "ist".
9. Click **Change**. This corrects the misspelled word.
10. Click on the word **Thus** in the Suggestions list and click **Change.**.
12. Click **Delete**. Word found two instances of the same word together (is is). Clicking the delete key will delete the second instance.
13. Select "believe" to replace the misspelled word "beleive" and **Change** it.
14. In the **Not in Dictionary** window, type a **eo** after the **K** in the highlighted word so that it reads: **Keoto**. Word cannot offer a suggestion for "Kto" so you need to manually type in the correction for the error.

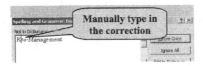

16. Click **Change**.
17. When the message box appears informing you that the **Spelling check is complete**, click **OK** as shown.

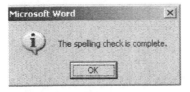

18. **Save** the active document.

2.8   Use the Thesaurus

U nder the **Review tab** on the Proofing command set, you will find the **Thesaurus** button that will help you quickly find synonyms for selected words. To use the Thesaurus, select the word you wish to replace and click the Thesaurus button on the Review Ribbon. The Research task pane will display on the right side of your screen. Click the arrow next to the desired word in the task pane and select **Insert** to replace the original word.

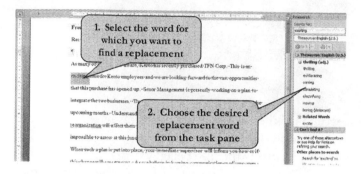

✓ Use the Thesaurus

1. **Make sure** the **Lesson2e.doc** file is active. Double-click the word **"inform"** in the last line of the memo paragraph. This selects the word you wish to look up.
2. Click the **Review** tab on the Ribbon.
3. Click the **Thesaurus** button on the Ribbon as shown. This displays the Research task pane and a list of synonyms.

4. Move your mouse point over the word **"update"** on the Research task pane. This displays a list arrow next to the word.
5. Click the arrow and choose **Insert** from the list as shown.

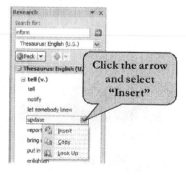

6. **Close** the task pane.
7. **Save** the document

2.9   Inserting Symbols

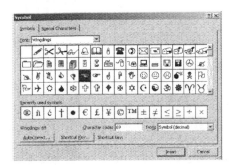

Microsoft Word supplies hundreds of useful, special characters that do not appear on your keyboard. Each font set contains its own set of symbols or characters. The **Windings** and **Monotype Sorts** contain a nice variety of useful characters. You can insert a recently used symbol by clicking the symbol in the **Recently used symbols** list in the **Symbol** dialog box. The **Special Characters** tab displays a list of common symbols such as the em dash, copyright and trademark symbols.

 Insert a Symbol into your Document

1.   **Make sure** the **Lesson2e.doc** file is active. Set the insertion point at the end of the title line, after the word **MEMO**
2.   Click the **Insert** tab on the Ribbon.
3.   Click the **Symbol** button on the Ribbon as shown and select **More Symbols**.

This displays the Symbol dialog box.

4.   Select **Wingdings** from the **Font** drop-down list as shown.

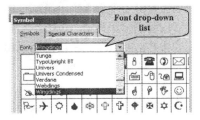

5.   In the **first row, seventh** column, click on the **Book** symbol.
6.   Click the **Insert** button.
7.   Click the **Close** button.
8.   Set the insertion point after the words **TFN Corp.** in the first line of the memo.
9.   Click the **Symbol** button on the Ribbon and select **More Symbols**.

---

10. Click on the **Special Characters** tab as shown. This displays commonly used symbols.

11. Select the **Registered** symbol from the symbol list.

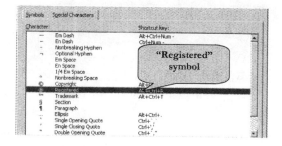

12. Click **Insert**.
13. **Close** the Symbol dialog box.
14. **Save** the document.

2.10 Using Undo and Redo

Word contains a powerful feature called **Undo/Redo** that allows you to reverse any editing action, including formatting. While entering data, you may have made a typo or even accidentally deleted a word or an entire sentence. You can reverse this action with the **Undo** command.

Each time you launch the Undo command, it will reverse your last action; thus clicking the Undo button 20 times will undo the last 20 actions. Rather than clicking the Undo button 20 times to undo multiple actions, clicking the arrow next to the Undo button allows you to quickly undo multiple past actions by navigating down the history list and selecting the number of actions you wish to undo.

Redo reverses the action of an Undo command.

Use the Undo and Redo Commands

1. **Make sure** the **Lesson2e.doc** file is active. Move your mouse pointer to the left of the word **To:** in the margin until the pointer transforms into an arrow, and then **Click** with your left mouse button. This selects the entire sentence beginning with the word "To:"

2   Press the **Delete** key to delete the entire sentence.

3. Click **3 times** (triple click) anywhere in the memo paragraph. This selects the entire paragraph.

4. Press **Delete**.

5. Click the **Undo** icon on the Quick Access Toolbar. This reverses the action of deleting the paragraph.

6. Click the **Undo** icon again. This reverses the action of deleting the "To:" line.

7. Click the **Redo** button. This reverses the action of the last Undo command.

8. Click **Undo**. This reverses the last action and restores the sentence.

9. Click the **Microsoft Office** button and select **Close**. **Save** any changes.

Lesson 3 - Formatting Text

3.1   Using Formatting Tools

One of the features of Microsoft Word is the ability to apply and modify **text formatting**. For example, you can modify the typeface (or font) of your text, change the size of your text, or emphasize text by applying bold, italics or underlining formats. When typing text in your document, each new character you type takes on the formatting of the previous character unless you apply new formatting. When creating a new paragraph (by pressing Enter), the first character takes on the formatting of the paragraph mark.

The quickest and easiest way to apply and modify text formatting is to use the Formatting Tools on the Home tab under the **Font group**. For an explanation of what a tool does; move your mouse pointer over a tool to display an informational box. The box will also display the **keyboard shortcut** for the command, if any.

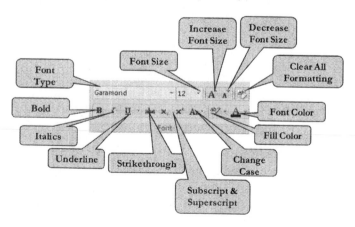

New in Word 2007 is the **Mini-Toolbar**. The Mini-Toolbar displays whenever you point to selected text and provides quick access to common formatting commands such as bold, italic, font color, font type, font size, fill color, increase indent, decrease indent and increase/decrease font size. If you wish to turn off this feature, you can do so from the Word Options dialog box.

Use Formatting Tools

1. Display the Open dialog box.
2. Open the **Lesson3a.doc file** found in your copy of the Course Docs folder
3. Click the **Home** tab on the Ribbon.
4. Select the words **Interoffice Memo**
5. Click on the arrow next to the **Font** drop-down list on the Ribbon to display a list of available typefaces.
6. Scroll down until you see **Arial,** and then **select it.** Notice that as you scroll through the fonts, the Live Preview feature displays how your text will appear if you apply that font.
7. Apply bold formatting to the selected text.
8. Apply a font size of 18 pt to the selected text.
9. Highlight the word **To:** in the first line of the memo.
10. Click the **Bold** icon on the Ribbon.
11. Select the entire paragraph of the memo.
12. Apply a font size of 12 pt to the selected text.
13. In the first line of the memo body, highlight the words **TFN Corp.**
14. Click the **Italics** icon on the Ribbon.
15. Click anywhere in the document to deselect the words TFN Corp.
16. Hold down the **Ctrl** key and **click** the last sentence of the memo body paragraph. This selects the last sentence in the memo body.
17. Click the **Underline** icon on the Ribbon.
18. Highlight the words **Keoto Management** in the last line of the memo.
19. Point to the text and then click the **Bold** button on the Mini-toolbar.

20. **Save and close** the active document.

3.2   Using the Font Dialog Box

The **Font Dialog Box** allows you to apply multiple formats (bold, italics, font size, font type, font color, etc.) to selected text at once. Additionally, you will find formats that are not available on the Formatting Toolbar. To apply multiple formatting to selected text, click the **Font Dialog Box Launcher** on the lower-right corner of the Font command set then make your desired selections.

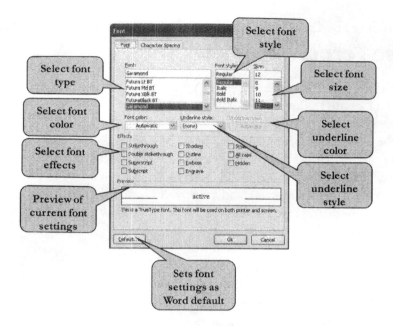

If you have worked with previous versions of Word, you may have noticed that the Text Effects tab is missing from the Font Dialog Box. With Word 2007, you can no longer apply text animation effects.

✓ Use the Font Dialog Box

1. Display the Open dialog box.
2. Open the **Lesson3b.doc** file found in your copy of the Course Docs folder.
3. Click the **Home** tab on the Ribbon.
4. Highlight the first two lines:

Rodney's Video
January Price Blowout

5. Click the Font Dialog Box Launcher.

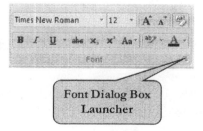

6. In the **Font Style** list box, click on **Bold.**
7. In the **Size** list box, scroll down to **22** and click.

8. Click on the **Font Color** arrow and select **Dark Blue** from the color palette (first row, fourth column).

9. Click **OK** to close the font dialog box and apply the changes.
10. Highlight the text: **$14.99!**
11. Hold down the **Ctrl key** and select the text as shown:
    $29.99!
    $9.99!
    Holding down the Ctrl key allows you to select non-adjacent text in a document.

12. Press **Ctrl + D** to display the Font Dialog Box.
13. In the **Font Style** list box, click on **Bold Italic.**
14. Click on the **Font Color** arrow and under the **Standard Colors** category, select **Red** from the color palette.
15. Click **OK** to close box and apply changes.
16. **Close** the Font dialog box to apply the changes.
17. **Save** the active document.

3.3   Using Format Painter

Using the **Format Painter** button on the Home Ribbon allows you to copy the formatting from one chunk of text and apply it elsewhere in your document. This feature copies all formats including font typeface, font color, alignment, etc. to the new object. You can copy all of the attributes of an object to **several** objects by **double-clicking** the Format Painter button then selecting the objects in succession.

✓ Use the Format Painter

1. **Make sure** the **Lesson3b.doc** file is active. Highlight the sentence which reads: **All previously viewed DVD's - *$14.99!*** You are going to apply formatting to the selected sentence, and then apply that formatting to the other sentences using the Format Painter button.
2. Apply bold formatting to the selected text.
3. Apply a 14 pt font size to the selected text.
4. Click the **Format Painter** button on the Ribbon. This activates the format painter button and picks up the formatting of the selected sentence.
5. Highlight the sentence which reads: **All new DVD's - *$29.99!*** This applies the formatting from the first sentence to the selected sentence.
6. **Double-click** the format painter button. Double-clicking the Format Painter button allows you to apply the formatting multiple times.
7. Highlight the sentence which reads: **Every VHS movie in the store - *$9.99!***
8. Highlight the sentence which reads: **Hurry…..Sales ends January 31st**
9. Click the **Format Painter** button to deactivate it.
10. Click on the text: ***$14.99!***
11. Activate the Format Painter.
12. Click on the word: **Hurry!** This applies the copied formatting to the word "Hurry!"

3.4 Using Character Effects

C haracter Effects allows you to add special effects to characters.. Character Effects include:

~~Strikethrough~~	Shadow	SMALL CAPS
~~Double strikethrough~~	Outline	ALL CAPS
^{Super}script	Emboss	Hidden (only appears on the screen – not printed)
$_{Sub}$script	Engrave	

Text effects are found in the Font tab of the **Font** dialog box.

✓ Use Character Effects

1. **Make sure** the **Lesson3b.doc** file is active. Highlight the text: ***$14.99*****!** in the first sentence as shown.

    ¶
    All·previously·viewed·DVD's·--*$14.99*¶
    ¶
    All·new·DVD's·--*$29.99!*¶
    ¶

2. Click the **Font Dialog Box Launcher** to display the Font dialog box.
3. Click the check box next to **Strikethrough**.

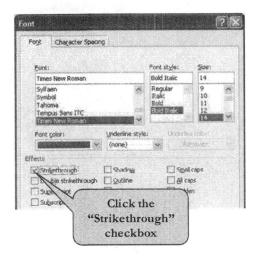

4. Click **OK**. This applies the character effects and closes the Font dialog box.
5. Set the insertion point at the end of the first sentence, behind the word ~~$14.99~~
6. Press **Ctrl + D** to display the Font dialog box.
7. **Uncheck** the box next to Strikethrough.
8. Close the Font dialog box. Click **OK**.
9. Press the **spacebar**, and then type: **$12.99** as shown.

    All·previously·viewed·DVD's·--*~~$14.99~~ $12.99*¶

10. Save the active document.
11. Click the **Microsoft Office button** and then click **Close** on the menu.

3.5   Adding a Drop Cap

A Drop Cap is a large dropped initial capital letter spanning several lines, usually at the beginning of the first paragraph of a chapter or section, that draws attention to that paragraph (such as at the beginning of this

---

paragraph, for example).

There are two types of Drop Caps: The **Dropped** style, where the Drop Cap is surrounded by the text in the paragraph as in the first example below, and the **In Margin** style, where the Drop Cap is placed in the margin, as in the second example below.

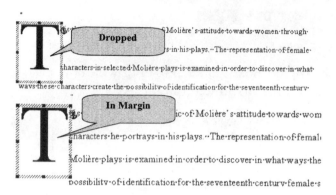

To add a Drop Cap, click anywhere within the paragraph, click the **Insert tab** and then click the **Drop Cap** button on the Ribbon. A Drop Cap Style list will display. To change Drop Cap options such as the font of the Drop Cap letter, the number of lines across which the drop cap will span or the distance the drop cap is to be placed from the text, select **Drop Cap Options** from the list to display the Drop Cap dialog box.

✓ Add a Drop Cap

1. Display the Open dialog box.
2. Open the **Lesson3c.doc** file found in your copy of the Course Docs folder.
3. Click anywhere within the paragraph.
4. Click the **Insert tab** on the Ribbon.
5. Click the **Drop Cap** button under the **Text command set** and choose **Drop Cap Options** from the list.
6. In the Position area, click the **Dropped** box .

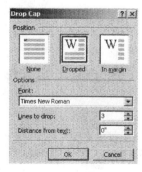

7. Click the **Font** drop-down list arrow and type **"Alge"** under until **Algerian** appears in the list. Click **Algerian**.
8. Click **OK**. This adds a Dropped style initial drop cap character to the first word of the paragraph.

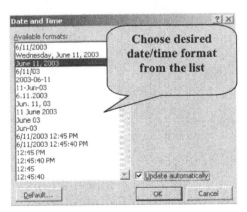

9. Click the **Drop Cap** button on the Ribbon and select **None** from the list. This removes the drop cap from the paragraph.
10. Click the **Undo** icon. This reverses the last action and restores the Drop Cap.
11. **Save** and **close** the active document.

3.6 Inserting the Date and Time

The **Date and Time** dialog box allows you to insert the current date and time into your document and choose from a variety of date and time formats. To have the date and time field update automatically to the current date and/or time every time the document is opened, click the **Update automatically** check box.

✓ Insert the Current Date and Time

1. Press **Ctrl + O** to display the Open dialog box.
2. Open the **Lesson3d.doc** file found in your copy of the Course Docs folder.

3. Place the insertion point in the beginning of the sentence before the words: **John S. Doe**

4. Insert two blank lines above the address.

5. Press the **Up Arrow key twice** to move the insertion point up two lines to where you want to insert the date.

6. Click the **Insert** tab on the Ribbon.

7. Click the **Date & Time** button on the Text command set.

8. Click on the **third** format from the top in the **Available formats** list.

9. Click the **Update automatically** checkbox, if it is **unchecked**. This sets the option to automatically update the date each time the document is opened.

10. Click **OK.** Then **save and close** the active document

Lesson 4 - Working with Paragraphs

4.1 Adding Borders to a Paragraph

A dding a line or **border** around a paragraph is one way to set the information in a particular paragraph apart from the rest of your document. Microsoft Word offers many different **line styles** to choose from. You also have the option of changing the color and the width of your borders or adding shadows and 3-D effects.

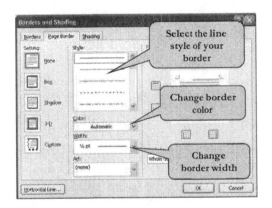

✓ Add Borders to a Paragraph

1. Display the Open dialog box.
2. Open the **Lesson4a.doc** file found in your copy of the Course Docs folder
3. Select the last paragraph, beginning with the word **Hurry** as shown.

> Hurry. Sales ends January 31st. Offer good only while supplies last. No valid with any other promotions.

4. Click the **Home** tab on the Ribbon. This switches to Page Layout commands.

5. Click the arrow next to the **Borders** button on the Paragraph command set and select **Borders and Shading** from the list (the last item).

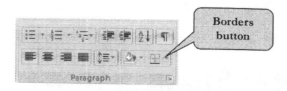

Borders button

6. Choose the **ninth line style** from the top in the **Style list** window.

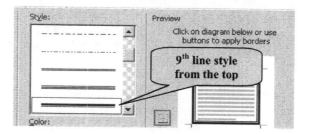

9th line style from the top

7. Under the **Setting** area, click the **Shadow** style.
8. Click the **Width** drop-down list, and then choose **2 ¼ pt**.
9. Click the **Color** drop-down list, and choose **Dark Blue** (1st row, 4th column).
10. Click **OK** to Close the Borders and Shading dialog box and apply the settings.

4.2 Adding Shading

Another way to set one paragraph apart from others is to apply a background color to the paragraph. Click the **Shading** button on the Home Ribbon and choose the desired color from the **Color** palette. To choose colors from a more extensive color palette, click the **More Colors** button.

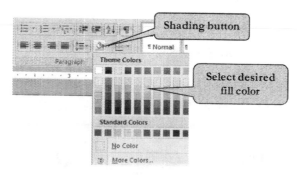

Shading button

Select desired fill color

✓ Add Shading to a Paragraph

1. **Make sure** the **Lesson4a.doc** file is active. Select the last paragraph beginning with the word **Hurry.**.

2. Click the **Shading** button on the Home Ribbon as shown to display the shading Color palette.

3. Click on the **fourth color in the third row** as shown. Notice that as you move your mouse pointer over the various colors, Word temporarily lets you preview the color.

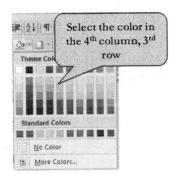

4. Click the Microsoft Office button and click **Close**. Click **Yes** to save changes.

4.3 Aligning Text

Alignment refers to the arrangement of text in relation to the left and right margins. For example, a paragraph that is left-aligned is flush with the left margin. There are four types of alignment that you can apply to a paragraph:

-   **Align Left** – text is flush with the left margin

-   **Align Right** – text is flush with the right margin

-   **Center** – text is positioned with an even space from the left and right margins

-   **Justify** – both edges of the paragraph are flush with the left and right margins (extra spaces are added between words to create this effect).

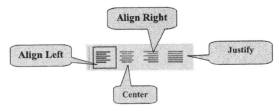

✓ Change Paragraph Alignment

1. Press **Ctrl + O**. This displays the Open dialog box.
2. Open the **Lesson 4b.doc** file found in your copy of the Course Docs folder
3. Select the first three lines of the letter, beginning with the words **Jan Koenig**.

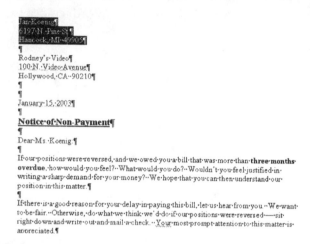

4. Click the **Align Right** button on the Ribbon. This aligns the selected text so that it is flush with the right margin.
5. Click anywhere in the line that reads: **Notice of Non-payment**
6. Click the **Center** button on the formatting toolbar.
7. Click anywhere in the paragraph that begins: **If our positions** The paragraph is presently left aligned, resulting in a jagged right-margin edge.
8. Click the **Justify** button. This aligns both edges of the paragraph so that they are flush with the left and right margins. Notice the extra space between words to create this effect.
9. Click anywhere in the paragraph that begins: **If there is a good reason**
10. Click the **Justify** button.
11. Save the active document.

4.4   Adjusting Line Spacing

Line Spacing refers to the amount of vertical space between each line of text in a paragraph. The default setting is single-spaced. You can change the amount of space between each line in a paragraph. There are several types of line spacing options from which to choose:

- **1.0 lines (Single)** – enough to accommodate a line of text with a small amount of white space between lines
- **1.5 lines** – One and a half times the single space amount.
- **2.0 lines (Double)** – Two times the single space amount
- **2.5 lines** – Two and a half times the single space amount
- **3.0 (Triple)** – Three times the single space amount

From the **Paragraph Dialog box**, you can also specify customized line spacing such as:

- **At Least** – The minimum amount of space (in points) between lines. Enter the point size in the **At** box. Space is increased to accommodate larger characters.
- **Exactly** - The amount of space (in points) between lines. Enter the point size in the **At** box. Space is **not** increased to accommodate larger characters.
- **Multiple** – Enter a multiple of the size of the font. Entering a multiple of 3 when a 10 point font is use results in 30 points between the lines.

You can set line spacing by clicking the **Line Spacing button** on the Home Ribbon and selecting the desired line spacing from the list.

✓ Change Line Spacing in a Paragraph

1. **Make sure** the **Lesson4b.doc** file is active. Select the two paragraphs that begin with the words: **If our positions**. Since you wish to change the spacing for multiple paragraphs, you must first select the paragraphs. If you were changing spacing for only one paragraph, you need only to click within the paragraph.

2. Click the arrow on the **Line Spacing** button as shown and choose **1.5**.

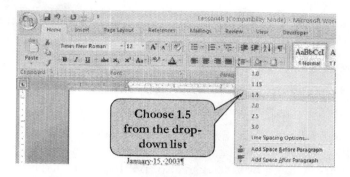

.3.   **Save** the document.

4.5   Adjust Spacing between Paragraphs

Y ou can tell Microsoft Word to add additional space (in points) before and/or after a paragraph. For instance, you may set your line spacing as single but want additional spacing between your paragraphs. Rather than creating this manually, you can add this setting in the **Before** and/or **After** boxes in the **Paragraph** dialog box, applying it to all paragraphs in your document.

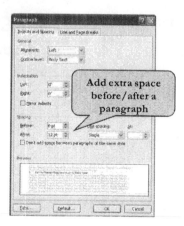

✓ Change Spacing Before/After Paragraphs

1.   **Make sure** the **Lesson4b.doc** file is active. Select the two paragraphs beginning with the words: **If our positions.**

2. Click the **Paragraph Dialog Launcher**.

Paragraph dialog launcher

3. Under the **Spacing** area, type: **12** in the **After** box as shown. This will add an extra 12 points of white space after the selected paragraphs.

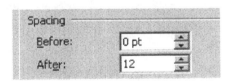

4. Click **OK** to closes the Paragraph dialog box.
5. Highlight the **paragraph mark** between the paragraphs as shown and then press the **Delete** key. This deletes the hard return from the document.

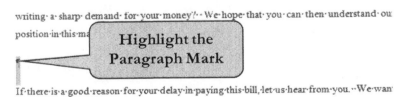

Highlight the Paragraph Mark

6. **Save** the active document.
7. Press **Ctrl + W** to close the active document.

Tip: You can also modify paragraph spacing from the **Page Layout** tab. Enter the before and after values under the Spacing area of the Paragraph command set.

4.6 Indenting Paragraphs

Paragraph indentation refers to the amount of extra white space from the left and/or right margins which you can add to a paragraph to set it apart from the other paragraphs in your document. Very often, you will see long quotations indented to set them apart from other text. Paragraph indentation options are located under the **Indents and Spacing** tab of the Paragraph dialog box.

✓ Add Left and Right Paragraph Indentation

1. Press **Ctrl + O** to display the Open dialog box.
2. **Open** the **Lesson4c.doc** file found in your copy of the Course Docs folder
3. Click anywhere in the second paragraph, that begins with the words **"You don't know"**
4. Click the **Paragraph Dialog Launcher** on the Ribbon.
5. Under the **Indentation** area, type **.5** in the **Left** box as shown

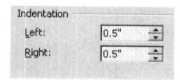

6. Press the **Tab** key and then type **.5** in the **Right** box as shown above. This sets an indentation of ½ inch from the right margin for the current paragraph.
7. Click **OK** to close the Paragraph dialog box.
8. Click the **Justify** button on the Ribbon. For an extra effect, you will justify your left and right margins.
9. Click anywhere in the last paragraph, that begins with the words **"Now the way"**
10. Display the Paragraph dialog box.
11. **Set an indentation** of ½ inch from the left margin for the current paragraph.
12. **Set an indentation** of ½ inch from the right margin for the current paragraph.
13. Close the Paragraph dialog box.
14. Click the **Justify** button on the formatting toolbar. For an extra effect, you will justify your left and right margins.
15. Click the **Microsoft Office** button and select **Close** from the menu. **Save** any changes.

> **Tip:** You can also modify paragraph indentation from the **Page Layout** tab. Enter the Left and Right values under the Indent area of the Paragraph command set.

4.7 Setting Tabs with the Ruler

When you press the Tab key, your insertion point automatically moves across the page. Tabs are an easy (and recommended!) way to align columnar data on a page. The default tab stops in Microsoft Word are set for every ½-inch. At some point, you will most likely need to change the default setting and add your own tabs. You can set tab stops by using either the horizontal ruler that appears on top of your screen or by using the Tabs dialog box. In this lesson, you will work with the horizontal ruler.

Before you begin working with tabs, you should know that there are several different types of tab stops. These are:

Tab Button	Type of Tab	Description
	Left Tab	Text is aligned along the left edge of the tab stop.
	Right Tab	Text is aligned along the right edge of the tab stop.
	Center Tab	Text is centered under the tab stop.
	Decimal Tab	Decimal numbers are aligned under the tab stop.
	Bar Tab	Places a vertical line at the specified position for each line in a document.

You choose the type of tab stop by clicking on the **Tab Alignment** button on the top left of your screen, to the left of the horizontal ruler. Clicking on the Tab Alignment button advances from one tab type to another until you see the desired tab type. Next, click the desired location of the tab on the **Horizontal Ruler**. (if the Horizontal ruler is not visible, click the **View/Show Ruler** button on top of the vertical scroll.

Once you have set a tab, you can easily adjust its location by clicking on the tab and then dragging it to a new location. While working with tabs, it's a good idea to show your paragraph marks so you can see the tab stops in your document. You can show or hide the Paragraph marks by clicking on the **Show/Hide Paragraph** button on the Ribbon.

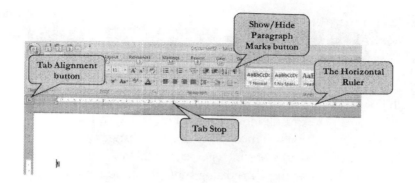

✓ Set Tab Stops with the Horizontal Ruler

1. Press the **Ctrl + N** keystroke combination to create a new blank Microsoft Word document.

2. Type: **Name**. This will be the first column heading.

3. If necessary, click the **Tab Alignment button** until the **Left Tab** appears.

4. Click at the **1.5 inch** mark on the **Horizontal Ruler**. The default tab is a Left tab.

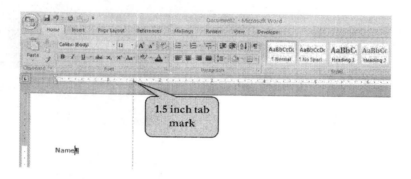

5. Press the **Tab** key.

6. Type: **Dept**. This enters the heading for the next column.

7. Click the **Tab Alignment button** until the **Right Tab** appears.

8. Click the **3 ½ inch** mark on the **Horizontal Ruler**. This sets a right tab at the 3 ½ inch mark.

9. Press the **Tab** key.

10. Type: **Salary**. This is the heading for the next column.

11. Click the **Tab Alignment button** until the **Decimal Tab** appears.

12. Set a decimal tab at the 4.5 inch mark.

13. Advance to the next tab stop.

14. Type: **Donation**. This is the heading for your last column.

15. Insert a new blank line.

16. Type: **Jim Harris** then press the **Tab** key.

17. Type: **Accounting** then press the **Tab** key.
18. Type: **$43,300** then press the **Tab** key.
19. Type: **$63.75** then press the **Enter** key. This Enters information for the donation column then inserts a new blank line.
20. Continue entering information, pressing the tab key to move between columns.

Name	→	Dept	→	Salary	→	Donation¶
Jim·Harris	→	Accounting	→	$43,300	→	$63.75¶
Jan·Nolen	→	HR	→	$125,200	→	$106.75¶
Dan·Brockton	→	Admin	→	$23,000	→	$8.00¶
Jennifer·Mann	→	Publications	→	$105,000	→	$3,000.00¶

¶

21. Observe the data. Notice that the data in the "Salary" column is right aligned (flush right) to the Right tab. The decimals in the "Donation" column are aligned underneath the tab.
22. Click the **Save** button. This opens the Save As dialog box because the document is unnamed. Locate your **Course Docs folder** and open the Word Tutorials folder
23. Type: **My Tabs** in the **File name** box.

File name:	My Tabs.doc	▼	Save
Save as type:	Word Document (*.doc)	▼	Cancel

24. **Save** the document.

4.8   Changing Tabs

C hanging the position of tabs couldn't be easier – simply click on the tab in the Horizontal Ruler and drag it to a new location! Note however, that if you have a columnar list of data with a hard return at the end of each line, you will need to first select all the rows of data before you move the tab; otherwise, you will change the tab position only for the sentence that contains the insertion point.

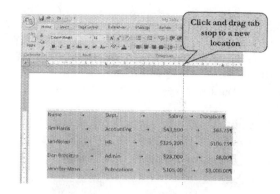

✓ Change the Position of Tabs

1. **Make sure** the **My Tabs.doc** file is active. **Highlight** the four rows of data under the heading row.

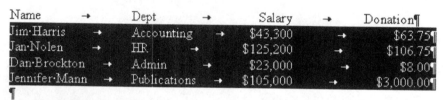

2. Click the tab stop for the **Salary** column at the 3 ½ inch mark and hold down the left mouse button.

3. Drag the tab stop to the **3.75** inch mark and release the mouse button.

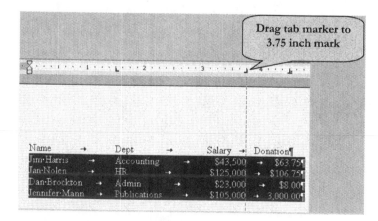

4. **Save** the active document.

4.9   Setting Tabs using the Tabs Dialog Box

I f you need to set more precise tabs, you can type in the exact postion of your tabs using the **Tabs** dialog box. With the tabs dialog box, you can also:

- Set the type of tab stop
- Set the default tab stops
- Add a leader (a series of characters such as dots that fills in the empty space between tabs)
- Clear all tabs at once

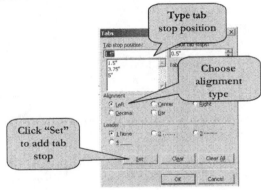

✓ Set a Tab Stop using the Tab Dialog Box

1. **Make sure** the **My Tabs.doc** file is active. Set the insertion point at the end of the last row of data
2. **Insert two blank lines** at the end of your document.
3. Display the **Paragraph dialog box**.
4. Display the **Tabs** dialog box.
5. Click the **Clear All** button. This removes any existing tab setting for the new paragraph.
6. Type: **1.75** in the **Tab stop position** box as shown.

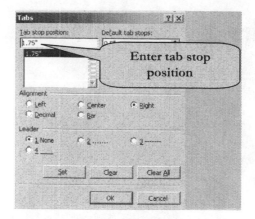

7. Click **Right** in the **Alignment** area as shown above.
8. Click **Set**. This inserts the tab stop.
9. Type: **2.94** in the **Tab stop position** box.
10. Click **Left** in the **Alignment** area.
11. Click **Set**.
12. Type: **4.06** in the **Tab stop position** box.
13. Click **Center** in the **Alignment** area.
14. Click **Set**
15. Click **OK** and observe the tab settings on the horizontal ruler.
16. **Save** and **close** the document.

Tip: You can also display the Tab dialog box by double-clicking on any tab stop on the Horizontal Ruler.

4.10 Creating a Bulleted List

A **Bulleted List** is a list of data that is preceded by a small round dot or bullet. The text is indented from the bullet to the first tab stop (or at .5 inches if no tab stops are set). Bullets make a list of items easier to read and sets the items apart from the other text in your document. To create a bulleted list, click on the **Bullets** button on the Home Ribbon. Click the bullets button again when you are finished with your list. To specify the type of bullet, click the arrow next to the Bullets icon and choose the desired bullet type from the gallery.

For more bullet options, such as setting the type of bullet, indentation, etc., click the arrow next to the Bullets button. Click **Change List Level** to modify bullet indentation or click **Define New Bullet** to create a new bullet type.

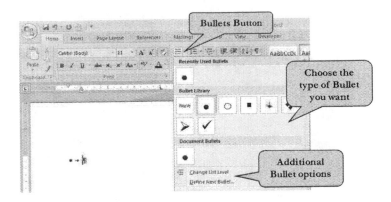

Create a Bulleted List

1. Display the Open dialog box.
2. **Open** the **Lesson4d.doc** file found in your copy of the Course Docs folder
3. Hold down the **Ctrl** key, and then press the **A** key.
4. Click the **Bullets button** on the Ribbon. This transforms the list of data into a bulleted list.

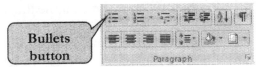

5. Set the insertion point after the word **Coffee**.
6. Press the **Enter** key to insert a new bulleted line item.
7. Type: **Flour** then Press **Enter**.
9. Click the **Bullets icon**. This turns off bulleting.
10. Select the entire bulleted list as shown. You will now change the bullet type.

11. Click the drop-down arrow next to the Bullets icon and choose the first bullet in the second row under bullet library.

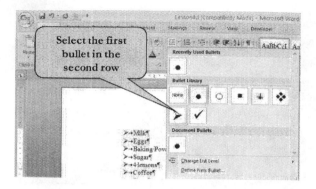

12. **Save** the active document.

4.11 Creating a Numbered List

I f your list of items needs to follow a particular order, such as step-by-step instructions for accomplishing a task, you will want to use a **Numbered List**. With a numbered list, each item in your list is preceeded by a sequential number. To turn on numbering, click the **Numbering** icon on the Home Ribbon.

For more numbering options, such as setting the number format, indentation, and starting number, click the arrow next to the Bullets button. To set the number at which to begin the list or to continue numbering from the previous list, choose **Set Numbering Value**. Choose **Change List Level** to modify number indentation or **Define New Number Format** to change the format of the numbers.

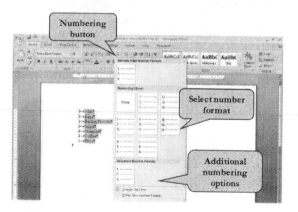

✓ Create a Numbered List

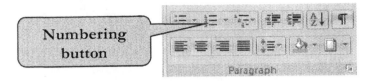

Numbering button

1. **Make sure** the **Lesson4d.doc** file is active. Select the entire list.
2. Click the **Numbering** icon on the Home Ribbon.
3. Set the insertion point after the word **Sugar**.
4. Press **Enter**.
5. Type **Baking Soda**.
6. Set the Insertion point after the word **Flour**.
7. Press **Enter**. This inserts a new blank.
8. Click the **Numbering** icon to turn off numbering.
9. **Insert** two new blank lines.
10. Click the **Numbering** icon. Notice numbering automatically continues from the previous list. You will change the number of your new list so that it begins at 1.
11. Click the drop-down arrow next to the Numbering button and choose **Set Numbering Value**.
12. Make sure that the **Start New List** radio button is selected. Restart numbering by typing **1** in the **Set Value to:** box.

13. **Close** the Bullets and Numbering dialog box.
14. **Close** and **save** the active document.

4.12 Creating a Hanging Indent

In addition to the left and right indentations you worked with earlier, you can also create a **Hanging Indent**. A hanging indent allows you to indent the subsequent lines of a paragraph by one or more tab stops. Hanging indents work well for bulleted and numbered lists, allowing you to line up text under the first line of the paragraph as well as anytime you want the rest of your paragraph to be indented from the first line of the paragraph. There are several ways to set a hanging indent:

- Use the Paragraph Dialog Box
- Use the keystroke combination **Ctrl + T**
- Hold down the **Shift** key and manually drag the **Hanging Indent Marker** on the Horizontal Toolbar
- Select **Hanging Indent** from the **Tab Alignment button** and then clicking on the Horizontal Ruler at the location where you want your hanging indent.

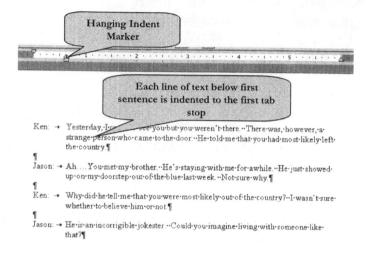

✓ Create a Hanging Indent

1. Press **Ctrl + O**. This displays the Open dialog box.
2. Locate your copy of the Course Docs folder and **Open** the **Lesson4e.doc** file.
3. Click anywhere in the first paragraph that begins with the word **Ken**.
4. Display the Paragraph dialog box.
5. Click the **Indents and Spacing** tab.
6. From the **Special** drop-down list in the indentation area, choose **Hanging** as shown.

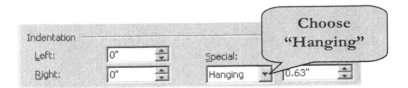

7. Click **OK**. This closes the Paragraph dialog box and applies a hanging indent.
8. Click anywhere in the second paragraph that begins with the word **Jason**.
9. Press the **Ctrl + T** keystroke combination. This applies a hanging indent to the second paragraph.
10. Select the last two paragraphs.
11. Hold down the **Shift** key and then **drag the Hanging Indent marker** on the Horizontal Ruler until the dialog text is lined up with the previous two paragraphs as shown. Release the Shift key. This manually sets a hanging indent for the last two paragraphs.

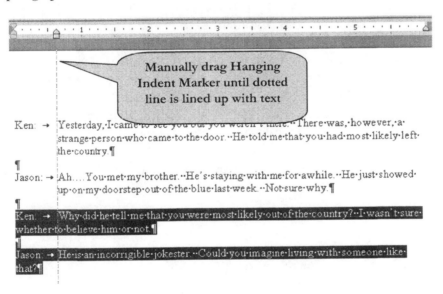

12. **Select** the entire document.
13. Press the keystroke combination **Ctrl + Shift + T** to remove the hanging indent from all four paragraphs.
14. Click the **Undo** button on the Quick Access Toolbar. This restores the hanging indents.
15. **Save and close** the current document.

Lesson 5 - Working with Pages

5.1   Creating a Header and Footer

Often, you may have information that you want to appear at the top or bottom of every page, such as page numbers, document name, a company name, a company logo, or the document location. **Headers** repeat information at the top of every page and **Footers** repeat information at the bottom of every page. You can add a Header or Footer to your document from the **Insert** tab. Click on the Header or Footer button to display a list of built-in headers or footers from which you can choose. Once the Header/Footer is activated, you can type your text directly into the Header/Footer window. Additionally, you can access the Ribbon, allowing you to insert a variety of special codes such as page number, current date and time, etc. Clicking on the **Go to Footer** or **Go to Header** button allows you to jump back and forth from Header view to Footer view.

✔ Create a Header and Footer

1. Open the **Walden Excerpts.doc** document found in your copy of the Course Docs folder
2. Click the **Insert** tab on the Ribbon.
3. Click the **Header** button on the Ribbon. This displays a gallery of available built-in headers.
4. Select the **Alphabet** header style.

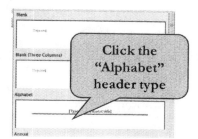

Click the "Alphabet" header type

5. Press the **Ctrl + A** keystroke combination. This selects all of the default Header text. You want to replace it with your own.
6. Type: **Walden Term Paper**
7. Click the **Go To Footer** button.
8. Click the **Date & Time** button on the Ribbon.
9. Click the **first** date format in the list and then click **OK**.

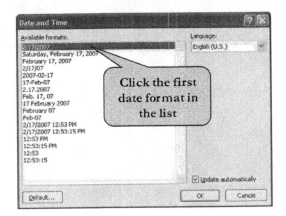

10. Use the **Ctrl + R** keystroke combination. This applies right alignment to the date code. You could also have clicked the right alignment button.
11. Click the **Close Header and Footer** button on the Insert Ribbon to return to Print Layout view.
12. Scroll up and down to observe the Header and Footer that you created. Notice that both the Header and Footer repeat on every page of the document.

5.2 Modifying a Header and Footer

Changing an existing Header or Footer is not complicated. Scroll until you can see the Header or Footer you wish to change, double-click the Header or Footer, and then make your changes. You can also click the **Header** or **Footer** button on the Insert Ribbon and then click **Edit Header** or **Edit Footer** from the menu.

✓ Modify an Existing Header or Footer

1. **Make sure** the **Walden Excerpts.doc** file is active. Scroll until you see the Header.
2. Double-click on the words **"Walden Term Paper"** This switches to Header view.

3.   Select the words **Walden Term Paper**
4.   From the **Font Size** drop-down list on the **Mini-Toolbar**, choose **10**.

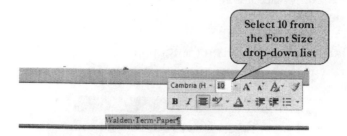

Select 10 from the Font Size drop-down list

5.   Press the **Ctrl + U** keystroke combination. This applies underlining to the selected Header. You could also click the Underline button on the Home Ribbon.
6.   Click the **Close Header and Footer** button on the Ribbon.
7.   **Save** the active document.

5.3   Setting Margins

Margins refer to the amount of white space between the text of the document and the left, right, top and bottom edges of the page. Margins can also be thought of as page boundaries — once the text reaches the boundary of the margin, it wraps to the next line or the next page.

Keep in mind that changing the margins of your document affects every page in your document – not just the active paragraph or page. To modify margins, click the **Margins** button on the Page Layout tab and make your selections.

Enter margin values in the appropriate boxes

✓ Create Custom Margins

1. **Make sure** the **Walden Excerpts.doc** file is active. Click the **Page Layout** tab on the Ribbon.
2. Click the **Margins** button as shown.

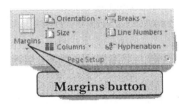

Margins button

3. Click **Custom Margins** from the list.
4. In the **Top** margin box, type: **1** as shown and then press **Tab**.

5. In the **Bottom** margin box, type: **1** and then press **Tab**.
6. In the **Left** margin box, type: **1.25** and then press **Tab**.
7. In the **Right** margin box, type: **1.25**.
8. Click **OK**.
9. Click the **Save** button on the Quick Access toolbar.

5.4 Setting Page Orientation

Microsoft Word allows you to change the **Page Orientation**; that is to say, the orientation of text – either wide or long – on the page. There are two choices of orienation – **Portrait** which prints across the shorter width (taller than longer) of the paper and **Landscape** which prints across the longer width (longer than taller) of the paper.

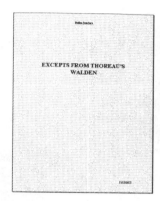

Landscape   Portrait

✓ Set Page Orientation

1. **Make sure** the **Walden Excerpts.doc** file is active. Click the **Orientation** button on the Page Setup group. This displays the Orientation menu.
2. Click **Landscape**.
3. Drag the **Zoom slider** on the lower-right and corner of your screen to the left to about **50%**. Observe that the page is wider than taller.

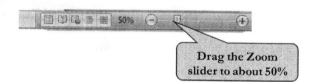

Drag the Zoom slider to about 50%

4. Click the **Zoom Level box** on the lower-right and corner of your screen and choose **100%** from the Zoom dialog box.

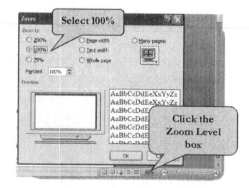

Select 100%

Click the Zoom Level box

5. **Save** the active document.

5.5   Setting Paper Size

Y ou may not always be working with the standard paper size of 8 ½" x 11". Microsoft Word can print on different paper sizes such as legal size (8 ½" x 14") or you can set the size of the paper yourself if you are working with non-standard paper size.   The default paper size in Microsoft Word is is 8 ½" x 11".

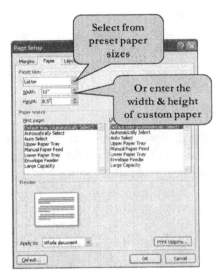

✓ Set a Custom Paper Size

1.   **Make sure** the **Walden Excerpts.doc** file is active. Click the **Page Setup Dialog Launcher** icon.

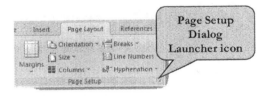

2.   Click the **Margins** tab.
3.   In the **Orientation** area, click on the **Portrait** box.
4.   Click the **Paper** tab.
5.   From the **Paper Size** drop-down list, select **Legal**
6.   Click **OK.**

7. Drag the **Zoom slider** on the lower-right and corner of your screen to the left to about **25%.** Observe that the page is displayed longer than the standard paper size.

8. Click the **Zoom Level box** on the lower-right and corner of your screen and choose **100%** from the Zoom dialog box. This restores the viewable area of the document to 100%.

9. **Save** the active document.

5.6 Inserting/Modifying Page Numbers

Y ou have already learned that you can add page numbers to your document in Header or Footer view. You can also add page numbers to your document by clicking the **Page Numbers** button on the Insert Ribbon, and then choosing the location from the list (top, bottom, page margins or current posiition) and then choosing the page number style you want from the galelry.

Word also provides numerous page number formatting options such as:

- Include chapter number with page number (i.e. 15-4, 15-5, etc.)
- Set the page number separator
- The number at which to begin page numbering
- Continue numbering from the previous sections (you'll learn more about sections in a later lesson)

To display the Page Number Format dialog box, click the the Insert tab, click the Page Number button and choose **Format Page Numbers** from the drop-down list.

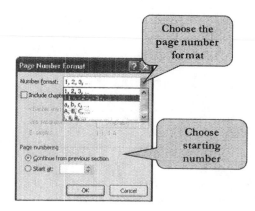

Choose the page number format

Choose starting number

✓ Insert Page Numbers

1. **Make sure** the **Walden Excerpts.doc** file is active. Click the **Insert tab** on the Ribbon.
2. Click the **Page Number** button under the Header & Footer command set.
3. Point to **Bottom of Page**.
4. Click the **Plain Number 2** from the gallery.

5. Click the **Page Number** button and select **Format Page Numbers** from the menu.
6. Choose the **second option** from the **Number format** drop-down list as shown.

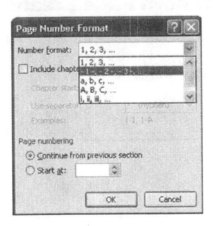

7. Click **OK**.
8. Click the **Close Header and Footer** button.

5.7   Page Breaks

When entering text into a document, Word automatically creates a new page when the text reaches the border of the bottom margin. There are times however when you will want to control the exact location where a page breaks. For example, after a title page, you may wish to begin the actual body of the document on a new page.

There are two way to insert a page break — press the keystroke combination **Ctrl + Enter** to insert a page break after the insertion point or you can click the **Page Break** button on the Insert Ribbon. To remove a page break, ensure that the codes are revealed by clicking the **Show/Hide** button on the Home Ribbon, and then press the **Delete** key.

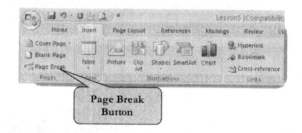

Page Break
Button

✔ Insert and Remove Page Breaks

1.   **Make sure** the **Walden Excerpts.doc** file is active. Set the insertion point **before** the section that begins **Where I lived…**
2.   Click the **Page Break** on the Insert Ribbon. This inserts manual page break at the insertion point.
3.   Set the insertion point before the words **Thoreau on Solitude**.
4.   Hold down the **Ctrl** key then press the **Enter** key (Ctrl + Enter). This inserts a page break after the insertion point.
5.   Scroll up to the page that begins with the words **Where I lived**
6.   Click the **Home** tab. If you cannot see the Page Break code, click the

   Show/Hide button ¶ on the Standard Toolbar.
7.   Select the **Page Break code** on the bottom of the page as shown and then press the **Delete** key. This removes the page break from the page.

5.8 Inserting a Watermark

Watermarks are faint text or graphic images that appear behind document text. Watermarks are often used to indentify the type or status of a document, such as "Confidential" or "Draft" or to add a company logo to the background. Watermarks are light enough so that they do not interfere with the reading of the document text and are intended for printed documents. You can choose from a gallery of pre-configured Watermarks or customize your own.

✓ Insert a Watermark

1. **Make sure** the **Walden Excerpts.doc** file is active. Click the **Page Layout** tab.
2. Click the **Watermark** button on the Page Background group. This displays a gallery of pre-designed watermarks.
3. Click the **Custom Watermark** option on the menu.
4. Click the circle (radio button) next to **Text watermark**.
5. In the box next to **Text:**, type: **DRAFT ONLY**

6.   Click **OK**. This closes the Printed Watermark dialog box.
7.   Scroll until you see the Watermark on the page. Observe the watermark. Notice that the Watermark appears on each page of the document.
8.   **Save** the active document.

5.9   Jumping to a Specific Page

When working in Word, you may at times wish to quickly jump to a specific page without having to scroll through the entire document, especially if you are working with longer documents. By using the **Go To** command (located under the Go To tab of the Find and Replace dialog box), you can jump to a specific page number. If you are working with sections, bookmarks, or footnotes, you can also use this command to find the item you are looking for.

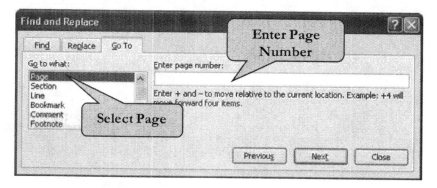

✓ Jump to a Specific Page in your Document

1.   **Make sure** the **Walden Excerpts.doc** file is active. Press the **Ctrl + Home** keystroke combination. This moves to the first page of the document.
2.   Press the **Ctrl + G** keystroke combination. This displays the Go To tab of the Find and Replace dialog box.
3.   Click in the **Enter page number:** box and type: **3**
4.   Click the **Go To** button. Word jumps to page 3 of the document.
5.   **Save** and close the active document.

Lesson 6 - Working with Document Sections

6.1 Inserting a Section Break

Section breaks allow you employ different page formatting in the same document. For example, you can print out one page in portrait orientation and another in landscape. Or you can have unique headers and footers on different pages.

There are four types of sections breaks that you can insert into your document:

- **Next Page** – forces the text following the break onto the next page.
- **Continuous** – does not change the location of the text following the break.
- **Even Page** – forces the text following the break onto the next even page.
- **Odd Page** – forces the text following the break onto the next odd page.

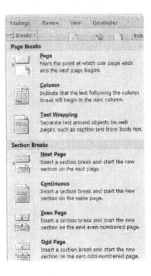

You can display Section Breaks on your screen by clicking the **Show/Hide** icon on the Paragraph area of the Home Ribbon to reveal Microsoft Word document codes.

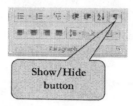

Show/Hide button

✓ Insert a Section Break

1. Display the **Open** dialog box.
2. Locate your copy of the Course Docs folder and open it.
3. **Double-click** the **Word Tutorials** folder.
4. **Open** the file named: **Walden Excerpts 2.doc**.
5. Set the insertion point at the first blank line before the title "**Thoreau Excerpts**"

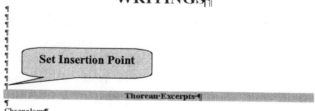

EXCERPTS·FROM·THOREAU'S·
WRITINGS¶

Set Insertion Point

Thoreau·Excerpts·¶
Chronology¶

6. Click the **Page Layout** tab on the Ribbon.
7. Click the **Breaks button** on the Page Setup group.

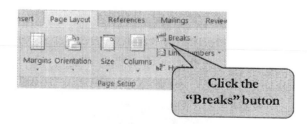

Click the "Breaks" button

8. Under the **Section break types** area, click **Next Page** as shown. Any text following the break will be forced onto the following page.

9. If the section break is not visible on your screen, click the **Show/Hide** button
¶ on the **Home Ribbon**. This reveals Word Codes, displaying the section break in the document.

10. **Save** the active document.

6.2 Setting Section Margins and Page Orientation

C hanging **margins** and **page orientation** for sections works nearly the same way as it does for the entire document. To limit the chamges to one section, the insertion point must be in the section and, if using the Page Setup dialog box, you must ensure that **This section** is selected in the **Apply to** drop-down box .

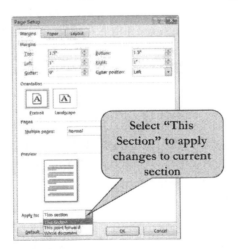

✓ Set Section Margins & Page Orientation

1. Make sure the **Walden Excerpts 2.doc** file is active. Set the insertion point before the **section break** in the first page of the document.

2. Click the **Page Layout** tab on the Ribbon.

3. Click the **Page Setup dialog launcher.**

4. Click the **Margins** tab.
5. In the **Left Margin** box, type: **2** as shown below. This sets the left margin at 2 inches.

6. In the **Top Margin** box, type: **3** as shown above.
7. Under **Orientation**, click **Landscape.**
8. Ensure that **This section** is selected in the **Apply to** box.
9. Click **OK** to close the Page Setup dialog box and applies the changes.
10. Press the **Page Down** key. The page orientation of the rest of the document is Portrait.

Tip: If using standard margins, you can use the **Margins button** on the Page Setup group on the Ribbon instead of the Page Setup dialog box. Just be sure that the insertion point is in the section that you want to modify.

6.3 Modifying Section Headers and Footers

Y ou can create headers and footers that apply to only a particular section of a document. To create/modify a section header or footer, click on the header and footer for that section and make your changes. Any headers or footers that you

---

create will appear on any subsequent pages of your document. You can avoid having a header or footer appear in subsequent sections by turning off the **Link to Previous** button on the Design Ribbon in each section that you do not want the header/footer to appear.

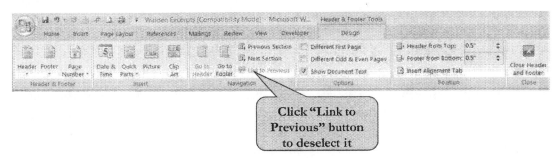

Click "Link to Previous" button to deselect it

✓ Modify Section Headers and Footers

1. Make sure the **Walden Excerpts 2.doc** file is active. **Double-click** the header on the second page of the document. This displays header/footer view for the second section of the document.
2. Click the **Link to Previous** button on the Navigation group. This allows you to create a new header for the current section without affecting the previous document section.
3. Select the text "**Thoreau Excerpts**"
4. Type: **Chronology**

5. Click the **Close Header and Footer** button.
6. Scroll to the first page of document then scroll downwards to view the rest of the document. Notice that the first page header is different from the rest of the document.
7. **Save** the current document.

6.4 Modifying Page Numbers in a Section Footer

Modifying page numbers in a section footer works the same way as modifying a section header. When working with page numbers, you also have the option of formatting the page number. For instance, the first page of your document may be a cover page. With page numbering, even if you choose not to display the page number on the first page, the second page will automatically begin numbering at page 2. You can modify the starting page number for a section by clicking **Format Page Number** on the Page Number menu.

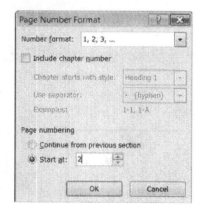

✓ Modify Page Numbers in a Section Footer

1.   Make sure the **Walden Excerpts 2.doc** file is active. Double-click the **header** on the second page of the document.
2.   Click the **Go to Footer** button on the Navigation group.

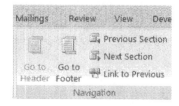

3.   Click the **Link to Previous** button. This allows us to create a new footer for the current section without affecting the previous document section.
4.   Click the **Page Number** button on the Header & Footer group.
5.   Point to **Bottom of Page** and then click the **Plain Number 2** style in the page number gallery. Notice that numbering automatically begins at 2.

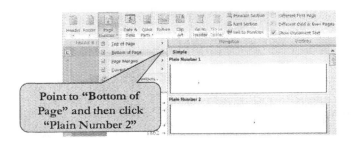

Point to "Bottom of Page" and then click "Plain Number 2"

6. Click the **Page Number** button and then click **Format Page Number** from the menu.
7. In the **Start at** box, type: **1** as shown.

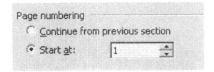

8. Click **OK.**
9. Click the **Close Header and Footer** button on the Ribbon.
10. Observe the footer. Notice that page numbering begins at 1.
11. **Scroll** up to the first page. Observe that the page number is not displayed on the first page.
12. **Save** the active document.

6.5   Removing a Section Break

Removing a Section Break works the same way as removing a page break — highlight the break code, and then press the **Delete** key. Or you can set the insertion point immediately after the section break then hit the **Backspace** key.
Remember - if your section break isn't visible on your screen, click the **Show/Hide** button on the Home Ribbon.

✓ Remove a Section Break

1. Make sure the **Walden Excerpts 2.doc** file is active. **Highlight** the Section Break on the first page.

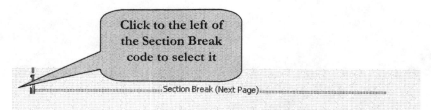

Click to the left of the Section Break code to select it

Section Break (Next Page)

2. Press the **Delete** key. Notice that the section formatting changes you made are now gone.

3. Click the **Microsoft Office button** and choose **Close** from the File Options menu. Click **Yes** when asked to save your changes.

Lesson 7 - Printing a Document

7.1 Previewing a Document

Before sending a document to the printer, it is a good idea to **Preview** the document to ensure that page breaks, margins, orientation, etc. are correct. Select **Print** from the File Options menu and then choose **Print Preview** in the second pane to display the active document in Print Preview mode. If you find yourself previewing your documents often, you may wish to add the Print Preview command to the Quick Access Toolbar by clicking the arrow next to the toolbar and then choosing Print Preview from the list.

Once in Print Preview mode, you have several additional options:

- Toggle the magnification of the document
- Display the current page of document
- Display multiple pages of the document
- Modify margins, page orientation and paper size.
- Set the Zoom percentage
- Send the document to the printer
- Shrink the document to fit

✔ Preview a Document Prior to Printing

1. Open the **Employment Letter.doc** document located in your copy of the Course Docs folder
2. Display the File Options menu.
3. Point to **Print** on the menu and then click **Print Preview** from the second pane.
4. **Click** on previewed page. Clicking on the document in preview mode toggles the zoom between 100% and the setting in the zoom box.
5. **Click** on the previewed page again. Word returns to original zoom.
6. Click the **Close Print Preview** button.

7.2 Setting Printer Options

Before you print your document, you may first want to set some **Printer Options**. For instance, you may need to specify which printer to use, the number of copies to be printed, or even designate Word to print only a specific range of your document. Printer options will vary, depending on the type of printer being used.

✓ Set Printer Options

1. **Make sure** the **Employment Letter.doc** file is active. Click the **Microsoft Office** button and then click **Print** to display the **Print** dialog box.
2. In the **Number of Copies** text box, enter 3 as shown.

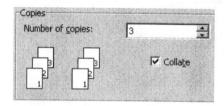

3. In the **Print Range** options dialog box, select **Current Page** as shown.

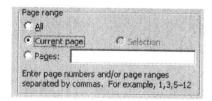

4. Click the **Cancel** button. This closes the Print dialog box without printing.

7.3 Printing an Envelope

Printing envelopes in Microsoft Word is straight-forward. Word will search your document guess at the mailing address based upon the active document. You can either use the address that Word comes up with or type your own in the **Delivery Address** box. Additionally, you can enter the **Return address** in the Return Address box.

After you enter the mailing information, you can either print the envelope immediately or **add it to the document** for later printing. If you are using a non-standard size envelope (the default is Number 10) or need to modify the font typeface or font size, click the **Options** button for additional envelope options.

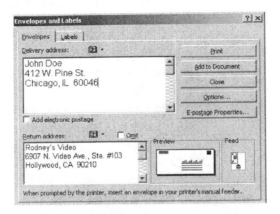

✓ Print an Envelope

1. **Make sure** the **Employment Letter.doc** file is active. Click the **Mailings** tab on the Ribbon.
2. Click the **Envelopes** button. This displays the Envelopes and Labels dialog box.
3. In the **Return address:** box, type in the following address as shown:

   Rodney's Video
   6907 N. Video Ave., Ste. #103
   Beverly Hills, CA 90210

4. Click the **Options** button.
5. Click the **Font** button under the Delivery Address area. This displays the Font dialog box.
6. Click **10** from the Font Size list and then click **OK.**
7. Click **OK.**
8. Click the **Add to Document** button. Click **No** if asked to save the current return address as the default. This adds the envelope to the current document and closes the Envelopes and Labels dialog box.

7.4   Printing Labels

Printing labels in Word is as easy as printing envelopes and is quite flexible. For example, you have the choice of printing either a single label or an entire sheet of labels with the same address.

You can choose from a wide variety of **label types**. This is found under the **Label Options** dialog box. From here, choose the label vendor (such as Avery) and the label product number that corresponds to the labels you will be using. If needed, select the printer tray you wish to use.

Like envelopes, you can choose to print your labels immediately or print them at a later time. If you wish to print your labels later and apply additional formatting such as changing the font, etc. choose the **New Document** option.

 **Print Labels**

1.   **Make sure** the **Employment Letter.doc** file is active. Click the **Mailings** tab on the Ribbon.
2.   Click the **Labels** button. This displays the Envelopes and Labels dialog box.
3.   Click the **Single label** radio button. This sets the option to print only one label using the address in the Address window.
4.   In the **Row** box, type: **3**

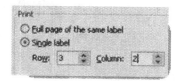

5.   In the **Column** box, type: **2**
6.   Click the **Options** button. This opens the Label Options dialog box.
7.   From the **Label Vendors** drop-down list, choose **Avery US Letter**.
8.   From the **Product number** list box, choose **5160 – Address** as shown.

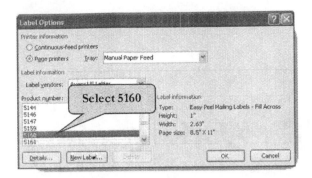

9. Click **OK**.
10. Click **Cancel**. This closes the Envelopes and Labels dialog box without printing.
11. **Save** and **close** the current document.

Lesson 8 - Working with Graphics

8.1 Adding Clip Art

Microsoft Office comes with a collection of images called **Clip Art** that you can use to make your documents more visually striking. Click the **Clip Art** button on the Illustrations group of the **Insert tab** on the Ribbon to display the **Clip Art Task Pane**. To browse clip art, enter a **keyword** in the **Search for:** text box.

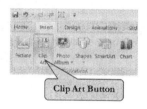

You can also insert clip art using the **Microsoft Clip Organizer** (the **"Organize Clips"** link at the bottom of the Clip Art Task Pane). Here, you can browse through clip collections, add clip art or catalog your clips.

✓ Insert Clip Art

1. Click the Microsoft Office button and then click **Open**.
2. Locate your copy of the Course Docs folder.
3. **Open** the **Course Docs** folder.
4. Double-click the **Word Tutorials** folder.
5. Click on the file named: **Camping Newsletter.doc** and click the **Open** button.
6. Click before the word **FROM** in the first line of the document.
7. Press the **Enter** key.
8. Press the **up arrow** key.
9. Click the **Insert tab** on the Ribbon.
10. Click the **Clip Art button** on the Illustrations group.

11. In the **Search for:** text box, type in: **Volleyball** and then click the **Go** button.

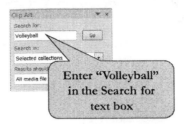

12. Click the volleyball image.

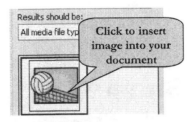

13. Click the Task Pane **Close button**.

14. **Save** the active document.

8.2 Adding Pictures from Files

In addition to Clip Art, you can also insert external **graphical images** into your documents from your computer drive, an external drive or a network drive. Microsoft Word supports a wide variety of graphical formats such as .jpg, .gif, .bmp, etc. Adding images can really add an extra touch to your documents.

 **Insert a Picture**

1. Make sure the **Camping Newsletter.doc** file is active. Set the insertion point at the blank line before the beginning of the third paragraph as shown.

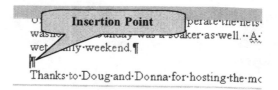

2. Click the **Picture button** on the **Insert Ribbon**.
3. Locate your copy of the Course Docs folder.
4. Double-click the **Course Docs** folder.
5. Double-click the **Word Tutorials** folder.
6. Click on the file named: **Canoe**
7. Click **Insert**.
8. **Save** the active document.

8.3   Adding Shapes

Word contains many powerful ready-made drawing tools such as lines, arrows, rectangles, circles, cubes, block arrows, callouts, stars and banners. Move your mouse pointer over any drawing icon to display an informational box explaining what the drawing tool is. These tools are located in the **Illustrations group** under the Insert Ribbon.

The Shapes are grouped for you by the following categories:

- Recently Used Shapes
- Lines
- Basic Shapes
- Block Arrows
- Flowchart
- Callouts
- Stars and Banners

One of the more common tools you will use is the **text box**. Text boxes allow you to place text anywhere on your document. Using text boxes as well as the other drawing tools can draw attention to particular areas of your document, helping you to convey your message more easily and effectively.

✓ Add a Shape

1. Make sure the **Camping Newsletter.doc** file is active. Set the insertion point before the line that begins: **Thanks to Doug**
2. Click the **Shapes** button on the Insert Ribbon.
3. Click the **Text Box** drawing tool under the Basic Shapes category (first shape in the Basic Shapes category).

4. Scroll up until the canoe photo that you inserted is visible. Move the mouse pointer over the canoe picture, about 2 inches from the right edge of the picture, about 1 inch down from the top.
5. Click and drag downward and to the right until your text box is about **1.5 inches high** and about **2 inches long**.

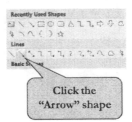

6. Click inside the text box and type: **Dan out for a ride**
7. Click the **Insert Ribbon**.
8. Click the **Shapes button** and then click the **Arrow tool** under the Lines category.

9. Move your mouse pointer (✛) to the bottom left of the text box.

---

10. Click and drag towards the person in the canoe until your arrow is about 2 inches long. Release the mouse button.

11. Click anywhere in the document to deselect the arrow to deselect the drawn object.

8.4 Formatting Drawn Objects

Chances are that after drawing your object, you will want to apply formatting to it so that it blends in with the rest of your document. The Shape Styles Group on the **Format Ribbon** contains several tools which allow you to modify such settings as line color, width and style, fill color, apply special effects such as shadows, bevel, glow, 3-D, etc. You can also apply a predesigned Shape Style to your object from the **Shape Styles gallery**. The selections available from the Shape Styles gallery will depend on the type of object selected.

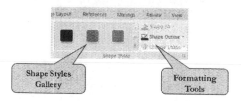

To apply formatting to your objects, you first need to **select the object** and then click on the appropriate formatting tool on the Drawing Toolbar. To apply formatting to more than one object at a time, hold down the **Ctrl** key and then select the desired objects.

✓ Apply Formatting to Drawn Objects

1. Make sure the **Camping Newsletter.doc** file is active. Click the **arrow** object that you drew in the last lesson.
2. Click the **More** button on the **Shape Styles** gallery on the Format tab.

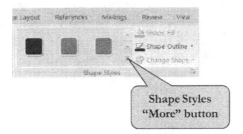

Shape Styles "More" button

3. Click the **Horizontal Gradient – Accent 2** thumbnail in the gallery (3rd row from the bottom, 3rd column).

Click the Horizontal Gradient – Accent 2 Thumbnail

4. With the arrow still selected, click the **Shape Outline** button.
5. Click the **red color swatch** in the color palette under the Standard Colors category.
6. Click the **Shape Outline** button again and point to **Weight**.
7. Click on ¾ **pt** in the gallery.
8. Click the **text box object** and then click the **Format tab**.
9. Click the **Shape Fill** button and select **Yellow**.
10. Click the **More button** on the **Text Box Styles** gallery.
11. Click the **Horizontal Gradient – Accent 2** style in the **third column, third row from the bottom**.
12. **Save** the changes.

Tip: You can see a preview of most formatting and styles by moving your mouse pointer over any gallery thumbnail or color swatch button. The effect will be temporarily applied to the selected object. This is an example of Word's Live Preview feature.

8.5 Resizing and Moving Objects

After you've drawn or inserted an object such as a graphic into your document, very often you will want to move it to another location on your document or change its width, length or height. In order to move or resize any object, you first must select that object. When you select an object, **sizing handles** appear on the object's border. Sizing handles allow you to change the size of the selected object. To move an object, move your mouse pointer over the border of the object or directly over a graphic until your mouse pointer turns into a 4-way black cross. Then, click and drag it to a new location.

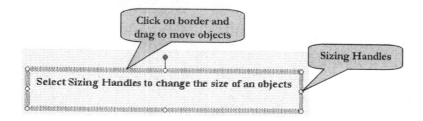

✓ Resize and Move an Object

1. Make sure the **Camping Newsletter.doc** file is active. Set the insertion point at the last blank line of the document.
2. Click the **Insert tab** on the Ribbon.
3. Click the **Picture button** on the Illustrations group.
4. Click on the file named: **Lake** in the Lesson Files folder.
5. Click **Insert**.
6. Select the **Lake graphic** that you just inserted.
7. Move your mouse pointer over the lower right sizing handle until the pointer transforms into a double arrow.
8. Click and drag **inward** until the picture is about 2 inches tall and 2 inches wide.
9. With the graphic still selected, click and drag until the insertion point is at the **blank line** above the sentence that begins with **Your board of directors**

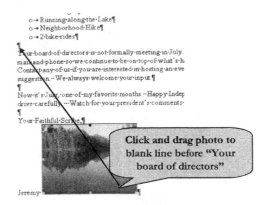

Click and drag photo to blank line before "Your board of directors"

10. Release the mouse button to move the graphic to the new location.
11. Press the **Ctrl + E** keystroke combination to center the graphic.
12. Click the **Save** the active document.

Tip: For a more precise measurement, you can also resize an object by entering in the desired dimensions in the Height and Width boxes in the Size group on the Insert Ribbon.

8.6   Adjusting Graphics

Once you have imported a graphic file into your document, you can modify various aspects of the image such as the brightness, contrast, color and more. Common picture adjustment options are available on the **Adjust** group of the **Format Ribbon**.

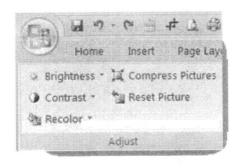

✓ Format a Graphic

1. Make sure the **Camping Newsletter.doc** file is active. Click the **Text Box** on the Canoe graphic.
2. Hold down the **Shift key**, and then click the **Arrow** object. This selects both the Text Box and Arrow graphics.
3. Press the **Delete** key.
4. Click the **Canoe** graphic.
5. Click the **Format** tab on the Ribbon.
6. Click the **Contrast** button on the Adjust group as shown and click **+10%**.

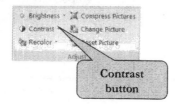

Contrast button

7. Click the **Brightness** button as shown and click **+20%** from the menu.
8. Click the **Picture Border** button on the Picture Styles group, point to **Weight** and click **1 ½ pt** as shown. This surrounds the picture with a 1 ½ pt border.
9. **Save** the changes.

8.7 Cropping Images

You can crop graphical images to remove unwanted portions of an image. To crop an image, click the **Crop button** on the format Ribbon, click on any crop handle bordering the image and drag inwards until the desired portion is removed. For a more precise measurement, you can use the **Size** dialog box by clicking on the Size Dialog Launcher. Enter dimensions in the appropriate boxes under the **Crop From** category.

Crop Tool

✓ Crop an Image

1. Make sure the **Camping Newsletter.doc** file is active. Click the Canoe graphic.
2. Click the **Format tab** on the Ribbon.
3. Click the **Crop** button under the Size group. Once the crop tool is activated, crop handles appear on the graphic.
4. Move your cursor over the left center crop handle, click and drag about one inch to the right.

5. Click the crop handle on the **right** center of the graphic and then drag about **one inch** to the left.
6. Type **3** in the **Height box** on the Size group.

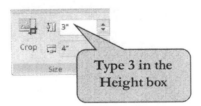

7. **Save** the active document.

8.8 Applying Quick Styles to an Image

Picture **Quick Styles** are a set of various formatting combinations that you can add to your images. These include 3-D effects, shadows, reflections, glows, bevel effects and more, all combined into one setting. To see the various Picture Quick Styles in action, select the graphic and then move your mouse point over the thumbnails in the styles gallery.

✓ Modify an Image with a Quick Style

1. Make sure the **Camping Newsletter.doc** file is active. Select the **Canoe** graphic.
2. Click the **Format tab** on the Ribbon.
3. Click the **More** button on the Picture Styles gallery.
4. Point to the **third style** in the **first row** (the Metal Frame style) to display a preview of the style.

5. Click the Metal Frame style.
6. **Center** the image.
7. **Save** the changes.

> **Tip:** You can also apply a Microsoft Office **Shape** to a picture. Click the Picture Shape button and choose the shape that you want. The image will appear in the shape and will be automatically cropped to fit into the shape.

8.9 Applying Image Effects

You can add some very interesting effects to your images using the **Picture Effects** tool on the Format Ribbon. You can add such effects as shadows, reflection, glow, soft edges and 3-D Rotation. To further customize your effects, click the **Picture Styles dialog launcher** to display the Format Picture dialog box.

You can also apply image effects to clip art and drawing objects.

✓ Apply Effects to an Image

1. Make sure the **Camping Newsletter.doc** file is active. Click the Canoe graphic.
2. Click the **Format tab** on the Ribbon.
3. Click the **Picture Effects button** on the Picture Styles group and point to **Glow**.
4. Click the **purple** glow effect in the last row.

Click the Purple glow effects in the last row

5. Click the **Picture Effects button,** point to **3-D Rotation** and select the **Off Axis 2 Left** effect under the Parallels group (2nd row, last column).

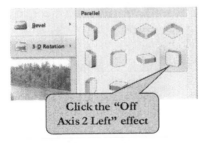

Click the "Off Axis 2 Left" effect

6. **Save** the changes.

8.10 Inserting WordArt

WordArt is a gallery of text styles and effects. With WordArt, you can add spectacular effects to the text of your documents – you can shadow it, bevel it, mirror it, and make it glow. As with text boxes, you can apply formatting to WordArt shapes and text.

The WordArt button is located on the **Insert Ribbon** on the **Text group** and will display the **WordArt Gallery** when clicked. From the Gallery, select the **style** of WordArt you wish to add and then type the text for your WordArt object.

From the **Format tab** (which displays when the WordArt object is selected), you can apply a variety of text effects by clicking the **Text Effects** button on the WordArt styles group.

 **Insert WordArt**

1. Make sure the **Camping Newsletter.doc** file is active. **Set the insertion point** at the last blank line of the document.
2. Click the **Insert tab** on the Ribbon.
3. Click the **WordArt** button on the Text group.

The WordArt
Button

4. Select the WordArt Style in the **2nd column, 3rd row** .

5. In the large text box, type: **See you at the next event!.**

6. Click **OK.**
7. Click the WordArt object that you just inserted, and then click **Edit Text** on the Text group of the Format Ribbon. To display the Edit WordArt Text dialog box.

8. Highlight the words: **at the next event.**
9. Type: **Next Month.**
10. From the **Font Size** drop-down list, select **32.**
11. Click **OK.**

12. With the WordArt object still selected, click the **Change Shape** button on the WordArt Styles group and click the **Wave 1** effect, in the 1ˢᵗ row, 5ᵗʰ column under the Warp category.

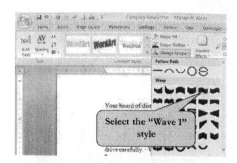

13. Click the **Insert** tab on the Ribbon.
14. Click the **Shapes button** on the Ribbon and click on the **Heart Shape** under the Basic Shapes category.

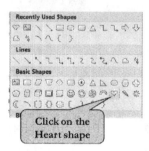

15. Click to the right of the WordArt object and draw the shape until it is about the same size as the WordArt object as. Release the mouse button.

16. Click on the Shape.
17. Click the **More button** on the Shape Styles group and click the Horizontal Gradient – Accent 2 style in the **3rd row from the bottom, 3rd column.**
18. Click the **Microsoft Office button** and choose **Close** from the File Options menu. Click **Yes** when asked to save your changes.

Lesson 9 - Columns and Tables

9.1 Creating Columns

With Microsoft Word, you can create newspaper-like columns in your document. You probably are most familiar with columns from your daily newspaper or even the newsletter that you receive in the mail.

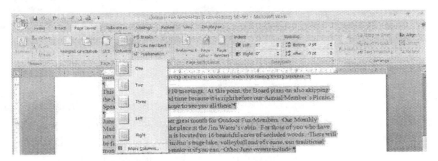

✓ Create Columns

1. Press the **Ctrl + O** keystroke combination to launch the **Open** dialog box.
2. **Locate** your copy of the **Course Docs** folder.
3. Double-click the **Word Tutorials** folder.
4. Open the file named: **Outdoor Fun Newsletter.doc**
5. Press the keystroke combination **Ctrl + A** to select the entire document.
6. Click the **Page Layout tab** on the Ribbon.
7. Click the **Columns button** on the Page Setup group and click **Three** from the Columns menu. This inserts the selected text into a three-column layout.
8. **Save** the active document.

9.2 Adding a Column Break

Notice that although you told Microsoft Word that you wanted three columns, you only ended up with two. This is because Word extends each column to the bottom of the page and then continues on the top of the next column. In our case, there was not enough text to fill up more than two columns.

You can force the start of a new column by inserting a **Column Break**. A column break terminates the column at the insertion point and begins any subsequent text in the next column. This is also handy if you find that our column breaks are in awkward places in the document. To delete a column break, select the break dotted line and press the **Delete** key

1. Make sure the **Outdoor Fun Newsletter** file is active. Set the insertion point at the beginning of the third paragraph, before the words **"This year's goal"**
2. Click the **Breaks** button on the Page Layout group to display the Breaks menu.
3. Click **Column**. This inserts the column break at the insertion point.
4. Set the insertion point at the beginning of the bulleted list in the second column, after the colon following the word **"include"**.

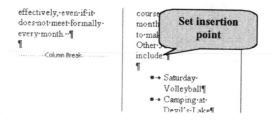

5. Click the **Breaks** button and then click **Column.**
6. **Save** the active document.

9.3 Modifying a Column Layout

You can make alterations to the column layout at any time. For instance, you may want to see what the layout would look like with two colums instead of three. Or perhaps you want to change the spacing between the columns. To change column layout, click anywhere in your column section, click the **Columns button** and then choose **More Columns**. Make any desired changes in the Column dialog box.

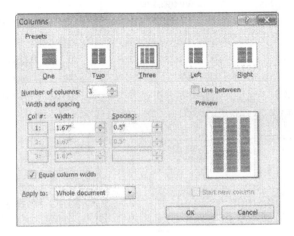

✓ Modify the Layout of Your Columns

1. Make sure the **Outdoor Fun Newsletter** file is active. Click anywhere in your document. To modify the column layout, you need to set the insertion point anywhere within your column area.
2. Click the **Columns button** and then click **More Columns**.
3. **Uncheck** the **Equal column width** checkbox. This sets the option to enter the column widths manually.
4. In the **Width** box for Column 1, enter: **2**.

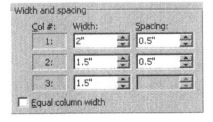

5. **Check** the **Line between** checkbox. This insets a line separator between columns.

---

6. Click **OK**. At this point, you might want to consider redoing the column breaks as now our columns appear uneven.
7. **Save** the active document.
8. **Close** the current document.

9.4 Creating a Table

Tables are a great way to organize and present columnar data. A table is organized in **rows** (the horizontal divisions) and **columns** (the vertical divisions). Data is entered into table **cells**, the intersection of the columns and rows. You can use tables whenever you need to present columnar data. In fact, some people like tables so much and find them so easy to work with that they often use them instead of tabs. To enter data into the table, click in the desired cell and begin type. Press the **Tab** key to navigate from one cell to the next.

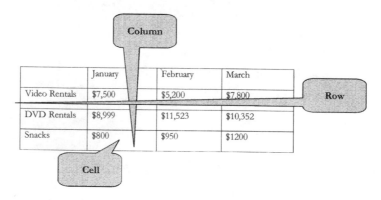

Sample Table in Microsoft Word

✓ Create a Table

1. Press the **Ctrl + N** keystroke combination to create a new blank document.
2. Click the **Insert tab** on the Ribbon.
3. Click the **Table button** on the Tables group. You can either drag on the grid to select the number of rows or columns, or click Insert Table to use the dialog box.
4. Click **Insert Table**.
5. In the **Number of Columns** box, type: **3** and then press the **Tab** key.

6. In the **Number of Rows** box, type: **4**
7. Click **OK.**
8. Place the insertion point in the **first row, second column** of the table

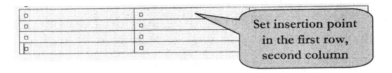

Set insertion point in the first row, second column

9. Type: **January**
10. Press the **Tab** key.
11. Type: **February**
12. Press **Tab**.
13. Continue typing text in the table.

	January	February	
Video·Rentals	$7,500	$5,200	
DVD·Rentals	$8,999	$11,523	
Snacks	$800	$950	

¶

14. Click the **Save** button. This displays the **Save as** dialog box.
15. In the **File Name** box, type: **My Table**.
16. **Save** .the document.

9.5   Inserting Rows and Columns

After creating a table, you may discover that you need another column or row. You can insert additional rows and columns anywhere in your table by using the **Row and Columns** tools on the **Layout** Ribbon. When adding rows or columsn, the table will automatically adjust to accommodate the new arrangement. When you insert a new row, the existing rows shift downward. When entering new columns, the existing columns shift to the right.

You can also quickly insert a new row at the end of a table by clicking in the last cell of the last row of the table, and then pressing the **Tab** key.

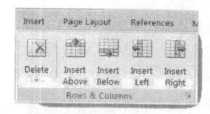

To add or delete columns and rows, click in the area of the table where you want to add or delete a row or column, and then choose from the following options from the Rows & Columns group:

- Insert Left (inserts columns to the left of the selected column)
- Insert Right (inserts columns to the right of the selected column)
- Insert Above (inserts rows above the selected row)
- Insert Below (inserts rows below the selected row)
- Delete (choose rows or columns)

You can also **right-click** in any table cell, point to insert, and then choose the desired command from the menu. To delete a row or a column, right-click and choose either **Delete Rows** or **Delete Columns**. To **Insert a Row at the End of a Table**, set the insertion point in the last cell of the last row of the table and press the **Tab** key. A new row is automatically inserted at the end of the table.

 Add Columns and Rows

1. Make sure the **My Table** file is active. Click in the **first column, third row** of the table (DVD Rentals)
2. Click the **Layout tab** on the Ribbon under Table Tools.
3. Click the **Insert Below** button on the Rows & Columns group.

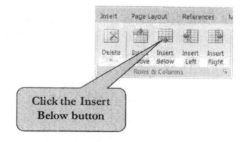

Click the Insert Below button

4. Set the insertion point after the text **$950**, in the last row and the last cell of the table.

---

5. Press the **Tab** key to insert a new row at the end of the table.
6. Click anywhere in the last column of the table.
7. Click the **Insert Right** button on the Rows & Columns group
8. Click in **the first row, fourth column** of the table.
9. Type: **March** and then press the **down arrow key.**
10. Type: **$7,800** and then press the **down arrow key.**
11. Type: **$10,532** and then press the **down arrow key.**
12. Type: **$3,895** and then press the **down arrow key.**
13. Type: **$1,200.**
14. Click in the blank cell below DVD Rentals (first column, fourth row).
15. Type: **DVD Sales** and then press the **Tab key.**
16. Type: **$2,100** and then press the **Tab key.**
17. Type: **$1,532**

	January	February	March	
Video·Rentals	$7,500	$5,200	$7,800	
DVD·Rentals	$8,999	$11,523	$10,532	
DVD·Sales	$2,100	$1,532	$3,895	
Snacks	$800	$950	$1,200	

The Completed Table

18. **Save** the changes.

9.6 Deleting Rows and Columns

Deleting rows and columns from your table is as easy as inserting them. Select the row or column you wish to delete, click the **Delete** button on the Layout Ribbon, and then choose either **Delete Rows** or **Delete Columns**. Other options on the Delete menu include deleting the entire table or deleting individual cells from a table.

✔ Delete Rows and Columns

1. Make sure the **My Table** file is active. Click anywhere in the blank row at the end of the table.
2. Click the **Delete button** on the Rows & Columns group and click **Delete Rows**.

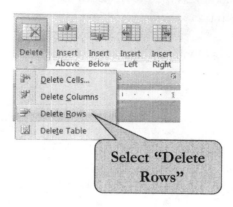

Select "Delete Rows"

3. Click anywhere in the **Match** column.
4. Click the **Delete button** on the Rows & Columns group and click **Delete Columns**.

5. Click the **Undo** icon on the Quick Access Toolbar as shown.
6. Move your mouse pointer to the left of the row that contains the words **"DVD Rentals"** until the pointer transforms to a right pointing white arrow .

¤	January¤	February¤	March¤	¤
Video·Rentals¤	$7,500¤	$5,200¤	$7,800¤	¤
DVD·Rentals¤	$8,999¤	$11,523¤	$10,532¤	¤
DVD·Sales¤	$2,100¤	$1,532¤	$3,895¤	¤
Snacks¤	$800¤	$950¤	$1200¤	¤

¶

7. Click and drag upward to select the second and third rows.

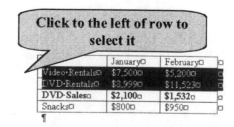

Click to the left of row to select it

	January¤	February¤	¤
Video·Rentals¤	$7,500¤	$5,200¤	¤
DVD·Rentals¤	$8,999¤	$11,523¤	¤
DVD·Sales¤	$2,100¤	$1,532¤	¤
Snacks¤	$800¤	$950¤	¤

¶

8. Click the **Delete button** on the Rows & Columns group and click **Delete Rows**.
9. Click the **Undo** button to reverse the delete action and restores the rows.
10. **Save** the active document.

9.7   Modifying Table Borders

The **Draw Borders** group, which can be found under the **Design tab**, allows you to change the borders of both the inside and outside lines of your table or remove the borders completely. Options include the border type, the border thickness (weight) and Pen color.

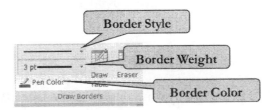

Once you have set the border formatting, click the **Borders button arrow** on the Table Styles group to apply it to your borders.

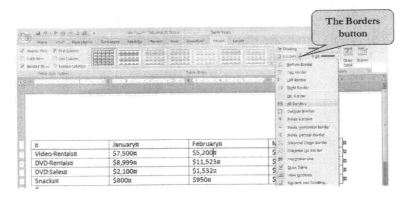

✔ Format Table Borders

1.   Make sure the **My Table** file is active. Click in the top row of the table. Click the **plus (+) symbol** that appears above the top left corner of the table. This selects the entire table.

	January¤	February¤	March¤	¤
Vid...ntals¤	$7,500¤	$5,200¤	$7,800¤	¤
	$8,999¤	$11,523¤	$10,532¤	¤
	$2,100¤	$1,532¤	$3,895¤	¤
	$800¤	$950¤	$1200¤	¤

Click the plus (+) symbol to select the entire table

2. Click the **arrow** on the **Borders button**.
3. Select **No Border**. This removes all borders from the table.
4. Click in the **last cell in the last row** of the table.
5. Press **Tab** to insert a blank row at the end of the table.
6. **Select** the new last row of the table.
7. Click the **Line Width** drop-down list and then select **3 pt** .

8. Click the **Pen Color** drop-down list and then click the **Dark Blue** color swatch under the Standard Colors category (second to the last color).

9. Click the **arrow** on the **Borders button** and click **Outside Borders** to add a 3 pt. blue outside border to the selected row.
10. Click the **arrow** on the **Borders button** again and click **Outside Borders**. This removes the border that was added.
11. Select the first row of the table.
12. From the **Line Weight** drop-down list, choose **1 pt**.
13. Click the **arrow** on the **Borders button** and click **Bottom Border**.
14. Click anywhere outside of the selected row to deselect the row.
15. Click in the top row of the table and then click the **plus (+) symbol** that appears above the top left corner of the table to select the entire table.
16. Click the **Pen Color** drop-down list and then click **Automatic**.
17. From the **Width** drop-down list, choose **1 ½ pt**.
18. Click the **arrow** on the **Borders button** and click **All Borders**.

9.8 Adjusting Column Width

When creating a new table in Word, all of the columns in your table are initially the same size. However, when entering data, you will quickly discover that some columns need to be wider than others in order to accommodate the data.

You can adjust column width by clicking and dragging the column border or the column margins to the desired length or, for a more precise measurement, use the Width box on the Cell Size group of the Layout Ribbon.

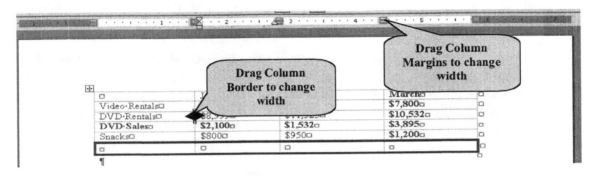

✓ Adjust Column Width

1. Make sure the **My Table** file is active. Move your cursor over the right border in the **January** column until your mouse pointer changes to a double vertical line with a double arrow through it.

2. Click and drag to the **left** until the column is about **one inch wide**.
3. Click on the right column boundary button on the vertical ruler for the **February Column**. Dragging to the left or right will adjust the width of the column.

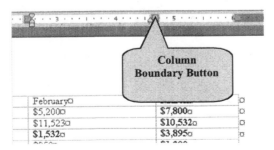

4. Click and drag to the **left** until the February column is about **one inch** wide.

5. Click anywhere in the **March** column.
6. Click the **Layout tab** on the Ribbon.
7. Type: **1.0** in the Column Width box on the Cell Size group. Press **Enter**.
8. **Save** the active document.

9.9   Adjusting Row Height

When entering data into a table, Word automatically expands the row height to accommodate the tallest entry. This is true even if you increase the font size. So the majority of the time, you will not need to bother with adjusting the row height.

However, there may be times when you want extra space between your rows for a visual effect. Adjusting row height is similar to adjusting column width. You can either use the click-and-drag method dragging the row's bottom border upward or downward until it is the desired width or, for a more precise measurement, use the Height box on the Cell Size group of the Layout Ribbon.

☐			March☐
Video·Rentals☐			$7,800☐
DVD·Rentals☐			$10,532☐
DVD·Sales☐	$2,100☐	$1,552☐	$3,895☐
Snacks☐	$800☐	$950☐	$1,200☐

Drag border up or down to change row height

✓ Adjust Row Height

1. Make sure the **My Table** file is active. Move your cursor over the bottom border of the **first row** until your mouse pointer changes to a double vertical line with a double arrow through it.

2. Click and Drag downward until the row height is about a half an inch.
3. **Save** the changes.

9.10 Formatting a Table

Word includes several **quick table styles** that you can add to your table. These table formats include preset colors and borders styles that you can instantly apply to your table. Under the Design tab under the Tables tab, you will see several Table Style thumbnails displayed on the Ribbon. Move your mouse pointer over any of these styles to see a preview of the selected style. Click the **Scroll Up** or **Scroll Down arrow** to scroll the style list. To view the entire Table Styles gallery, click the **More Styles** button.

You can further modify the formatting of your table by modifying table style options such as hiding or displaying the header row, adding special formatting to the first or last columns, or displaying banded rows or columns, in which the even rows or columns are formatted differently from the odd rows and columns.

To remove a table style, click the **More button** on the Table Styles group and choose **Clear** from the menu. The table will display in the default table format.

✓ Apply a Quick Style to a Table

1. Make sure the **My Table** file is active. Click anywhere inside of the table to select it.
2. Click the **Design tab** on the Ribbon.
3. Move your mouse pointer over the third Table Styles thumbnail from the left in the Table Styles group to display a preview of the Table Style.

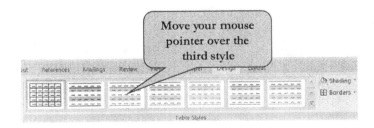

---

4. Click the **Scroll Down** arrow on the Table Styles group to display the next row of thumbnails.
5. Click the third Table Style thumbnail from the left in the Table Styles group.

9.11 Merging and Splitting Cells

T here are times when you may wish to combine two or more cells into a single larger cell that spans several columns. For example, you may have a title row as the first row of your table and you wish to center the title horizontally over the other cells in your table. To combine several cells into one, select the cells you wish to merge then use the **Merge Cells** command on the Layout Ribbon.

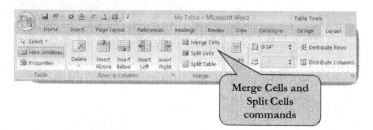

Merge Cells and
Split Cells
commands

Likewise, individual cells can be split into smaller cells by using the **Split Cells** command from the Table menu.

✓ Merge Cells in a Table

1. Make sure the **My Table** file is active. Click anywhere in the first row of the table. This selects the row above which you want to insert a new row. You will use the new row as a Title Row.
2. Click the **Layout tab** on the Ribbon.
3. Click the **Insert Above** button on the Rows & Columns group.
4. Select the new row. In this case, you want to merge all of the cells in the first row into one larger cell.
5. Click the **Merge Cells** button on the Merge group.
6. Type: **First Quarter Sales 2007**.

First·Quarter·Sales·2007¤				¤
¤	January¤	February¤	March¤	¤
Video·Rentals¤	$7,500¤	$5,200¤	$7,800¤	¤
DVD·Rentals¤	$8,999¤	$11,523¤	$10,532¤	¤
DVD·Sales¤	$2,100¤	$1,532¤	$3,895¤	¤
Snacks¤	$800¤	$950¤	$1200¤	¤

7. Press the **Ctrl + E** keystroke combination to center the title in the cell.
8. **Save** the active document.

Tip: You can also right-click and choose **Merge Cells** from the menu to merge the selected cells.

9.12 Changing Text Orientation and Alignment

When entering data into a cell, the default text alignment is top left with horizontal orientation. However, you can change both the alignment and orientation of the text within a cell from the **Alignment** group on the contextual **Layout Ribbon**. Using the alignment tools, you can realign the contents of your table cells both horizontally and vertically as well as change the direction of text within the cells.

Table Alignment tools

To change the alignment of text within a cell, click the desired button on the Alignment group. You can also evenly distribute the height and width of your columns and rows by clicking the Distribute Rows or Distribute Columns button on the Cell Size group.

To change the orientation of text within a cell, click the **Change Text Direction** button on the Alignment group. Each time you click the icon, the text will change orientation. The three choices are: vertical left, vertical right and original position. Click the icon until the desired alignment is displayed.

✓ Change the Alignment and Orientation of Text

1. Make sure the **My Table** file is active. Highlight the three cells which contain the text: **January, February** and **March**

First-Quarter-Sales-2007¤				¤
¤	January¤	February¤	March¤	¤
Video·Rentals¤	$7,500¤	$5,200¤	₂00¤	¤
DVD·Rentals¤	$8,999¤	$11,523¤		
DVD·Sales¤	$2,100¤	$1,532¤		
Snacks¤	$800¤	$950¤		

> **Highlight the January, February & March cells**

2. Click the **Align Center** button (second row, second column) on the Alignment group. As your move your mouse pointer over the Alignment tools, an informational box displays, telling you what each tool us used for.
3. Click the **Text Direction** button on the Alignment group.

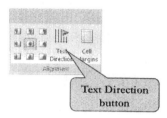

> **Text Direction button**

4. **Save** the changes.

First-Quarter-Sales-2007¤			
¤	January¤	February¤	March¤

9.13 Totaling Rows and Columns

Word allows you to **total the data in your tables** by clicking the **Formulas** button on the Layout Ribbon. By default, Word will propose the **=SUM(ABOVE)** or **=SUM(LEFT)** formulas, which will sum the cells above the selected cell or the to the left of the selected cell. You can also use other aggregate functions in your formula, such as AVERAGE, MIN, MAX, and COUNT. Simply replace the word "SUM" with the word for the aggregate function you want to use.

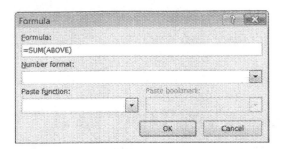

It is important to note that when adding new rows or columns to a table, the formula will not automatically update. To update the formula, right-click the formula and choose **Update Field** from the menu.

Total Rows and Columns in a Table

1. Make sure the **My Table** file is active.
2. Click in the blank cell under the **January** column.
3. Click the **Formula button** on the Data group.
4. Ensure that the formula in the Formula box reads: **=SUM(ABOVE)**.

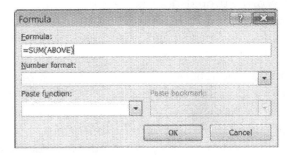

5. Click the **Number Format arrow** and then choose **#,##0** from the list. This specifies a number format with a comma and no decimal places.
6. Press the **Home** key to move the insertion point to the beginning of the number format.
7. Type the dollar symbol: **$**

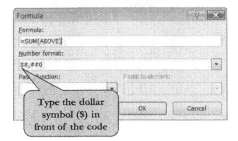

Type the dollar symbol ($) in front of the code

8. Click **OK.**
9. Click the **Microsoft Office button** and choose **Close** from the File Options menu. Click **Yes** when asked to save your changes.

9.14 Converting Text to a Table

A handy feature in Word is the ability to create a table from existing text. This saves the trouble of having to retype it should you wish it in table format. To convert text to a table, select the text, click the **Table button** on the **Insert Ribbon** and click **Convert Text to Table**.

✓ Convert Text to a Table

1. Press the **Ctrl + O** keystroke combination.
2. Locate your copy of the Course Docs folder.
3. **Open** the **Course Docs folder** folder.
4. Double-click the **Word Tutorials** folder.
5. Click on the file named: **Customer List** and then click the **Open** button.
6. Press the **Ctrl + A** keystroke combination to select all of the text in the document.
7. Click the **Insert tab** on the Ribbon.
8. Click the **Table button** on the Tables group.
9. Click **Convert Text to Table**.
10. Ensure that **7** is displayed the **Number of Columns** box.
11 Click the **AutoFit to Contents** radio button under the AutoFit behavior area.
12 If necessary, click the **Tabs** radio button.

13. Click **OK.** .Save and close the active file

NAME: *Sarah Connor*

Word Quiz

1. What are two ways to create a new document?

   Office button and open new / Ctrl + N

2. What are two ways to access the Microsoft Word Help System?

   Click the help icon in the upper right corner or F1

3. What are two methods for copying and pasting text?

   Select text 1. right click "copy", right click "paste"

   2. Ctrl + C (copy) Ctrl + V (paste)

4. Name three formatting effects that you can apply from the Formatting Toolbar.

   Styles, shadow effects, color

5. What are the 4 types of alignment that you can apply to a paragraph? How do you change a paragraph alignment?

   Left, right, center, justified

   Select paragraph (indents + spacing) drop down box under general next to alignment

6. How can you insert page numbers into your document?

   Insert tab - page number on header + footer options

7. What is a page break? How do you add one to your document?

   a page break indicates where the text will end of one page to continue on the next. Insert tab - Page break on pages options

8. You inserted a section break between page 1 and page 2. You want the margins of page 2 to be different than those of page one. How can you accomplish this?

   Page layout tab - breaks (section) on the page setup options. Open page setup change margins. Tick apply to this section.

9. Name three options you can set in the Print Dialog box.

   Name of printer
   How many copies
   what pages

Fundamentals of MS Office 2007

An Introduction to Excel 2007

Table of Contents

Lesson 1 - Excel Basics

1.1 Examining the Excel Environment

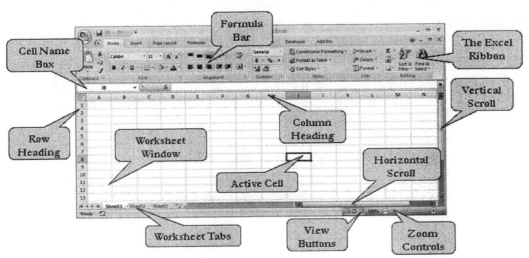

The Excel Working Environment

When you first launch Microsoft Excel, the application displays a blank worksheet along with the parts of the Microsoft Excel screen shown above. If you have worked with previous versions of Excel, you will immediately notice that the user interface has been completely redesigned.

The menu and toolbar system have been replaced by the **Ribbon**. The Ribbon is designed to help you quickly find the commands you need in order to complete a task. On the Ribbon, the menu bar has been replaced by **Command Tabs** that relate to the tasks you wish to accomplish. The default Command Tabs in Excel are: **Home, Insert, Page Layout, Formulas, Data, Review** and **View**.

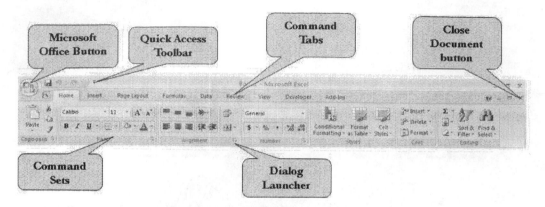

Different command icons, called **Command Sets,** appear under each Command Tab. Each command set is grouped by its function. For example, the Insert tab contains commands to add tables, charts, illustrations, links and text objects to your spreadsheet. **Contextual Commands** only appear when a specific object is selected.

On the bottom of many of the Command Sets is a **Dialog Launcher** that, when clicked, will launch a dialog box for that set of commands.

To the right of the **Microsoft Office icon** (from where you access file options), is the **Quick Access Toolbar.** This toolbar contains by default the Save, Undo, and Redo commands. In addition, clicking the drop-down arrow to the right allows you to customize the Quick Access Toolbar to add other tools that you use regularly. You can choose from the list, those tools to display on the Quick Access Toolbar or select **More Commands** to add commands.

As you can see on the **worksheet window,** the columns are labeled with letters of the alphabet while the rows are numbered. These numbers and letters are very important when working with formulas because they provide a means of referring to a particular cell. This is called a *cell reference.* For example, if you wanted to refer to the cell in the first row and the first column, the cell reference would be **A1.** You will work much more with cell references later.

1.2   Opening an Existing Workbook

I f you have worked with previous versions of Excel, you will notice that the **File > Open** command on the menu is no longer available. Instead of the word "File", the **Microsoft Office Button** indicates where the file menu commands are now located.

Click the Microsoft Office Button to access File commands

As you will quickly discover, there are several ways to accomplish the same task in Microsoft Excel. Many commands under the File Options menu have an equivalent keyboard command. For instance, to open an existing workbook in Microsoft Excel, you can use the keystroke combination **Ctrl + O** that bypasses the File Options menu to directly display the Open dialog box. To display the File Options menu, you can use the **Alt + F** keystroke combination rather than clicking the Microsoft Office button.

✓ Open a File

1. Click the **Microsoft Office Button** on the top left of your screen. This displays the **File Options** menu.
2. Click **Open** in the left pane to display the Open dialog box.
3. Search for your copy of the Course Docs folder.
4. Open the **Excel Tutorials** folder.
5. Select the **Lesson 1.xls** file. You will use this file throughout Lesson 1.
6. Click the **Open** button.

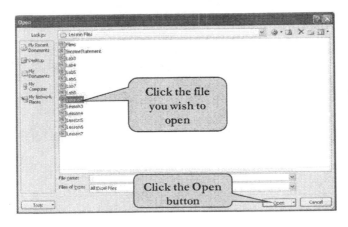

Click the file you wish to open

Click the Open button

1.3 Navigating a Worksheet

To move from one location to another in Excel, click in the cell that you want to activate. That cell then becomes the **active cell**. Excel also provides both **horizontal and vertical scroll bars**. In addition to changing position in the worksheet by clicking with your mouse, there are several methods for navigating a worksheet using your keyboard. Some of these are:

Method	Action
Move Left	Left Arrow Key
Move Right	Right Arrow Key or Tab Key
Move Down	Down Arrow Key
Move Up	Up Arrow Key
Move to cell A1	Ctrl + Home keys
Move to last cell containing data	Ctrl + End keys
Move to beginning of a row	Home
Move down one screen	Page Down
Move up one screen	Page Up
Move to the next sheet in workbook	Ctrl + Page Down
Move to the previous sheet	Ctrl + Page Up

1.4 Moving Between Workbooks

Each new workbook that you open is represented by a button on the **Windows Taskbar**. To move between open documents, you click the appropriate button on the Taskbar. You can also move between other open applications such as Word or PowerPoint by clicking on the appropriate document button on the Taskbar. To jump to another Excel workbook, you can click on the **View tab** and then click the **Switch Windows** button. The subsequent list displays all currently open Excel documents. Click on the document you wish to make active.

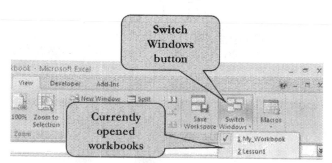

You can also use the **Alt + Tab** keystroke combination to scroll through all open documents as well as other open applications. With the Alt key held down, continue to press the Tab key until the desired document or application is selected.

1.5 Setting Excel Options

In previous versions of Excel, you could set preferences for specific program settings from the Options dialog box. The Options command has been moved to the **Excel Options** button on the File Options menu.

From the Excel Options dialog box, you can specify such options as setting a default location to save files, setting the default file format, setting display options and much more.

You may wish to spend some time browsing through the Excel Options dialog box and set any preferences that may help you work with less effort.

✓ Set Excel Options

1. Make sure the **Lesson1.xls** file is active. Click the **Microsoft Office Button** to display the File Options menu.
2. Click the **Excel Options** button at the bottom of the dialog box.
3. Click the **Popular** category in the left pane.
4. Under the **Creating New Workbooks** area, click the **Font Size arrow** and choose **12**. This sets a new default font size for all new Excel workbooks.

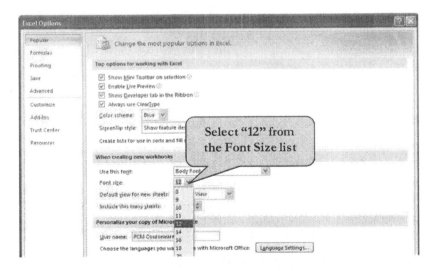

5. Click **OK**. This displays a message telling you that your changes will not take effect until you close and restart excel.
6. Click **OK**.

1.6 Switching between Views

Views control how your document appears on the screen. You can quickly switch views by clicking on one of the **View Buttons** located on the lower left hand corner of the document window. You can also switch between views by clicking the **View** tab and then clicking the desired View command button on the Ribbon.

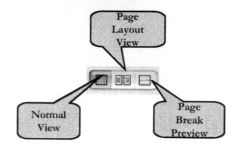

The available views are:

- **Normal View**   Used for entering, editing and formatting data. In Normal view, headers, footers, backgrounds and other objects are not visible.

- **Page Layout View**   New in Excel 2007, this view is used for entering, editing and formatting text, while displaying graphics, headers/footers, objects, margin borders, etc.

- **Page Break Preview**   Displays the worksheet with marked page breaks, allowing you to change their position.

To Switch between Views Click the appropriate view button on the lower left hand corner of your screen **or** click the **View** tab and then click the desired View command button on the Ribbon

1.7 Using Help

The **Help system** is designed to provide **assistance** to users whether you are online or offline and to bring all available resources to you as quickly as possible. To access the Help system, press **F1** or click the **Help icon** on the upper right-hand corner of the Excel window.

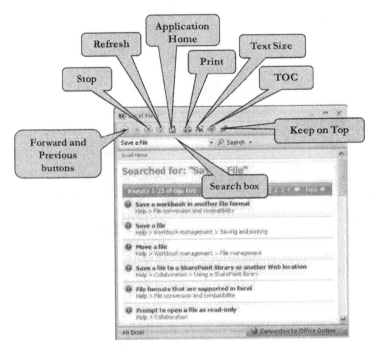

The Help system toolbar includes the familiar Back, Forward and Stop commands. Additionally, you will find the new **Refresh** tool, which allows you to update the content of the Help window. The **Application Home** tool brings you to the Excel starting point, where you can browse through information related to the Microsoft Excel application. The **TOC** tool displays a listing of available help topics. If you wish to increase or decrease the text size in the Help window, click the **Text Size** tool. Another nice feature on the Help toolbar is the **Keep on Top** tool that allows you to keep the current Help page open while you work.

✓ Use the Help System

1. Make sure the **Lesson1.xls** file is active. Click the **Microsoft Office Excel Help icon** on the upper right-hand corner of the screen.

2. In the **Search box**, type: **Save a file**.

3. Press **Enter**. The results are displayed in the Search Results pane.
4. Click the **Save a file** link in the Search Results pane.
5. Click the **Table of Contents** button on the toolbar. This displays a listing of Microsoft Excel help topics in a new pane.

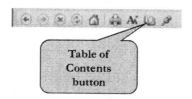

6. Click the **Table of Contents** button to hide the Table of Contents.
7. Click the Excel Help **Close button**.

Lesson 2 – Working with Data

2.1   Entering Text and Numbers

Data that you enter into an Excel worksheet can be either text, numbers or a formula. Text that is entered into cells is often referred to as **labels** and is not included in formulas. Numbers can be either test or numerical **values**. When entering numbers into a cell, Excel automatically treats them as values and aligns them to the right edges of the cell. If you wish a numerical value to be treated as text – that is to say, to take on the same formatting as labels (which are left-aligned), you can precede the numerical value with an apostrophe ('). Thus, to enter the year as text, you would type: **'2006**.

To enter data, click on the cell into which you wish to enter data (this becomes the **active cell**) and begin typing. Once you are finished, press **Enter** to confirm your entry. Any time you wish to clear a cell into which you have begun typing, press the **Esc** key **or** the **X** key to the left of the formula bar.

You will begin by **creating a blank new worksheet** and entering sales information for a video store.

✓ Enter Text or Numbers into a Cell

1. Launch Excel.
2. Click in cell **A1**. This makes A1 the active cell.
3. Type **Stores** then press Tab.
4. Type **Q1** and then press Tab.
5. Type **Q2** and then press Tab.
6. Type **Q3** and then press Tab.
7. Type **Q4** and then press Tab.
8. Click in cell **A2** and type **New York**. Press the down arrow key.
9. Type **San Francisco** and then press the down arrow key.
10. Type **Dallas** and then press **Enter**.
11. Click in cell **B2** and type **14381** and then press **Tab**.

12. Continue entering values as shown until your worksheet contains the data as listed below. Press **Tab** to move from one column to the next.

	A	B	C	D	E
1	Stores	Q1	Q2	Q3	Q4
2	New York	14391	11524	16979	21075
3	San Franci	22987	25424	24552	29780
4	Dallas	15344	17045	19024	23242

13. **Save** the workbook. Name it **Lesson2** and store it in your Course Docs folder.

✓ Change Column Width:

Notice that in **Cell A3**, the end of your store location is cut off since column A is not wide enough to accommodate the text. To widen the column, you must perform the following steps:

1. Move your cursor to the column heading between **Column A & B** until your cursor becomes a 4-way black arrow.
2. Click on the line between Column A & B and drag to the right until all of the text in Cell A3 is visible.

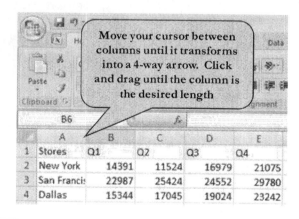

2.2 Entering Simple Formulas

Formulas perform calculations such as addition, subtraction, multiplication and division in your spreadsheet. You type the formula in the cell where you wish the result to appear. The result of the formula appears in the cell. The formula will appear in the formula bar.

To tell Excel that you are about to enter a formula, you must begin with an equal sign. For instance, if you wished to find the total for the numbers 8 and 12, you would enter: **=8+12** in the active cell.

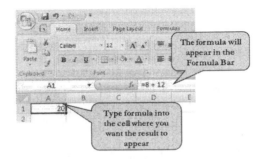

Valid mathematical operators that you can use in your formulas include:

    +   Addition
    -    Subtraction
    *   Multiplication
    /   Division

In addition to performing calculations on actual numbers (= 11 + 2 + 5), you can perform calculations on the value of cells by using **Cell References** in your formula. If you wanted to find the total of the cells A3, B6 and C7, you would enter the formula: **=A3 + B6 + C7.**.

In your worksheet, you will create formulas to total the sales values for each quarter.

✓ Create a Simple Formula

1. Make sure the **Lesson2.xlsx** file is active. Click in cell **F1** and type the word **Total**.
2. Press the **Down Arrow key**.
3. Type **=B2 + C2 + D2 + E2.** This enters a formula that sums the sales values for the New York store.
4. Press the **Enter** key.
5. Click in cell **F3**.
6. Type: **=B3 + C3 + D3 + E3.** This enters a formula that sums the sales values for the San Francisco store.
7. Press the **Enter** key.
8. **Save** the worksheet.

2.3 Choosing Formula Cell References Manually

If you want to build a formula that uses several different cell references in a large worksheet, it could be easier to select the cells manually, rather than try to remember the cell addresses. This can be accomplished by typing the **equal sign (=)**, and then selecting the cells that you want to include in the formula with your mouse.

✓ Choose Cell References Manually

1. Make sure the **Lesson2.xls** file is active. Click in cell **F4**.
2. Press the **=** key. This begins the formula.
3. Click in cell **B4**.
4. Type **+**.
5. Click in cell **C4**. This selects the next cell in your formula.
6. Type **+**
7. Click in cell **D4**.
8. Type **+**
9. Click in cell **E4**.
10. Press the **Enter** key. This confirms your formula entry.
11. Click in cell **F4** and observe the formula window.
12. Click the **Save** button.

2.4 Using AutoSum

If you wish to perform a common calculation such as SUM on a contiguous range of data, you can use the **AutoSum** button (located on the Home Ribbon). Clicking on the AutoSum button automatically selects a range of cells (vertical or horizontal) and calculates the total of all cells in that range. That is to say, when the cell that contains the SUM function is at the end of a row or column, Excel always uses that entire column or row in the calculation. However, if any cell in the range contains a blank row or column, the range to be totaled stops there. If Excel does not choose the range of cells you wish to use, you can choose the range manually by clicking on the first cell of the range and dragging to the last cell of your range.

The AutoSum button

If you wanted to total the values from **B3 to B18**, clicking the AutoSum button while having B19 as the active cell would automatically enter the following formula in cell B19: **=SUM(B3:B18)**. This tells Excel to sum the values in the B3 to B18 range.

The AutoSum feature includes other functions in addition to the **SUM** function. By clicking on the arrow to the right of the AutoSum button, you can choose the **AVERAGE, COUNT NUMBERS, MIN,** or **MAX** functions instead of the **SUM**. These functions will be discussed in more detail in a later chapter.

✓ Calculate Totals with AutoSum

1. Make sure the **Lesson2.xlsx** file is active. Click in cell **A6** and type **Total.**
2. Click in cell **B6** and click the **AutoSum** button on the **Home Ribbon**. The range B2 to B5 is selected. To change the range that Excel uses, you can manually select your desired range.
3. Press the **Enter** key to confirm the formula.
4. To select the range C2 to C5, click in cell **C6** and then click the **AutoSum** button on the Home Ribbon.
5. Press the **Enter** key.
6. Click in cell **D6** and then click the **AutoSum** button on the Home Ribbon. Notice that AutoSum selected cells B6 to D6, which is not what you want. You will need to manually select the cells you want to total.
7. Press the **Esc key**. This cancels the operation.
8. Click in cell **D2**.
9. **Click and hold down** your left mouse button and drag down to cell D6.

	A	B	C	D	
1	Stores	Q1	Q2	Q3	Q4
2	New York	14391	11524	16979	
3	San Francis	22987	25424	24552	
4	Dallas	15344	17045	19024	
5					
6	Total	52722	53993		
7					

Select the cell range D2 to D6

10. Click the **AutoSum** button on the Home Ribbon.
11. Click in cell **E2**.
12. **Click and hold down** your left mouse button and drag down to cell E6.
13. Click the **AutoSum** button on the Home Ribbon.
14. Click in cell **F2**.
15. **Click and hold down** your left mouse button and drag down to cell F6.
16. Click the **AutoSum** button on the Home Ribbon.
17. **Save** the document.

2.5 Changing & Deleting Data

To delete the contents of a cell, click in the cell to activate it and then press the **Delete** key. This erases the entire contents of that cell. If you wish to simply replace the contents of the cell, you do not need to press the delete key — just begin typing and the contents will be automatically overwritten by whatever you type.

There are times, however, when you do not wish to delete the entire contents of a cell but only wish to change part of the cell's contents. For example, you may have discovered an error in a formula you entered and wish to modify it. Rather than retype the entire formula, it would be easier just to edit the existing formula.

✓ Change the Contents of a Cell

1. Make sure the **Lesson2.xlsx** file is active. Click in cell **A6**.
2. Type: **Grand Total** and then press **Enter**.
3. Click in cell **A2**.
4. Click in the formula bar after the **k** in New York.

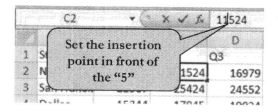

5. Press the spacebar and then type **City.**
6. Press **Enter**.
7. Double-click in cell **C2**. This enables edit mode in cell C2.
8. Position the I-beam pointer in front of the **5** and then press the **Backspace key**. This deletes the 1 in front of the 5 in cell C2.

9. Type **2.** This enters the number 2 between the 1 and 5 in cell C2.
10. Press **Enter**.
11. **Save** the worksheet.

2.6 Using Undo/Redo

Excel contains a powerful feature called **Undo/Redo** that allows you to reverse any editing action, including formatting. While entering data, you may have accidentally activated the wrong cell and inadvertently replaced the data in that cell. You can reverse this action with the **Undo** command.

Each time you initiate the Undo command, it will reverse the last action that you did; thus, clicking the Undo button 20 times will undo the last 20 actions as if they had never occurred. Rather than clicking the Undo button 20 times to undo multiple actions, clicking the arrow next to the Undo button allows you to quickly undo multiple past actions by navigating down the history list and selecting the number of actions you wish to undo.

Redo allows you to reverse the action of an Undo command.

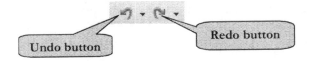

Undo button

Redo button

✓ Use the Undo and Redo Commands

1. Make sure the **Lesson2.xlsx** file is active. Click in cell **A4** and then press the **Delete** key.
2. Type the word **Total.**
3. Press **Enter.**
4. Click the **Undo** button on the Quick Access Toolbar. Excel reverts to the previous action – an empty cell.
5. Click the **Undo** on the Quick Access Toolbar again. Excel restores the cell to its original contents.
6. Click the **Redo** button on the Quick Access Toolbar.
7. Click the **Undo** button on the Quick Access Toolbar.

2.7 Using Find and Replace

You can find specific information in an Excel worksheet or workbook by using Excel's **Find and Replace** feature. Once you find the search entry, you can replace it with the desired text or number, or move on to find the next occurrence of the data.

By clicking on the **Options** button in the Find and Replace dialog box, Excel presents additional search options such as the ability to search in the active worksheet or the entire workbook as well as the choice to search in formulas, values and cell comments.

✓ Use Find and Replace

1. Make sure the **Lesson2.xls** file is active. Click in cell **A1**.
2. Click the **Find & Select** button on the Home Ribbon and select **Find** from the list. This displays the Find and Replace dialog box.
3. Enter **24552** in the **Find what:** text box.

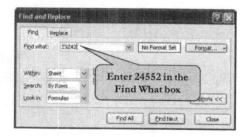

4. Click on the **Find Next** button to find the first occurrence of the search value in cell D3.
5. Click on the **Replace** tab.
6. Enter **26552** in the **Replace with:** text box.

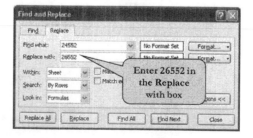

7. Click on the **Replace** button.
8. Click the **Close** button.
9. **Save** the worksheet.

2.8 Using the Go To Command

Excel's **Go To** command, located under the Find & Select command button, allows you to quickly jump to a specific cell or select a cell range (including named ranges) in your worksheet. This can come in especially handy if you want to select a long range of cells in a large worksheet.

The **Special** button on the Go To dialog box also allows you to select other areas of your worksheet, such as formulas, comments, blank cells within your data range, constants (non-formula entries) and more.

✓ Use the Go To Command

1. Make sure the **Lesson2.xlsx** file is active. Press the **Ctrl+Home** keystroke combination.
2. Press the **Ctrl + G** keystroke combination.
3. Type: **C1:C6** in the Reference box and then click **OK**.
4. Press the **Ctrl+Home** keystroke combination.
5. Click the **Find & Select** button on the Home Ribbon and select **Go To** from the list.
6. Click the **Special** button.
7. Click the **Formulas** radio button as shown and then click **OK**. This highlights all cells that contain formulas.

8. Click in cell **A1**. This activates cell A1 and deselects the highlighted cells.

2.9 Spell Checking Your Worksheet

Excel has a built-in **spelling and grammar checker** that automatically checks for errors as you type. Microsoft Excel will use its built-in dictionary to offer suggestions for any errors it finds. You can then choose the correct spelling of the word from the Suggestions list or add the word to the dictionary so that Excel will not flag the word in the future.

When Excel finds a questionable spelling error, a dialog box displays, prompting for a suggested action:

- **Ignore Once** – Ignores this instance of the spelling error.
- **Ignore All** – Ignores all instances of the spelling error
- **Add to Dictionary** – Adds the word in question to the built-in dictionary so that it will not be flagged in the future.
- **Change** – Changes the instance of the spelling error to the selected suggestion.
- **Change All** – Changes all instances of the spelling error in the document to the selected suggestion.
- **AutoCorrect** – Adds the error and the correction to the error to Excel's AutoCorrect list so that Excel will automatically correct the error in the future.

✓ Check Spelling and Grammar in a Worksheet

1. Make sure the **Lesson2.xlsx** file is active. **Double-click** in cell **A4**.
2. Delete the **s** in the word **Dallas** and then press the **Enter** key.
3. Press the **Ctrl+Home** keystroke combination.
4. Click the **Review tab** on the Ribbon.
5. Click the **Spelling Icon**. This begins the spell checking process.
6. Click **Dallas** in the **Suggestion List Box** and then click the **Change** button. This changes Dalla to Dallas.

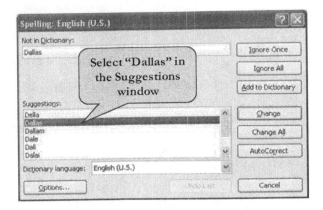

7. Click **OK** and Click the **Save** button.

2.10 Inserting Symbols

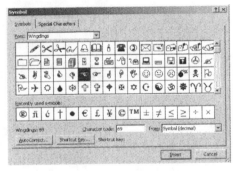

Microsoft Excel supplies hundreds of special characters (that do not appear on your keyboard) for use in your documents. Each font set contains its own set of symbols or characters. The **Windings** and **Monotype Sorts** contain a nice variety of useful characters.

You can insert a recently used symbol by clicking the symbol in the **Recently used symbols** list in the **Symbol** dialog box. The **Special Characters** tab displays a list of common symbols such as the em dash, copyright and trademark symbols.

✓ Insert a Symbol into your Worksheet

1. Make sure the **Lesson2.xlsx** file is active. Click in **A8**.
2. Click the **Insert tab** on the Ribbon.
3. Click the **Symbol** button on the Text command set.
4. Click on the **Special Characters** tab. Commonly used symbols are displayed.

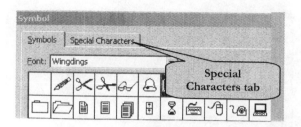

5.   Select the **Copyright Symbol** and then click **Insert.**

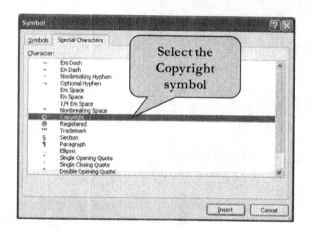

6.   Click **Close**.
7.   Type: **2007 Rodney's Video** and then press **Enter.**
8.   Press the **Ctrl + S** keystroke combination to save the changes.
9.   Click the **Microsoft Office** button and then click **Close** from the menu.

Lesson 3 – Editing a Worksheet

3.1　Working with Ranges

A range is a related group of cells. In Chapter 2, you looked at the SUM function where Excel totals a group of cells. If you wanted to retrieve a total for the cells B2 to B15, the formula would be written as:

=SUM(B2:B15)

Here, the formula B2:B15 designates all cells in the **B2 to B15 range**. This is an example of a **contiguous** range, that is to say, a group of cells that are next to each other in the same row or column.

There are several reasons why you might want to select a range in Excel:

- Apply the same formatting quickly to a group of cells
- Use the range in a function such as SUM or AVERAGE
- Apply a function or formula to several columns/rows at once
- Designate a group of cells as a print area
- Designate a group of cells for sorting

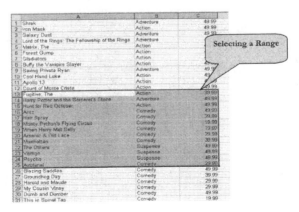

You can select a range in a variety of ways: To **select a Contiguous Group of Cells:** click in the first cell of the group. With the left mouse button held down, drag in the desired direction to select the range. To select an entire Row or Column, click the column heading or row heading. To select additional rows or columns, hold down the left mouse button and drag in the desired direction. To select an entire Worksheet, click the **Select All** button (above row 1 and to the left of column A).

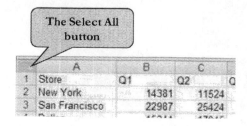

To Select a Non-contiguous range of cells, click in the first cell you wish to select. Hold down the **Ctrl** key and select any additional non-adjacent cells.

✓ Select Groups of Cells

1. Open the **Lesson3.xlsx** workbook in your Course Docs folder.
2. Click on the **Column Heading** for Column B. This selects Column B entirely.

3. Click on the **Row Heading** for **Row 3**.

4. Click in **cell C2**.
5. Press and hold down the left mouse button and drag to **cell E4**.
6. Select **cell B2**.
7. Hold down the Ctrl key. Click on **cells C4, D2, E6 and F4**. Excel enables you to select a non-contiguous range of cells.
8. Click on the **Select All** button. This selects the entire worksheet.
9. Click in **cell A1** to deselect the selected cells.

3.2   Copying and Pasting Data

When you want to **duplicate data** in several locations, whether it be another worksheet, another workbook or another application, you can save time by using Excel's **copy command** rather than retyping the data you want to duplicate. When you copy data, it is placed on the **clipboard** (an area in memory that holds copied items). You can then insert the selection into another location by using the **Paste** command.

When you paste the contents of the clipboard into your worksheet, the **Paste Options Button** appears. When you click the button, a list appears, allowing you to decide how the information is pasted into your document. For instance, when pasting from another document, you could choose to change the formatting of the pasted text to match the current document.

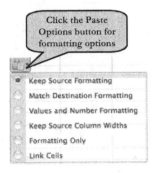

✓ Copy and Paste Data

1. Make sure the **Lesson3.xlsx** file is active. Click the **Home tab** on the Ribbon.
2. Click in Cell **A1**.
3. Hold down the left mouse button and drag to cell **B6**.
4. Click the **Copy icon** in the Clipboard group on the Home Ribbon .
5. Click on the **Q1** worksheet tab on the bottom of the screen and then click in cell **A1**. Switches to the Q1 worksheet and makes A1 the active cell.
6. Click the **Paste icon** on the Home Ribbon .
7. Widen column **A** to accommodate the text.
8. Click on the **Yearly Totals** worksheet tab and press the escape key. Excel returns to the original worksheet and clears the worksheet of the copy range.
9. Select the cell range **A1:A6**.
10. Hold down the **Ctrl** key and select the cell range **C1:C6**.

	A	B	C	D	E	F	
1	Store	Q1	Q2	Q3	Q4		
2	New York	14381	11524	16979	21075	63959	
3	San Francisco	22987	25424	24552	29780	102743	
4	Dallas	15344	17045	19024	23242	74655	
5							
6	Total	52712	53993	106705	74097	241357	
7							
8							

A1:A6 and C1:C6 non-contiguous ranges

11. Click the **Copy** button on the Ribbon.
12. Click on the **Q2** worksheet tab on the bottom of the screen and click in cell **A1**.
13. Click the **Paste** button on the Ribbon.
14. Click on the **Yearly Totals** worksheet tab and then press the escape key.
15 **Save** the worksheet.

> **Tip:** You can also **right-click** on selected text and then choose Copy from the menu. Right-click and choose Paste after you have set the insertion point where you want to insert the copied text.

3.3 Using the Office Clipboard

The **Office Clipboard** allows you to assemble data from several locations in the same document or from different Office documents, and then paste the items one at a time into any Microsoft Office document. Unlike the Windows clipboard which holds only one item, the Office Clipboard can store up to 24 items that you have cut or copied.

To use the Office Clipboard feature, ensure that the Clipboard Task Pane is visible by clicking the **Clipboard Dialog Launcher** on the bottom right corner of the Clipboard command group. Then, use the standard copy or cut commands. Each item, up to 24, that you copy or cut will be individually placed in the Clipboard for your later use.

Once you exit Excel, all items from the Office Clipboard are removed.

✓ Use the Office Clipboard

1. Make sure the **Lesson3.xlsx** file is active. On the **Home** tab in the **Clipboard** command group, click the **Clipboard Dialog Box Launcher**.
2. Click the **Clear All** button.
3. Select the cell range **D1:D6**.
4. Click the **Copy** button on the Ribbon.
5. Select the cell range **E1:E6** and click the **Copy** button on the Ribbon. This places the selection on the Office Clipboard above the previous entry.
6. Click on the **Q3 worksheet** tab on the bottom of the screen and click in cell **B1**.
7. **Click the second item** in the Office Clipboard. This pastes the Q3 data into the Q3 worksheet.

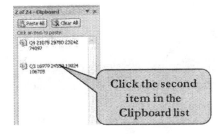

8. Click on the **Q4** worksheet tab on the bottom of the screen and then click in cell **B1**.
9. **Click the 1ˢᵗ item** in the Office Clipboard.
10. Click the **Clear All** button in the Office Clipboard Task Pane. If you want to remove only a specific item from the office clipboard, move your mouse pointer over the item to be deleted, click the arrow that appears next to the item and select **Delete** from the list.
11. Click on the **Yearly Totals** worksheet tab and hit the escape key.
12. Click the **Close button** on the Office Clipboard pane.
13. **Save** the worksheet.

3.4 Cutting and Pasting Data

When you wish to move data from one location to another, rather than duplicating data like you did in the previous lesson, use Excel's **Cut and Paste** commands. By using the Cut and Paste commands, the data is deleted from its original location and moved to the new location. Like the copy command, the data is stored temporarily on the Windows clipboard.

Using the **Cut and Paste commands** allows you to rearrange worksheet cells, rows and columns with ease.

✓ Cut and Paste Data

1. Make sure the **Lesson3.xlsx** file is active. Select the cell range **A1:F6**.
2. Press the **Ctrl + X** keystroke combination. This cuts the selection
3. Click in cell **B8**.
4. Press the **Ctrl + V** keystroke combination to paste the selection

	A	B	C	D	E	F	G	H
1								
2								
3								
4								
5								
6								
7								
8		Store	Q1	Q2	Q3	Q4		
9		New York	14381	11524	16979	21075	63959	
10		San Francisco	22987	25424	24552	29780	102743	
11		Dallas	15344	17045	19024	23242	74655	
12								
13		Total	52712	53993	106705	74097	241357	
14								
15								

The Pasted Data

5. Click the **Save** icon.

Tip: You can also **right-click** on selected text and then choose Cut from the menu. Right-click and choose Paste after you have set the insertion point where you want to insert the copied text.

3.5 Copying and Moving Cells using Drag-And-Drop

Instead of using the Cut/Copy and Paste commands, you can also move and copy cells or ranges of cells using the **drag-and-drop** method. That is to say, you can manually move the contents of cells to another location by first selecting the cell range and then dragging the cells with your mouse to the new location. To copy cells instead of moving, hold down the **Ctrl** key as you drag.

✓ Copy or Move a Range using Drag-and-Drop

1. Make sure the **Lesson3.xlsx** file is active. Select the range **B8:G13**.
2. Move your mouse pointer over the **top border of the range** until the pointer changes to a 4-way black arrow.
3. Click and drag until the top left corner rests in cell **A1**.
4. Release the mouse button.
5. With the range still selected, move your mouse pointer over the **bottom border of the range** until the pointer changes to a 4-way black arrow.
6. Press and hold the **Ctrl** key, then **click and drag** until the top left corner rests in cell **A11**.

	A	B	C	D	E	F	G
1	Store	Q1	Q2	Q3	Q4		
2	New York	14381	11524	16979	21075	63959	
3	San Franc	22987	25424	24552	29780	102743	
4	Dallas	15344	17045	19024	23242	74655	
5							
6	Total	52712	63993	106705	74097	241357	
7							
8							
9							
10							
11	Store	Q1	Q2	Q3	Q4		
12	New York	14381	11524	16979	21075	63959	
13	San Franc	22987	25424	24552	29780	102743	
14	Dallas	15344	17045	19024	23242	74655	
15							
16	Total	52712	63993	106705	74097	241357	
17							

Duplicated Range

7. Release the mouse button and the Ctrl key.
8. **Undo** the last action.
9. **Save** the worksheet.

3.6 Changing Column Width

When typing data into a cell, you often find that the column is not wide enough to accommodate the text and often, the end of your text will either be cut off or will continue into the next cell. In such a case, you will want to **adjust the column width** by clicking on the boundary of the right side of the column heading and dragging until the column is the desired width.

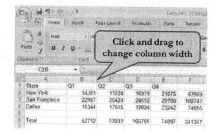

Rather than change the size of a column manually, you can use Excel's **Column Width** commands in which you enter **precise values** for column width.

✓ Change the Width of a Column

1. Make sure the **Lesson3.xlsx** file is active. Move your mouse pointer over the **boundary** of the right side of the column heading until the mouse pointer changes into a black cross with a double arrow.
2. Click and hold the mouse button down and **drag** until the column is the desired width.

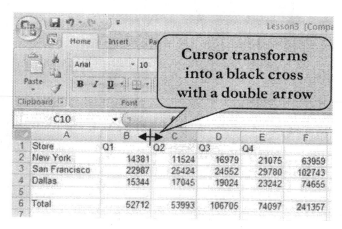

✓ Change the Size of a Column using the Column Width Command

1. Make sure the **Lesson3.xlsx** file is active. Click on the column heading for **Column A**. This selects Column A.
2. Click on the border between **Column A and Column B** as shown.

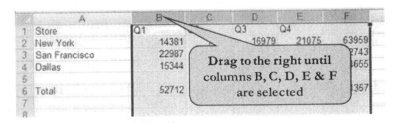

3. Click and drag until Column A is about **2 inches wide**
4. **Save** the changes.

Autofit

You can also use Excel's **Autofit** feature. This allows you to automatically change the width of a column or height of a row to accommodate the widest or tallest entry.

✓ Change the Size of a Column or Row using Autofit:

1. Make sure the **Lesson3.xlsx** file is active. Select **Column B**.
2. Click and drag to the right until **Columns B, C, D, E & F** are selected.

	A	B	C	D	E	F
1	Store	Q1		Q3	Q4	
2	New York		14381	16979	21075	63959
3	San Francisco		22987			7743
4	Dallas		15344	Drag to the right until		655
5				columns B, C, D, E & F		
6	Total		52712	are selected		357
7						
8						

3. Double-click on the border between **Columns C & D** in the column heading. This autofits all selected columns.
4. Save the active workbook.

3.7   Changing Row Height

At times, you may want a particular row to stand out by increasing the font size such as in a worksheet title heading. In this case, you would also need to adjust the row height to accommodate the taller text of the increased font size. The process for changing the width of columns works the same way for changing the height of rows – click on the boundary of the bottom of the row heading and drag until the row is the desired height.   Just as you saw with changing column width, you also change the size of a row or column (rather than dragging manually) by using Excel's **Row Height** command in which you enter **precise values** for row height.

✓ Change the Height of a Row using the Row Height Commands

1.   Make sure the **Lesson3.xlsx** file is active. Click on the row heading for **Row 1**.

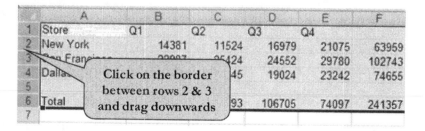

2.   Click and then drag downwards until **Rows 1-6** are selected.
3.   Click on the border between **Rows 2 and 3** in the row heading and drag downwards about **1/4 of an inch**.

4.   **Save** the worksheet.

3.8 Inserting and Removing Rows and Columns

To change the appearance of your worksheet, you can insert additional columns and rows or delete existing ones. When you insert a new column into your worksheet, existing columns shift to the right. When inserting new rows, existing rows shift down.

✓ Insert/Remove a Column or Row

1. Make sure the **Lesson3.xlsx** file is active. Click on the Heading for **Row 4**.
2. **Right-click** and then choose **Insert** from the menu.
3. Click in cell **A4** and type: **Milwaukee**.
4. Press the **Tab** key and type: **41224**
5. Press the **Tab** key and type: **42655**
6. Press the **Tab** key and type: **38972**
7. Press the **Tab** key and type: **45268**
8. Select the **Row Headings** for **Rows 1 and 2**.
9. Click the **Insert button** on the Cells group on the Ribbon.

10. Click the **Row Heading** for Row 1.
11. **Right-Click** and choose **Row Height** from the menu.
12. Enter **21** in the Row Height dialog box as shown.

13. Click **OK**.
14. Click in cell **A1**.
15. Type: **Quarterly Sales for FY 2002**.
16. Press **Enter**.
17. Click the Row Heading for **row 4** and press the **Delete** button on the Ribbon. Deletes row 4 from the worksheet.
18. Press the **Ctrl + Z** keystroke combination. This reverses the last action.
19. **Save** the current worksheet.

3.9 Copying Data and Formulas with AutoFill

You can copy data and formulas to adjacent cells using the **AutoFill** feature. To use the AutoFill feature, select the cell whose data you wish to copy and then move your mouse pointer over the cell's **fill handle**, the small black box on the lower right corner of the cell. Your mouse pointer will transform into a black cross. Then, click and drag to the adjacent cell(s) where you wish to copy the data. Once the action is completed, the **AutoFill Options** button will appear, giving you the option of copying just the data, copying the formatting only, or copying the data without the formatting.

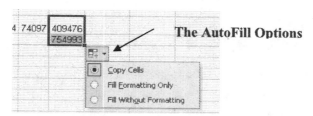

Use AutoFill to Copy Data and Formulas or to Create a Series

You can use AutoFill to create a series or a sequence of values. For instance, you can quickly fill cells that follow a sequence of 5, 10, 15, etc. You need only provide an example of a couple of entries to show Excel the pattern for the series. For a series such as a sequential date, you need only provide one example — Excel will automatically increment the date by one day.

✓ Use AutoFill to Create a Series

1. Make sure the **Lesson3.xlsx** file is active. Click in cell **F5**.
2. Observe the formula in the formula bar. The formula sums the values from B5 to E5.
3. Move your mouse pointer over **the fill handle** (the box on lower right of cell) until the pointer transforms into a black cross.
4. **Click and hold** the left mouse button and drag the contents down to **cell F6**.
5. Click in cell **F6**. Activates cell F6.
6. Observe the formula bar. Formula cell references are automatically updated to your new cell location (the formula now sums the values from B6 to E6).
7. Click on the column heading for **Column A**.
8. **Right-click** and choose **Insert** from the menu.
9. Click in cell **A3** and type: **Store #**. Press **Enter** to confirm the entry.
10. Type **1** in cell **A4** and then press **Enter**.
11. Type **2** in cell **A5** and then press **Enter**.
12. Select cells **A4 and A5**.
13. Move your mouse pointer over the **Fill Handle** on the bottom right of cell **A5**.
14. Click and drag down to cell **A7**. **Release** the mouse button.
15. **Save** the current worksheet.
16. Press **Ctrl + W** to close the workbook

Lesson 4 – Formatting a Worksheet

4.1 Formatting Text

One powerful feature in Microsoft Excel is the ability to format the text in your worksheet. For instance, you can modify the typeface (or font) of your text, change the size of your text, or emphasize text by adding bold, italics or underlined formatting.

Some common text formatting options are:

- Changing the font style (typeface)
- Changing the font size
- Adding bold, italic and underlined formatting
- Adding Borders
- Increasing/Decreasing Font Size

The quickest and easiest way to apply and modify text formatting is to use the Formatting Tools on the Home tab under the **Font group**. To change text emphasis, select the cell or cell range you wish to format then click on the appropriate button (Bold, Italics or Underline). To change the font or font size, select the text then choose the desired option from the font or font size drop-down list. For an explanation of what a tool does, move your mouse pointer over a tool to display an informational box. The box will also display the **keyboard shortcut** for the command, if any.

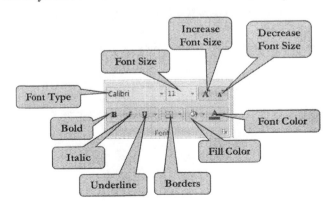

New in Excel 2007 is the **Mini-Toolbar**. The Mini-Toolbar displays whenever you right-click on selected cells and provides quick access to common formatting commands such as bold, italic, font color, font type, font size, fill color, increase and decrease indent. If you wish to turn off this feature, you can do so from the Excel Options dialog box.

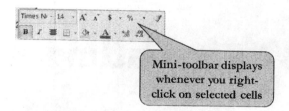

Mini-toolbar displays whenever you right-click on selected cells

✓ Use Formatting Tools

1. Open the **Lesson4.xlsx** file found in your Course Docs folder
2. Click the **Yearly Totals** worksheet tab.
3. Make B1 the active cell.
4. Click the **Bold** formatting button **B** on the Home Ribbon.
5. Change the typeface to Times New Roman.

6. Click on the **Font Size** drop down list and choose **14**. Notice that as you move your mouse pointer over the different font sizes and font styles, the data in your worksheet displays a preview of the selected font or font size.
7. Press the **Ctrl + S** keystroke combination. This saves your changes.

4.2 Using the Format Cells Dialog Box

The **Format Cells Dialog Box** allows you to apply multiple formats (bold, italics, font size, font type, font color, etc.) to selected text at from one interface. Additionally, there are formats that are not available on the Ribbon. To apply multiple formatting to selected text, click the **Font Dialog Box Launcher** on the lower-right corner of the Font command set and then make your desired selections.

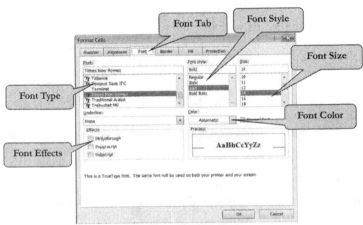

The Font Dialog Box

✓ Use the Format Cells Dialog Box

1. Make sure the **Lesson4.xlsx** file is active. **Select** the cell range A3:G3.
2. Click the **Font Dialog Box Launcher**
3. In the **Font Style** window, select **Bold**.

4. Click the **Underline** drop down list, choose **Single** as shown above.
5. Click **OK**.
6. Click the **Save** button on the Quick Access toolbar.

4.3 Formatting Values

The Ribbon contains many options for applying **number formatting**. Buttons for the three most common number formats – **Currency Style, Percent Style** and **Comma Style** can be found on the Number group on the Home Ribbon. Two additional buttons allow you to increase and decrease the number of decimal places.

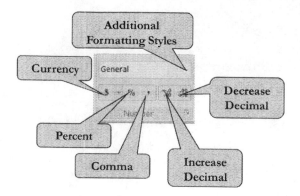

You click the drop-down list on the Number group to choose value formatting options (date, time, text, fraction, etc.). The **Number** tab of the **Format Cells dialog box** contains many additional options.

✓ Format Values

1. Make sure the **Lesson4.xlsx** file is active. Select the cell range **C4:G7**.
2. On the **Number group** on the Home Ribbon, click the **Comma Style** button.
3. Click the **Decrease Decimal** button twice. Decimal places will not be displayed.
4. Press **Ctrl + 1** and click on the **Number** tab.
5. Select **Number** from the **Category** list. Notice that you can set the number of decimal places and add a comma from here as well.

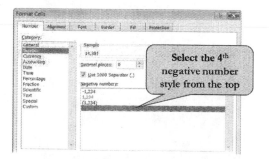

6. In the **Negative Number** list box, choose the fourth style from the top **(1,234.10)** as shown above. Negative numbers will be displayed in red color and surrounded with parentheses.
7. Click **OK**. This closes the Format Cells dialog box and applies the changes.
8. Select the cell range **C9:G9**.

9. Click the **Number** Dialog Launch button.
10. Select **Currency** from the **Category** list.
11 In the **Negative Number** list box, choose the fourth style from the top (1,234.10). This will display negative number in red color and surround them with parentheses.
12. Click **OK**. This closes the Format Cells dialog box.
13. Select cell **G1** and enter the date **12/31/2002**.
14. Press **Enter**. Excel automatically applies a date format to the cell.
15. Activate cell G1.
16. Click the **Number** Dialog Launch button.
17. Under **Category** click on **Date**.
18. Choose the **March 14, 2001** style. This selects the mmmm/dd/yyyy format.
19. Click the **Font Tab** on top of the Formatting Cells dialog box.
20. Apply **Bold** and **Italic** formatting to the cell.
21. Click **OK** to close the Format Cells dialog box.

Notice that when you changed the last row to Currency, your values are no longer displayed. Instead, the cell is populated with the pound sign (or commonly referred to as "the railroad tracks"). This occurs when a numerical value is longer than the cell can accommodate. To solve this problem, you need only increase the width of your columns.

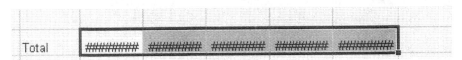

1. Make sure the **Lesson4.xlsx** file is active. Select the Column Heading for columns **C, D, E, F & G**.
2. **Double-click** on the border between any two of the selected columns (mouse pointer will transform into a black cross). This Applies AutoFit which sizes the column to accommodate the longest data value.

3. **Save** the current workbook.

4.4   Using the Format Painter Button

Using the **Format Painter** button on the Home Ribbon allows you to copy the formatting from one cell or cell range to another. This procedure copies all formats including font typeface, number formatting, cell and font color, alignment, etc. to the new cell range. To copy the formatting to several locations, **double-click** the Format Painter button. It will then continue to be activated until you click its icon to deactivate it.

✓ Copy Formats from One Cell or Cell Range to Another and Copy Column Widths from One Column to Another

1. Make sure the **Lesson4.xlsx** file is active. Select the cell range **C9:G9**.
2. Apply bold formatting to the selected range.
3. Activate the Format Painter.
4. Click in cell **G4** and hold down the left mouse button.
5. Drag from cell **G4:G7**. This selects the range to be formatted.
6. **Release** the mouse button to Apply the formatting from C9:G9 to G4:G7.
7. Click in Cell **G9**. This makes G9 the active cell.
8. **Double-click** the **Format Painter** button. You want to apply the formatting in G9 to more than one area.
9. Click the **Q1** worksheet tab.
10. Click in Cell **B6**. This applies the formatting to cell B6 in the Q1 worksheet.
11. Click the **Q2** worksheet tab.
12. Click in Cell **B6**. This applies the formatting to cell B6 in the Q2 worksheet.
13. Click the **Format Painter** button to deactivate it.
14 **Save** the workbook.

4.5 Alignment and Text Wrapping

When entering data into cells, the default alignment is left-aligned along the bottom for text and right-aligned along the bottom for numbers. Excel supplies many other alignment options from which to choose – left alignment, right alignment, center alignment, as well as horizontal and vertical alignment options.

The alignment options are available on the **Alignment group** on the Home Ribbon:

Alignment commands

Other alignment options are available from within the **Format Cells** dialog box.

✓ Change the Alignment of Data within Cells

1. Make sure the **Lesson4.xlsx** file is active. Switch to the Store Sales worksheet.
2. Select the cell range **C4:F7**.
3. Click the **Center** Alignment Button on the Home Ribbon.

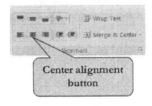

Center alignment button

4. Select the cell range **C3:F3**.
5. Click the **Alignment Dialog Launcher**.
6. In the **Degrees** text box, type **28** to change the orientation of the text to 28 degrees.
7. Click **OK** to close the Format Cells dialog box.
8. Activate the **Yearly Totals** worksheet.
9. Select the cell range **B4:B7**.
10. Click the **Wrap Text** button on the Alignment group on the Ribbon. This wraps the text within a cell so it does not cross adjoining cells or get cut off.
11. Select the cell range **A3:G3**.
12. **Center the text** within each cell.
13. **Save** the active workbook.

4.6 Merging Cells and Centering Text

With Excel's **Merge Cells and Center Text** feature, you can combine the contents of several cells into one **merged** cell. For instance, you may have a lengthy title that spans several cells. The Merge Cells and Center Text feature will combine the extra cells into one large cell and center the text within the new cell. You can change the text alignment by choosing **Left** or **Right** alignment from the Home Ribbon or by choosing additional options from the **Format Cells dialog box**.

Once the cells have been merged, they can be returned to their original state by clicking the **Merge and Center** button with the merged cell selected.

✓ Merge Cells and Center Text

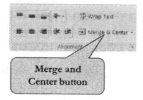

Merge and
Center button

1. Make sure the **Lesson4.xlsx** is active. Select the cell range **B1:F1**.
2. Click the **Merge and Center** button on the Alignment group on the Ribbon. This merges cells B1 to F1 into one cell and centers the text across the range.

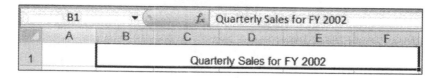

3. **Save** the active workbook.

4.7 Adding Cell Borders

You can separate or outline cells by applying borders (left, right, top or bottom) to the edges of the cells. Border options can be found under the **Borders button** on the Font group on the Home Ribbon or under the **Border tab** of the **Format Cells dialog box**. The Format Cells dialog box contains additional border options such as line style and border color.

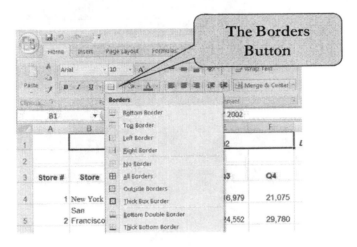

✓ Apply Cell Borders

1. Make sure the **Lesson4.xlsx** file is active. Select the cell range **B9:G9**.
2. Press the **Ctrl + 1** keystroke combination to display the **Format Cells** dialog box.
3. Click the **Border Tab**.
4. Choose the third **Line Style** from the bottom in the second row to select the line style (thickness and type).

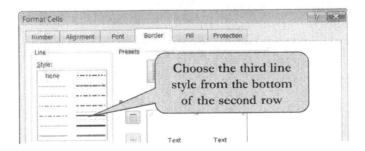

5. Click the Top Border in the **Sample Window**. This applies the line style to the top border.

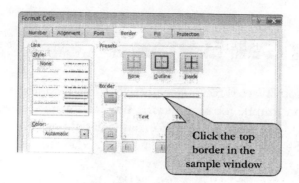

6. Click **OK** and then Enter. A top border has been applied to the selected cell range.
7. Select cell **B1**.
8. Click the **Drop Down Arrow** on the **Borders Button** to see the border choices

9. Apply a **bottom border** to your title.
10. **Save** the active workbook.

4.8 Applying Colors and Shading to Cells

To make a particular cell or cell range stand out, you can apply patterns and background colors to the cells in your worksheet. **Background color options** are located under the **Fill tab** of the Format Cells Dialog box (you can also click the Fill Color button on the Home Ribbon on the Font group then choose the desired background color from the color palette). Additionally, you can change the color of the fonts in your worksheet by changing the **foreground color** of a selected cell or cell range. Excel's **Color Palette** provides a wide variety of colors from which to choose.

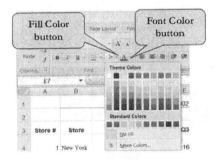

✓ Apply a Background and Font Color to Cells

1. Make sure the **Lesson4.xlsx** file is active. Click in cell **B1**.
2. Display the **Format Cells** dialog box.
3. Click on the **Fill** tab.
4. Click on the **green** color (seventh column, fourth row)). This applies a green background to the cell.

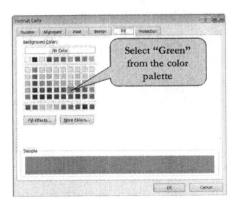

5. Click **OK** to close the **Format Cells** dialog box.
6. Select the cell range **C9:G9**.
7. Click on the arrow on the **Font Color Palette** button ![A] on the Ribbon.
8. Change the **font color to dark blue**.
9. **Save** the current worksheet.

4.9 Applying Cell Styles

Another way to format a cell is to use one of Excel 2007's styles from the **Cell Styles Gallery**. A Cell Style is a collection of formats such as, font type and size, shading, font color, background color, and more. Click the **Cell Styles** button on the styles group on the Home Ribbon to display a variety of pre-defined formats that you can quickly apply to your cells. As you move your mouse pointer over any of the styles in the gallery, the formatting of your worksheet will change to reflect what your cells would look like.

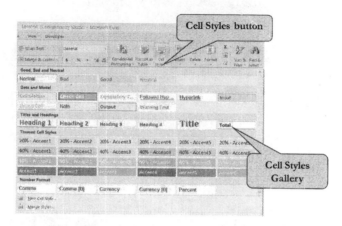

As you work more with Excel, you will most likely develop your own preferred formats for particular worksheets. Rather than manually setting these formats over and over, you can store these formatting options in Excel's **Cell Style Gallery**. You should consider adding any special cell formatting that you plan to use in the future. Cell Styles can be a real time-saver if you find yourself applying the same formatting over and over.

To Apply an Existing Style, select the cells to format. Click the **Cell Styles** button on the Styles Group on the Ribbon and move your mouse pointer over any of the styles to preview how the formatting will look on your worksheet.

✓ Create a Style

1. Make sure the **Lesson4.xlsx** file is active. Click the **Store Sales** worksheet tab.
2. Make **C3** the active cell.
3. Click the arrow on the **Font Color** button on the Home Ribbon to display the Font Color Palette.
4. Choose **Dark Red** (fifth row, sixth column).
5. Open the **Fill Color** Palette.
6. Choose **Gray-25%** from the color palette as shown.

7. Click the **Italics** button on the Home Ribbon to italicize the cell value.
8. Click the **Cell Styles** button on the Styles group on the Home Ribbon to display the Cell Styles gallery.

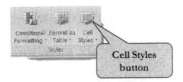

9. Click **New Cell Style** on the bottom of the gallery to display the Style dialog box.
10. Type **My Heading** in the **Style Name** text box.
11. Click **OK** to close the Style dialog box.
12. Select the Cell Range **D3:F3**.
13. Click the **Cell Styles** button on the Ribbon. This displays the Cell Styles gallery.
14. Click on **My Heading** under the **Custom** area.

15. **Save** the active document.

4.10 Hiding and Unhiding Rows and Columns

Sometimes you may wish to remove a row or column from view but not permanently delete it from your worksheet. For instance, you may wish to print out only relevant rows or columns. Excel allows you to temporarily hide a row or column from view using the **Hide command**. When a row or column is hidden, the row heading or column heading disappears from view as well. Hidden cells can still be included in calculations.

To unhide a column or row, you must first select the rows or columns adjacent to the hidden one(s) before using the unhide command

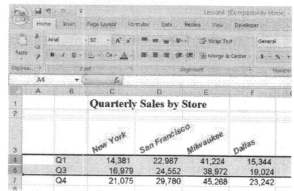

Hidden Row 5 Disappears from View

✓ Hide and Unhide Rows and Columns

1. Make sure the **Lesson4.xlsx** file is active. Click the **Store Sales** tab on the workbook.
2. Select rows **4, 5 and 6**.
3. **Right-click** and choose **Hide** from the menu. Notice that row numbering does not change.

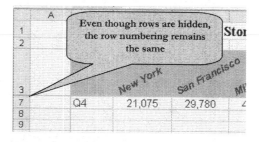

4. Select rows **3 and 7**.
5. **Right-click** and choose **Unhide** from the menu.
6. **Save and Close** the Lesson4 workbook.

4.11 Freezing and Unfreezing Rows and Columns

If you have a large worksheet, you may wish to keep the data labels of your rows and/or columns in view as you scroll. To accomplish this, freeze rows and/or columns in place by using the **Freeze Panes** command on the View Ribbon. The frozen columns or rows will be bordered by a thin black line. When scrolling downward, any rows that are frozen will remain on the top of the screen in view as you scroll. Likewise, as you scroll to the right, any columns that are frozen will remain on the left of the screen in view as you scroll.

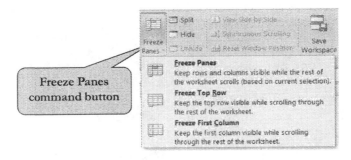

✓ Freeze/Unfreeze Rows or Columns

1. Open the **Films.xlsx** workbook found in your copy of the Course Docs folder.
2. Make **B2** the active cell.
3. Switch to **View commands and tools.**
4. Click the **Freeze Panes** button under the Window group.
5. Click **Freeze Panes.** This Freezes the all rows above B2 and all columns to the left of B2.
6. **Scroll down** to observe the frozen row. Row 1 stays in place as you scroll downwards.
7. Scroll to the right to observe the frozen column. Column A stays in place as you scroll to the right.

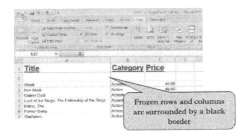

8. Click the **Freeze Panes** button under the Window group and select **Unfreeze Panes.**

4.12 Inserting and Removing Page Breaks

When the data in your worksheet does not fit on one printable page, Excel automatically inserts page breaks, dependent on the page setup of the document (margins, paper size, etc.). The automatic page breaks appear as dashed lines on the worksheet. In the example below, any data after column E and row 50 will print on a separate page. You can adjust these page breaks manually by displaying your worksheet in **Page Break Preview** and then adjusting the page break borders by dragging the thick page break borders to a new location.

You can also insert a **manual page break** in your worksheet by clicking the **Breaks** button on the **Page Layout tab** and then choosing **Insert Page Break** from the menu. This will override the automatic page breaks.

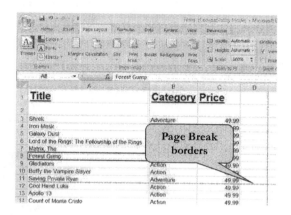

✓ Insert and Remove a Manual Page Break

1. Make sure the **Films.xlsx** file is active. Select **Row 25**.
2. Click the **Page Layout tab** on the Ribbon.
3. Click the **Breaks** button under the Page Setup group. This displays available Breaks commands.

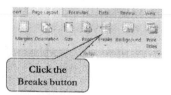

4. Select **Insert Page Break** from the menu to insert a page break below Row 24.
5. Select **Row 50**.
6. Insert a **manual page break**.
7. Press the **Ctrl + Home** keystroke combination to move to cell A1.
8. Click the **Page Layout View button (the center button)** on the lower right hand corner of your screen. This allows you to view your workbook as it will appear when printed.

9. Click the **Zoom Level** button on the lower-right corner of the worksheet window and select **50%**. Click **OK**. Observe the manual page break after row 24.
10. Press the **Page Down** key.
11. Press the **Page Down** key again. Excel moves to the third page of the worksheet.
12. Click **Normal View button (the first button)** on the lower right hand corner of your screen.
13. Select **Row 25**.
14. Click the **Breaks button** and select **Remove Page Break** from the Breaks menu.
15. Click the **Breaks button** and select **Reset All Page Breaks** from the Breaks menu. This removes any additional manual page breaks in the worksheet.
16 **Save and close** the active workbook.

Lesson 5 – Page Setup and Printing

5.1 Adjusting Margins

Margins refer to the amount of white space between the text of the worksheet and the left, right, top and bottom edges of the page. Margins can also be thought of as page boundaries — once the text reaches the boundary of the margin, it wraps to the next line or the next page.

Keep in mind that changing the margins of your document affects every page in your document – not just the active paragraph or page. To modify margins, click the **Margins** button on the Print Layout tab and make your selections.

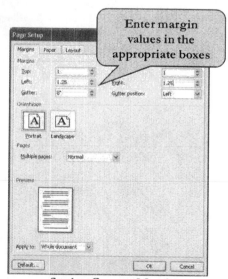

Setting Custom Margins

✓ Create Custom Margins

1. Open the **Lesson5.xlsx** workbook found in your Course Docs folder.
2. From Normal View, click the **Page Layout** tab on the Ribbon.

3. Click the **Margins** button.

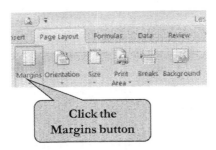

Click the
Margins button

4. Click **Custom Margins** from the list.
5. Double-click in the **Top** margin box, type: **1.5** as shown and then press **Tab**.

6. In the **Bottom** margin box, type: **1.5** and then press **Tab**.
7. In the **Left** margin box, type: **1.5** and then press **Tab**.
8. In the **Right** margin box, type: **1.5**.
9. Under the **Center on Page** area, click the checkbox next to **Horizontally**.
10. Click the **Print Preview** button. This displays the document as it will be printed.
11. Click the **Next Page** button on the Ribbon.
12. Click the **Close Print Preview** button on the Ribbon.
13. Click the **Save** button on the Quick Access toolbar.

5.2   Setting Page Orientation

Microsoft Excel allows you to change the **Page Orientation**. There are two choices of orienation – **Portrait** which prints across the shortest width (taller than longer) of the paper and **Landscape** which prints across the longest width (longer than taller) of the paper.

Portrait

Landscape

✓ Set Page Orientation

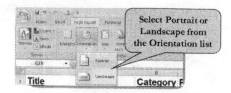

1. Make sure the **Lesson5.xlsx** file is active. Click the **Orientation** button on the Page Setup group.
2. Click **Landscape**.
3. Click the **Page Layout** view button on the lower-right corner of your screen.
4. Drag the **Zoom slider** on the lower-right and corner of your screen to the left to about **50%**. Observe that the page is wider than taller.

5. Click the **Zoom Level box** on the lower-right and corner of your screen and choose **100%** from the Zoom dialog box. Click **OK**.

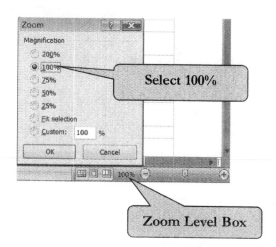

6. Click the **Save** button.

5.3   Setting Paper Size

Y ou may not always be working with the standard paper size of 8 ½" x 11". Luckily, Microsoft Excel can print on many different paper sizes such as legal size (8 ½" x 14"), A4, A3, etc.

The default paper size in Microsoft Excel is is 8 ½" x 11". This is the standard paper size for most documents.

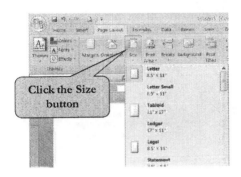

✓ Set a Non-Standard Paper Size

1.   Make sure the **Lesson5.xlsx** file is active. Click the **Page Setup Dialog Launcher** icon. Rather than choose from the Size list, you will set your paper size from the Page Setup dialog box.

2.   Click the **Page** tab.
3.   In the **Orientation** area, click on the **Portrait** radio button.
4.   From the **Paper Size** drop-down list, select **Legal**
5.   Click **OK.**
6.   Drag the **Zoom slider** on the lower-right and corner of your screen to the left to about **25%.** This reduces the size of the viewable area to 50% of the normal size. Observe that the page is displayed longer than the standard paper size.
7.   Click the **Zoom Level box** on the lower-right and corner of your screen and choose **100%** from the Zoom dialog box. Click **OK.**
8.   Click the **Save** button on the Quick Access toolbar.

5.4   Defining a Print Area

Left to its own devices, Excel will print all the data that is in the currently active worksheet. You can however, force Excel to use a defined print area for the worksheet. Start by selecting the cell range that you want to print. Then, click the **Print Area** button under the Page Set up group on the Page Layout Ribbon and choose **Set Print Area** from the list.

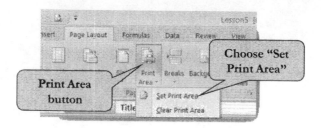

To delete a print area, click the Print Area button and choose **Clear Print Area**.

✓ Define a Print Area

1. Make sure the **Lesson5.xlsx** file is active. Select the cell range **A1:A80**.
2. Click the **Print Area** button on the Page Layout Ribbon and choose **Set Print Area**. This sets A1:A80 as the range of cells to be printed.
3. Press **Ctrl + F2**. This displays the worksheet in Print Preview view.
4. Click the **Close Print Preview** button.
5. Click the **Print Area button** and choose **Clear Print Area**.

5.5 Printing Worksheet Titles

If your worksheet spans several pages, you may wish to repeat one or more rows or columns as titles on each page. For example, if working with an income/expense statement, your first column might contain a category title with each month spanning to the right of your worksheet. You can repeat rows and columns on each page from Sheet tab of the Page Setup dialog box.

✓ Print Rows or Columns on Every Page

1. Make sure the **Lesson5.xlsx** file is active. Click the **Print Titles** button on the Page Layout Ribbon.
2. Click in the **Rows to Repeat at top** text box.

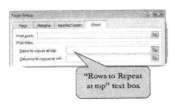

"Rows to Repeat at top" text box

3. Click on the **Collapse Dialog Box** button to the right of the **Rows to repeat at top** text box.
4. Select the row heading for **row 1**.
5. Click the **Display Dialog** Box.
6. Click the **Gridlines** check box in the **Print** area. You can also set gridlines options from the Sheet Options area of the Page Layout Ribbon.
7. Click **OK**.
8. Press **Ctrl + F2**. Excel displays the document as it will be printed.
9. Click the **Next Page** button. Notice the Worksheet title row is displayed on the top of page 2.
10. Click the **Close Print Preview** button.

> **Note:** You can also type in the range of the rows or columns to repeat manually in the appropriate box.

5.6   Forcing a Worksheet to Fit

If you want to reduce the size of data on a printout, you can use the **Scale to Fit** tools on the Page Layout Ribbon. This is especially helpful if your data spans more than one page in width or height and you wish to shrink it so that it fits on one page. Reducing the scale of your printout allows you to fit more rows and columns on each page. Be careful though – reducing the scaling too much can result in a printout that is unreadable.

✓ Force a Worksheet to Fit on a Specified Number of Pages

1. Make sure the **Lesson5.xlsx** file is active. Click the **Width** drop-down arrow under the Scale to Fit group and select **1 Page**. This specifies that the width of the document is to be reduced so that it fits on one page.

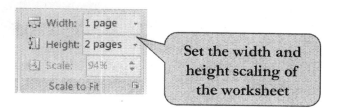

2. Click the **Height** drop-down arrow under the Scale to Fit group and select **2 Pages** as shown above. This specifies that the height of the document is to be reduced so that it fits on two pages.
3. Click the **Microsoft Office** button.
4. Point to **Print** and select **Print Preview**.
5. Click the **Next Page** button. The size of the document has been reduced so that it fits on two pages. You can also press the Page Down or Page Up keys to navigate in Print Preview view.
6. Click the **Close Print Preview** button to return to Page Layout view.

Tip: You can also set worksheet scaling from the Page tab of the Page Setup dialog box

5.7 Inserting Headers and Footers

When you want to automatically print certain information on the top or bottom of every page, you can insert a **Header** or a **Footer** into your document. The information in the header section will appear at the top of every printed page while the information in the footer section will appear at the bottom of every printed page. If your worksheet contains more than one page, you should consider adding a header and/or footer. Creating a header or footer is accomplished by using the **Header/Footer Tab** of the **Page Setup dialog box** or from the **Insert Ribbon**

The Header & Footer Tools Ribbon

Excel comes with several pre-defined headers and footers (page numbers, current date, sheet name, file name, author, etc.) that you can add to your worksheets. You can add your own text in the left, center or right section of the Header or Footer window. The Header and Footer Tools Ribbon contains a set of icons that allow you to insert page numbers, insert total pages, insert the date and time, insert the file name, sheet name or file path, insert a picture from a file and format a picture.

✓ Add a Header and Footer to a Worksheet

1. Make sure the **Lesson5.xlsx** file is active. Click on the **Insert** tab on the Ribbon.
2. Click the **Header & Footer** button under the Text group.

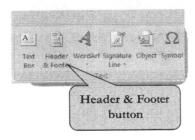

Header & Footer button

3. Click in the **Center Section** Box.
4. Type **Rodney's Video**
5. Click in the **Right Section box** and type your first and last name
6. Click the **Go To Footer** button.

7. Click in the **Right Section box**.
8. Type the word **Page** and then press the space bar.
9. Click the **Page Number** button. This inserts the page number code after the word "Page".

Page Number button

10. Click in the **Left Section box**.
11. Click the **File Path** button. This inserts the path and file name of the document in the left footer section.

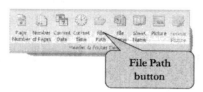

File Path button

12. Select the **File Path code**.

Select the File Path code

&[Path]&[File]
Footer

13. Click the **Home** tab.
14. Select **8** from the **Font Size drop-down list** and click the **Bold** button on the Ribbon.
15. Click the **Design tab** under the Header & Footer tools on the Ribbon.

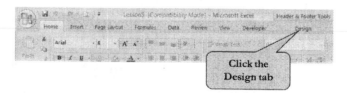

Click the Design tab

16. Click the **Go To Header** button.
17. Highlight the text **Rodney's Video**.
18. Click the **Home** tab.
19. Select **8** from the **Font Size drop-down list** and click the **Bold** button on the Ribbon.
20. Click anywhere in your worksheet.
21. Press **Ctrl + F2** and click the **Zoom** button to zoom in.
22. Click the **Close Print Preview** button.

5.8 Printing a Worksheet

Before you print your worksheet, you may first want to set some **Printer Options**. For instance, you may need to specify which printer to use, the number of copies to be printed, or even designate Excel to print only a specific range of your document. Printer options may vary, depending on the type of printer being used.

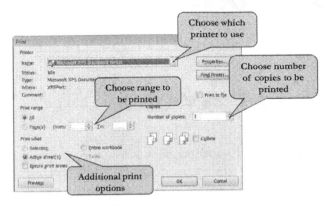

✓ Set Printer Options & Print a Worksheet

1. Make sure the **Lesson5.xlsx** file is active. Click the **Microsoft Office** button and then click **Print**. You can also press the Ctrl + P keystroke combination to display the Print dialog box.
2. In the **Copies** box, enter 3 as shown.

3. In the Pages box of the Print range area, type **1-3**.

4. Click the **Cancel** button.
5. **Save** any changes and close the workbook

Lesson 6 – Formulas and Functions

6.1   Relative References

As you have seen, when you copy a formula to a new location, the formula automatically adjusts to its new location. For example, suppose you have the following formula in cell D3:   **=B3 * C3.** If you copy this formula down to cell D4, Excel will automatically change this formula to read: **=B4 * C4.**

This is called a **Relative Cell Reference**. When a formula is copied to a new location, it will reference the new cells based on their **relative location** to the original cells containing the formula. Relative Cell References are the default type of references in Excel.

✓ Use Relative References

1.   Open the **Lesson6** workbook found in your Course Docs folder.
2.   Click the **Income Statement** worksheet tab.
3.   Set cell H5 as the active cell.
4.   Apply bold formatting to cell H5.
5.   Type: **Total**.
6.   Click in cell **H6**.
7.   Type in the following formula: **=B6+C6+D6+E6+F6+G6** and then press **Enter.**
8.   Make **H6** the active cell.
9.   Click on the lower right **Fill Handle** of cell H6 and drag downwards to cell **H10**. Release the mouse button. This copies the formula in H6 to cells H7 to H10.
10. Click in cell **H6** then click in cell **H7.** Observe the formula bar. Notice the formula is automatically updated to its new location.

6.2 Absolute References

There are times when you do not want the cell reference to change when you copy or move cells to a new location. In such a case, you would need to enter the cell reference as an **Absolute Reference**. Absolute cell references are preceded by a $ (dollar sign) in front of both the column reference and the cell reference.

As an example, suppose you have the following formula in cell D3: **=B3 * C3**

If you copy this formula down to cell D4, you would have: **=B4 * C3**

The first part of this formula (B4) is a **relative** cell reference, which automatically adjusted to its new location. The second part of the formula (C3) or the **absolute** cell reference did not change after being copied — it still refers to the original cell location of C3.

✓ Use Absolute References

1. Make sure the **Lesson6.xlsx** file is active. Switch to the Time Sheet worksheet.
2. Make C4 the active cell.
3. Enter the following formula: **=B4 * H1** and then press **Enter**. Since the pay rate does not change, you will make this reference an Absolute Reference.
4. Select cell **C4**.
5. Click on the lower right **Fill Handle** and drag downwards to cell **C12**. Release the mouse button. This copies the formula in C4 to cells C7 to C12.
6. Click in cell **C6** and observe the formula bar. Notice that reference to the pay rate in cell H1 did not change and is still H1. However, the relative reference to cell B4 automatically updated to the new location.
7. **Save** the workbook.

6.3   Mixed References

In this lesson, you will work with a combination of Absolute and Relative cell references.

You can also use a combination of Absolute and Relative cell references in your formulas. This is called a **Mixed Reference**. You have the choice of making either the column or the row absolute, such as $D3 (column is absolute, row is relative) or F$6 (column is relative, row is absolute). The row or column preceded by the $ (the absolute reference) would not change when copied or moved, whereas the row or column reference not preceded by the $ (the relative reference) would automatically adjust to its new location.

As an example, suppose you have the following formula in cell D3: **=$B3 * C3**. If you copy this formula down to cell E4, you would have: **=$B4 * D4**

The $B4 portion of the formula contains a **Mixed Reference** — the row adjusts automatically to the new location (from row 3 to row 4) but the column address will continue to reference column B.

✓Use Mixed References

1. Make sure the **Lesson6.xlsx** file is active. Switch to the **Estimate worksheet**.
2. Click in cell **C7**.
3. Multiply the monthly estimate in cell B7 by 12 months.
4. Press **Enter**.
5. Select cell **C7**.
6. Copy the formula in C7 to cells D7 and E7.
7. Select the cell range **C7:E7**.
8. Copy the formulas to the cell range C7 to E11.

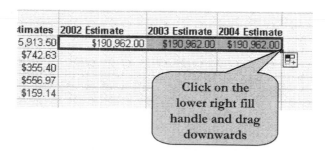

9. Click in cell **E9** and observe the formula bar. Notice that in the first part of the original formula ($B7), the formula still references column B but the column has adjusted the row reference to the new location.
10. **Save** the active workbook.

6.4 Copying Formulas

We have been working so far with copying formulas to adjacent cells. You can also copy formulas to non-adjacent cells using the **Copy & Paste** method. The cell references will automatically update depending on the type of cell reference – Relative, Absolute or Mixed.

1. Make sure the **Lesson6.xlsx** file is active. Switch to the Income Statement worksheet.
2. Make **H6** the **active** cell.
3. Press **Ctrl + C** to place the contents of cell H6 on the Clipboard.
4. Select the cell range **H16:H19**.
5. Press **Ctrl + V**. This inserts the formula into the new cell range (H16:H19). Observe the data as illustrated.

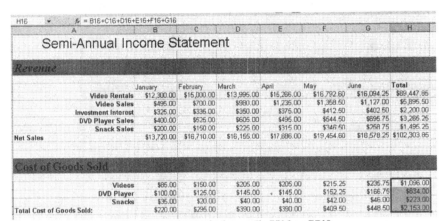

The Formula copied to cells H16 to H19

6. Select the cell range **H28:H35**.
7. **Insert the formula** into the new cell range (H28:H35).
8. **Save** the active workbook.

6.5 MIN, MAX, COUNT and AVERAGE Functions

I n an earlier lesson, you learned how to enter the **SUM** function using the **AutoSum** button. There are also several other functions available using the AutoSum feature. These are:

- **SUM**   Totals the values in a selected range
- **AVERAGE**   Computes the average of the values in a selected range
- **MIN**   Returns the lowest value in a selected range
- **MAX**   Returns the highest value in a selected range
- **COUNT NUMBERS**   Totals the number of cells with values in a selected range

✓ Enter Additional Functions using AutoSum

1. Make sure the **Lesson6.xlsx** file is active. Make cell **I5** the active cell and **apply bold** formatting.
2. Type: **Average**.
3. Press **Enter**.
4. Select the cell range **B6:G6**. As you did not want your Totals column to be included in your average, you must manually select the desired range you wish included in your formula.
5. Click the **arrow to the right of the AutoSum button** on the Home Ribbon.
6. Click on **Average** as shown.

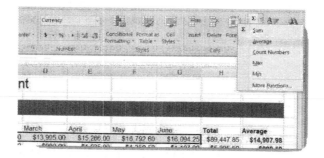

7. Select cell **I6**.
8. Click the **Fill Handle** on cell I6 and drag downwards to cell I11.

	January	February	March	April	May	June	Total	Average
Video Rentals	$12,300.00	$15,000.00	$13,995.00	$15,266.00	$16,792.60	$16,094.25	$89,447.85	=AVERAGE(B6:G6)
Video Sales	$495.00	$700.00	$980.00	$1,235.00	$1,358.50	$1,127.00	$5	AVERAGE(number1, [number2],
Investment Interest	$325.00	$335.00	$350.00	$375.00	$412.50	$402.50	$2,200.00	
DVD Player Sales	$400.00	$525.00	$605.00	$495.00	$544.50	$695.75	$3,265.25	
Snack Sales	$200.00	$150.00	$225.00	$315.00	$346.50	$258.75	$1,495.25	
	$13,720.00	$16,710.00	$16,155.00	$17,686.00	$19,454.60	$18,578.25	$102,303.85	

Average Function for Cells B6:G6

✓ Entering Functions Manually

In addition to using the **AutoSum** button for the above functions, you can also type in these functions manually, directly into the desired cell. The format is:

=Function name, cell range surround by parentheses.

For example, if you wanted to find the **Average** from the cell range B3 to B8, you would enter the following formula in cell B9: **=AVERAGE(B3:B8)**

To include non-contiguous cells in a formula, separate each cell or range by a comma. For example, if you wanted to find the **Average** for cells B3:B8, D3:D8 and cell F5, the formula would read:
=AVERAGE(B3:B8, D3:D8, F5)

6.6 The Insert Function Button

I n addition to the five functions discussed in the last section, there are many other pre-defined functions available to you in Excel such as: financial functions, logical functions, date and time functions and statistical functions, just to name a few of the available categories.

To access Excel's pre-defined functions, click the **Insert Function Button,** located to the left of the Formula Bar or on the **Formulas Ribbon.** The Insert Function dialog box allows you to choose from a wide array of handy functions.

Once you have chosen the desired function, the **Function Arguments** dialog box opens, prompting you for each argument. You can type the cell address directly into the argument boxes or you can click the **Collapse Dialog Box** button and select the cell or cell range to be included in the arguments.

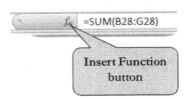

Insert Function button

✓ Enter a Function Using the Insert Function Feature

1. Make sure the **Lesson6.xlsx** file is active. Press **Ctrl + G** and type in **I28** in the Reference box. Press **Enter.** This makes I28 the active cell.
2. Open the Insert Function dialog box.

3. Select **Statistical** from the **Select a Category** combo box.

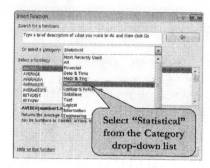

4. In the **Select a Function** list box, highlight **AVERAGE**.

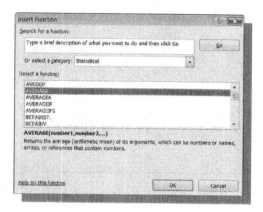

5. Click **OK**.
6. In the **Number1** text box, type in **B28:G28**. Click **OK**. This provides the cell range B28:G28 as the function argument (the range to be included in the calculation).

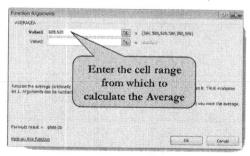

7. **Copy the formula** to the cell range I28 to I35.
8. Click the Microsoft Office button and select **Close** from the menu. **Save** any changes.

Lesson 7 – Modifying Workbooks

7.1 Adding and Deleting Worksheets

When creating a new workbook, Excel provides you with three default worksheets, named Sheet 1, Sheet 2 and Sheet 3. To insert additional worksheets, use the **Insert Worksheet** icon at the end of the sheet tabs. Excel will insert a new worksheet at the very end of the sheet tab. To specify where you want to insert a new sheet, click on the **worksheet tab** of the sheet to the left of which you want to insert a new sheet, **right-click** on the active sheet tab and then choose **Insert** from the menu.

To delete a worksheet, click the **Delete arrow** on the Home Ribbon and choose **Delete Sheet**. Excel will delete the active worksheet.

✓ Insert and Delete a Worksheet

1. Open the **Lesson7.xlsx** workbook found in your Course Docs folder.
2. **Right-click** on the **Time Sheet** worksheet tab and select **Insert** from the menu. Click **OK**. This inserts a new worksheet to the left of the Time Sheet worksheet.
3. Click the **Insert Worksheet icon** at the end of the worksheet tabs.
4. **Right-click** on the **Sheet 2** worksheet tab and select **Delete** from the menu. This removes the Sheet 2 worksheet from the workbook.
5. Activate the Estimate worksheet.
6. Click the **arrow** on the **Delete button** on the Home Ribbon and choose **Delete Sheet** from the menu. This displays a warning box informing you that data may exist in the worksheet.
7. Press the **Delete** button.

7.2 Copying Worksheets

You can copy an entire worksheet in Excel, including all of its data and formatting by using the **Move or Copy Sheet** command from the menu. Excel provides a **sequential number** after the worksheet name to allow you to distinguish between the new sheet and the original sheet. For example, if you copied a sheet named June Sales, the new copied sheet would be named June Sales (2). You can copy a worksheet to any workbook that is open, to the current workbook or to a new workbook file. You can also copy a worksheet manually by pressing and holding the **Ctrl** key and then dragging the worksheet tab with your mouse to the new location.

✓ Copy a Worksheet

1. Make sure the **Lesson7.xlsx file** is active. Activate the Time Sheet worksheet.
2. Right-click and choose **Move or Copy Sheet** from the menu.
3. Select **Lesson7.xls** under the **To book:** combo box.
4. Select **Time Sheet** from the **Before sheet:** list box. This sets the position of the new sheet to the left of the Time Sheet worksheet.

5. Click the **Create a copy** checkbox as shown above.
6. Click **OK**. This closes the Move or copy dialog box and makes a copy of the Time Sheet worksheet.

7.3   Renaming Worksheets

Excel by default provides the generic names of Sheet 1, Sheet 2 and Sheet 3, etc. to worksheets. To rename a worksheet, **double-click on the tab** of the worksheet to receive the new name and then type the desired name. Another way to rename a worksheet is to **right-click on the worksheet tab**, select **Rename** from the menu, and then type the new name.

✓ Rename a Worksheet

1. Make sure the **Lesson7.xlsx file** is active. Double-click the **Time Sheet (2)** worksheet tab.
2. Type **John's Time Sheet**
3. Press **Enter.**
4. Right-click on the **Time Sheet** worksheet tab.
5. Choose **Rename** from the pop-up menu.
6. Type **Melissa's Time Sheet** and then press **Enter.**

The Renamed Worksheets

7. **Save** the worksheet.

7.4   Repositioning Worksheets

After you begin creating worksheets in your workbook, you may decide that the worksheets are not in the order that you would like. You can rearrange the worksheets in your workbook by clicking the tab of the worksheet you would like to move and then dragging it to the new location. As you drag, a small black arrow appears marking the new location of the sheet should you release the mouse button.

✓ Reposition a Worksheet

1. Make sure the **Lesson7.xlsx** file is active. Click and hold the left mouse button on the **Sheet 1** worksheet tab.
2. Drag **Sheet 1** until the black arrow is to the right **Melissa's Time Sheet.**

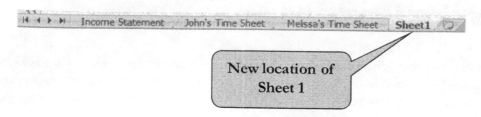

New location of Sheet 1

3. Release the mouse button.

Tip: You can also move worksheets from the Move or Copy dialog box.

7.5 Grouping Worksheets

Excel allows you to work on several worksheets simultaneously by **grouping** them together. When worksheets are grouped, any formatting, data entry or changes you make to the active sheet are made to every sheet in the group. Grouping sheets is a quick way to apply formatting to or delete several sheets at once. When multiple worksheets are grouped together, [Group] appears in the title bar on top of the worksheet window.

✓ Group and Ungroup Worksheets

1. Make sure the **Lesson7.xlsx** file is active and make John's Timesheet the active worksheet.
2. Double-click in cell **A1**.
3. Highlight the words: **Melissa Edwards**.
4. Type: **John Browne** and then press **Enter**.
5. Press and hold the **Ctrl** key and click on the **Melissa's Time Sheet** tab. This adds the Melissa's Time Sheet worksheet to the group. Notice that the worksheet tab is highlighted in white and the word [Group] appears in the Title Bar.
6. Click in cell **J1** and type in today's date. Press Enter This enters the date into both worksheets.
7. Select the cell range **A4:C12** and change the font size to **12**.
8. Center the text in the selected cell range.
9. Click on the **Income Statement** worksheet tab.
10. Click on the **Melissa's Time Sheet** worksheet tab and observe the changes. The changes that you made in "John's Time Sheet" worksheet were also made in "Melissa's Time Sheet" worksheet.
11. **Save** the active workbook.

7.6   Changing Worksheet Tab Colors

Excel provides the option of **applying colors** to your worksheet tabs. This can be useful if you have a large workbook comprised of many worksheets. You might want to give each worksheet in a particular group a different color. The tab color only appears when the worksheet is not the active worksheet.

✓ Change the Worksheet Tab Color

1. Make sure the **Lesson7.xlsx** file is active. Make John's Timesheet the active worksheet.
2. Add the Melissa's Time Sheet worksheet to the group.
3. Click the **Format** button under the **Cells group** and point to **Tab Color**. This displays the Format Tab Color Palette.
4. Choose **Red** from the color palette (second color in the Standard Colors area).
5. Click the **Income Statement** worksheet tab. This ungroups the worksheets and makes the Income Statement worksheet the active sheet.
6. **Save** your changes and **close** the workbook file.

7.7   Using 3-D Formulas & References

When you want to create a formula which uses data from several worksheets, you create a **3-D Formula**. A 3-D Formula is created using **3-D References**, that is to say, references to cells in a different worksheet. To create a 3-D Reference, the format is:

'Sheet Name'!Cell Name

For example, suppose you have three sheets named **2000, 2001 and Yearly Totals**. In the Yearly Totals sheet, you want to calculate the sum of the values in cell C18 from both the 2000 and 2001 sheets. Thus, your formula in the Yearly Totals worksheet would be:

='2001'!C18 + '2000'!C18

To use a function such as **SUM, AVERAGE,** etc. in your 3-D formula, the format is:

=SUM('Sheet1:Sheet2'!C12:C35)

You can create your 3-D formula yourself by typing it into the cell or you can manually select the appropriate worksheets and cells to include in your formula.

✓ Create a 3-D Formula

In this exercise, you will first create a formula using the grouping method and then a formula by manually selecting the cell range in each sheet to be included in the formula. Using the Grouping method, you need only select the cell range in one of the grouped sheets.

1. Make sure the **Lesson7.xlsx** file is active. Open the **IncomeStatement** worksheet.
2. Make the **Semi-Annual** worksheet the active worksheet
3. In cell **B7**, type: **=Sum(**
4. Click the **Q1** tab to switch to the Q1 Worksheet
5. Group the Q1 & Q2 Worksheets
6. Select the cell range **B6:D6**
7. Click in the **Formula Bar** after **D6** and type: **)** This completes the formula.
8. Press **Enter**
9. Click in cell **B7**. Observe the 3-D formula.
10. Click in cell **B8** and type: **=**
11. Click the **Q1** Tab
12. Click in cell **E7**
13. Click in the **Formula Bar** after **E7** and type: **+**
14. Switch to the Q2 Worksheet.
15. Activate cell E7 in the Q2 worksheet.
16. Click in the **Formula bar** after **E7** and press **Enter**
17. **Copy the formula** to cells B9:B12.
18. **Save** the Active workbook.
19. **Close** the workbook.

Lesson 8 – Working with Charts

8.1 Creating a Chart

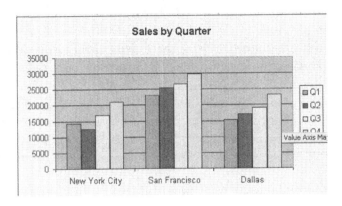

A **chart** is a graphical representation of data and is an effective way to illustrate relationships and trends in data. Charts can be powerful tools that provide data analysis and data comparisons.

Excel can create a wide variety of charts — bar charts, line charts, pie charts, column charts, etc. and Excel 2007 makes creating charts easy with new charting tools. To insert a chart, select the data you want to include in your chart, click the chart type button on the Insert Ribbon and then choose the chart type you want from the gallery.

✓ Create a Chart

1. Open the **Lesson8.xlsx** workbook found in your Course Docs folder.
2. Click on the **Sheet 1** tab.
3. Select the cell range **A4:E7**.
4. Click the **Insert** tab on the Ribbon.
5. Click the **Column button** on the Charts group to display a gallery of all Column Chart types.

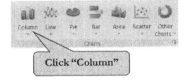

6. Click the **Clustered Column** chart type (the first selection under the 2-D Column category).

Click the "Clustered Column" chart type

8.2   Moving a Chart

When you insert a chart in another worksheet, the chart is embedded and can be moved and resized like a standard graphical object. Most of the time, you will not be satisfied with the placement of the chart in the worksheet and will want to move it to a more desirable location. In order to move a chart, you must first activate it by clicking on the chart's white area or on the border of the chart object. Do not click on an object such as the plot area (the gray section) or a data series because you will select that particular area rather than the entire chart. Once the chart is activated, click inside the chart area, hold down your mouse button and drag the chart to the new location.

Another option for moving a chart is using the **Cut and Paste** method. Select the chart and click the **Cut** button on the Home Ribbon (or press Ctrl + X). Then, select the cell where you wish to paste your chart and click the **Paste** button on the Home Ribbon (or press Ctrl + V).

✓ Move a Chart by Dragging

1. Make sure the **Lesson8.xlsx** file is active. Click anywhere on the **White Chart Area** and hold down your left mouse button.
2. Drag the chart until the left corner of the chart's border (which appears as you drag) rests in cell **A12**

3. Release the mouse button.
4. Click the **Save** button.

8.3 Resizing a Chart

You can change the size of an embedded chart by holding your mouse pointer over any of the chart's sizing handles until the pointer transforms into a double arrow. Then, drag either inwards or outwards, depending on whether you want to decrease or increase the size of the chart. As you drag, you will see a dark bordered outline which represents the size of chart.

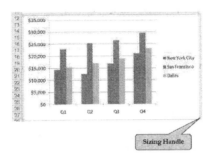

✓ Resize a Chart

1. Make sure the **Lesson8.xlsx** file is active. Click anywhere on the **White Chart Area**.
2. Position your mouse pointer over the **lower right sizing handle** until the pointer transforms into a double arrow.
3. **Click and drag** the chart **outward and down** until the lower right edge of the chart is **flush with cell G33**.

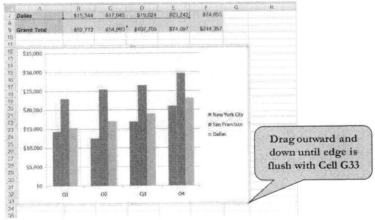

4. Release the mouse button.
5. Save the workbook.

8.4   Changing the Layout and Style

A fter creating your chart, three Ribbons appear under Chart Tools when the chart is selected: **Design, Layout** and **Format**, from where you can format your chart, apply various styles and change the chart layout.

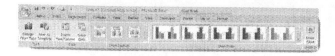

From the **Design Ribbon**, you can apply various predefined chart layouts and chart styles as well as change the chart type and modify the existing chart data. There are a wide variety of chart styles both in 2-D and 3-D formats that you can apply from the Chart Styles group on the Ribbon. Click the **More button** to display a gallery of all available chart styles.

For each chart type, you can also apply a preset layout from the **Chart Layouts** group. Again, clicking the More button on the Chart Layouts group will display a gallery of all available layouts.

✓ Change the Layout and Style of a Chart

1. Make sure the **Lesson8.xlsx** file is active. **Click** on the **border** of the chart. This selects the chart and displays the Design, Layout and Format Ribbons.
2. Click the **Design** tab under **Chart Tools** on the Ribbon.
3. On the **Chart Layouts** group, click the **third thumbnail** as shown.

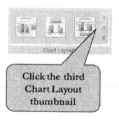

Click the third
Chart Layout
thumbnail

4. Click the **More** button on the **Chart Styles** group.

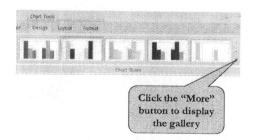

Click the "More"
button to display
the gallery

5.   Click the **last style** in the **last row** (Style 48).
6.   On the **Chart Layouts** group, click the **first thumbnail**.
7.   Click the **Save** button on the Quick Access toolbar.

8.5   Labeling Chart Elements

After creating your chart, you may wish to customize the various elements of your chart, depending on the chart layout you have chosen. Labeling a chart element inserts a small text box on or near the chart element. For instance, you may wish to display or reposition a chart title, axis titles, the chart legend or add data labels. To add or modify a chart element, click the **Layout tab** under Chart Tools, click the button for the label you want to add or modify on the Labels area and then make your selection.

You can then format the actual text of the labels by clicking inside the text box, drag selecting the existing text and then typing your changes.

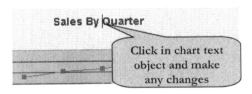

✔ Add/Modify a Chart's Labels and Change Chart Text

1.   Make sure the **Lesson8.xlsx** file is active. Click on the border of the chart.
2.   Click the **Layout tab** under Chart Tools.
3.   Click the **Chart Title** button on the Ribbon and choose **Centered Overlay Title** from the menu.

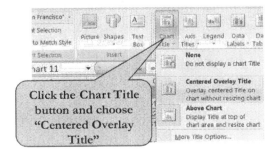

4.   Click the **Chart Title** button again on the Ribbon and choose **Above Chart** from the menu.
5.   Select the text in the **Chart Title** box and type: **Sales by Store** as shown.

Sales by Store

6.   Click the **Axis Titles** button on the Ribbon, point to **Primary Horizontal Axis Title** and choose **Title Below Axis** from the menu.
7.   Select the text in the **X-Axis Title** box, type: **Quarter**.
8.   Click the **Axis Titles** button on the Ribbon, point to **Primary Vertical Axis Title,** and choose **Horizontal Title** from the menu.
9.   Select the text in the **Value axis box** and type: **Sales**.
10. Click the **Data Labels** button on the Ribbon and click **Outside End** from the menu. This inserts the data values above the data series.
11. Click the **lower-right sizing handle** and drag to the right and downward until the right edge rests in cell **H34**
12. **Save** the workbook.

8.6   Formatting Chart Text

You can format any text object on your chart, such as the chart title and chart axis labels using the formatting techniques that you have already learned. You can change the text or apply various formatting such as bold, italics, font size, font type, text alignment, and colors and patterns. You can use the **Mini-Toolbar** that displays when you right-click on highlighted text or any of the commands on the Font group on the Home Ribbon.

You can use the **Format Object dialog box** that allows you to apply a wide variety of formatting from one location. Right-click the object and choose Format [Selected Object] from the menu. Click the desired tab in the left pane and make your selections.

✓ Format Chart Text

1.   Make sure the **Lesson8.xlsx** file is active. **Right-click** any of the values on the Value Axis (the vertical axis on the left) and select **12** from the Font Size drop-down list on the Mini-Toolbar.

Click "12" in the Font Size list on the Mini-Toolbar

2. Click the **Sales By Store** text object on top of the chart.
3. Click the **Home tab** on the Ribbon.
4. Click the **Font Size** drop-down list and select **24**.
5. Click the **Font Color** button on the Ribbon and click the **Yellow** color swatch under Standard Colors.
6. Click the **Quarter** text object.
7. Click the **Font Size** drop-down list and select **14**.
8. Click the **Sales** text object.
9. Click the **Font Size** drop-down list and select **14**.
10. Right-click on the Chart Title (Sales by Store) and click **Format Chart Title** from the menu.
11. Click on the **Border Color** tab.
12. Click the **Solid Line** radio button.
13. Click the **Color** button and choose **Orange** from the Theme color category.

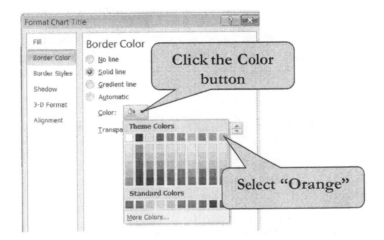

14. Click **Close**.
15. Click anywhere in the worksheet to deactivate the text box.

8.7   Formatting Chart Elements

From the **Format tab**, you can apply formatting such as fill color and (solid, gradient, picture or texture) and borders as well as visual effects such as shadows, reflection, glow, and bevel to the individual elements of your chart. In order to do so, you must first select the object and then choose the formatting you wish to apply. For instance, if you wanted to change the fill color for one of the bars for a specific data series, you would select one of the bars, click the Shape Fill button on the Ribbon and choose the desired color from the color palette.

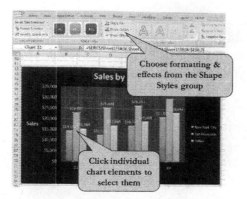

Use the **Shape Fill, Shape Outline or Shape Effects** buttons on the Shape Styles group to apply effects to your chart shapes. The Shape Styles gallery also includes some interesting effects. To add effects to the text on your chart, the **Text Fill, Text Outline or Text Effects** buttons on the WordArt group.

Another handy way to format chart elements is by using the Format Selection button on the Design Ribbon. When clicked, the **Format Object dialog box** appears. Here you can apply multiple format settings.

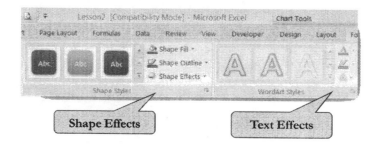

✓ Apply Formats to Chart Elements

1. Make sure the **Lesson8.xlsx** file is active. Click on the border of the chart.
2. Click the **Format tab** under Chart Tools.
3. **Click** any of the values on the Value Axis (the vertical axis) and click the **Format Selection** button under the Current Selection group.

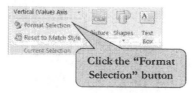

4. Click the **Number** category in the left pane.
5. In the **Category** box in the right pane, select **Number** as shown. This Changes the number formatting of the data series from Currency to Number.

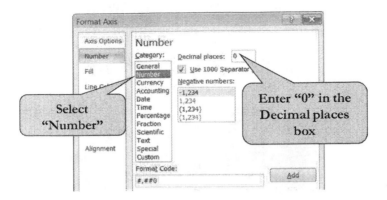

6.   In the **Decimal places** box, type: **0**. Click **Close**.
7.   With the value series still selected, click the **More** button on the **WordArt Styles** gallery.
8.   Click the gallery style in the fourth row, second column.

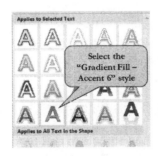

9.   Click on the **Sales text box**.
10. Click the **More button** on the Shape Styles gallery.

11. Click the blue Shape Style in the **last row, second column** (Intense Effect – Accent 1).
12. Click on the **Quarter text box**.
13. Click the first **Shape Style** in the Shapes Gallery on the Ribbon. The most recently used style is displayed first in the Shape Style gallery.

14. Click on any of the **orange bars** for **New York City** (the leftmost bar in each group).

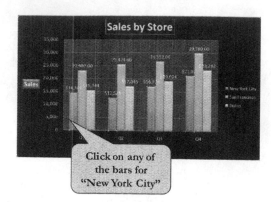

15. Click the **Shape Fill** button on the Shapestyles group and click the **Purple** color swatch under the Standard Colors category.
16. Click on any of the **orange bars** for **San Francisco** (the center bar in each group).
17. Click the **More button** on the Shape Styles gallery.
18. Click the red Shape Style in the **last row, third column** (Intense Effect – Accent 2).
19. Click on the **dark gray plot area** of the chart.

20. Click the **Shape Effects** button on the Shape Styles group.
21. Point to **Glow** and click the glow style in the last row, last column.

22. Click the **Save** button on the Quick Access toolbar.

8.8 Changing the Chart Type

E xcel offers many different chart types to aid you in communicating different types of information. Once your chart is created, you can change the type of chart (to a pie chart, line chart, area chart, etc.). To change the chart type, click the **Change Chart Type** button on the Type group under **Design tab** under Chart Tools to display the Chart Type dialog box. From there, you can choose from a wide array of chart types.

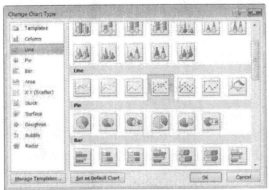

Change Chart Type dialog box

✓ Change the Chart Type:

1. Make sure the **Lesson8.xlsx** file is active. Click anywhere on the chart.
2. Click the **Design tab** on the Ribbon.
3. Click the **Change Chart Type** button on the Type group as shown.

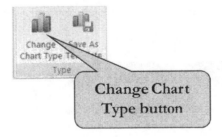

Change Chart Type button

4. Click **Line** in the left pane.
5. Click the **fourth** chart type from the left in the right pane in the **Line category (Line with markers)**

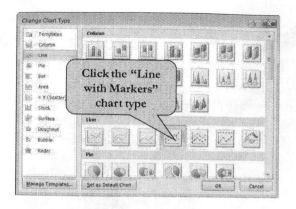

6. Click **OK**.
7. Click the **Change Chart Type** button on the Type group.
8. Click **Bar** in the left pane.
9. Click the **first** chart type from the left in the right pane in the Bar category (**Clustered Bar**)
10. Click **OK**.
11. Click the **Layout** tab on the Ribbon. This switches to chart layout tools and commands.
12. Click the **Data Labels** button in the Labels group and select **None**.
13. Click the **Save** button.

8.9 Showing and Hiding Gridlines

Gridlines are horizontal or vertical lines displayed in the plot area that help you to visualize the value point values in a chart. There are two types of gridlines: **Major gridlines and Minor gridlines**. Major gridlines are displayed at each value on an axis while minor gridlines occur between the values of an axis. To display or hide gridlines, click the **Gridlines** button on the Axes group under the Layout tab.

Depending on the chart style, gridlines can help improve the readability of a chart; however, they should be using sparingly so as not to make your chart appear too cluttered.

✓ Modify Chart Gridlines

1. Make sure the **Lesson8.xlsx** file is active. Click anywhere on the chart.
2. Click the **Layout tab** on the Ribbon.
3. Click the **Gridlines button** on the Axes group on the Ribbon as shown.

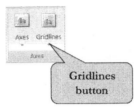

4. Point to **Primary Horizontal Gridlines** and choose **Major & Minor Gridlines**.
5. Click the **Gridlines button** on the Ribbon, point to Point to **Primary Vertical Gridlines** and choose **Major & Minor Gridlines**.
6. Click the **Gridlines button** on the Ribbon, point to Point to **Primary Vertical Gridlines** and choose **Major Gridlines**.

8.10 Customizing Axes

For most charts, data is plotted along the **horizontal (X) axis** and along the **vertical (Y)** axis (3-D charts contain a (Z) axis as well). **Categories** are generally plotted on the horizontal axis and **values** are plotted on the vertical axis. Thus, the x-axis is referred to as the **category axis** and the y-axis is referred to as the **value axis**. You have already seen that you can change various formatting options such as font type, color and size, alignment of text, formatting of numbers, patterns, etc. of both category and value axis data.

When you create a chart, Excel automatically creates a default scale for the horizontal and vertical axis. Sometimes, the default scale is not ideal and your chart will prove difficult to read. The Axis command button on the Layout group allows you to display values in thousands, millions, etc. Additionally, you can set the minimum and maximum values for the value axis, as well as the major and minor units of measurement (you will need to turn on minor gridlines as you learned in the last lesson for the minor gridlines to display) from the Format Axis dialog box.

If axis readability is an issue, you may wish to also consider changing the axis alignment from the Format Axis dialog box.

Format Axis Dialog Box

✓ Format the Category and Value Axis

1. Make sure the **Lesson8.xlsx** file is active. Click anywhere on the chart.
2. Click the **Design tab** on the Ribbon.
3. Click the **Change Chart Type** button on the Type group.

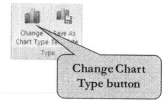

Change Chart
Type button

4. Click **Column** in the left pane.
5. Click the **first thumbnail** in the column category (Clustered Column) and then click **OK.**
6. Click the **Layout tab** on the Ribbon.
7. Click the **Axes button** on the Axes group on the Ribbon as shown.

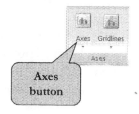

Axes
button

8. Point to **Primary Vertical Axis** and click **Show Axis in Thousands**.
9. Click the **Axes button** on the Axes group again.
10. Point to **Primary Vertical Axis** and click **Show Default Axis**.
11. Click on any of the values for the **Vertical Value Axis**.

12. Click the **Format Selection** button on the Current Selection group as shown.

13. Click **Axis Options** in the left pane.
14. Click the **Fixed** button next to **Maximum**.
15. Change the **Maximum** to **30000**.

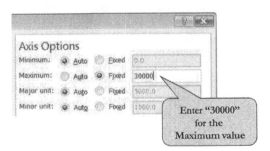

16. Click the **Fixed** radio button next to Major Unit and change the **Major Unit** to **10000**.
17. Click **Alignment** in the left pane.
18. In the **Custom Angle** box, type: **20**
19. Click **Close.**
20. Click the **Save** button.

8.11 Creating a Pie Chart

Pie Charts show the relative size of parts in a whole. Each data series in a pie chart has a unique color (or pattern) and the data will be sorted with largest numbers appearing first. Pie charts have no x-axis or y-axis and have only one data series. Because of this, your data values should be arranged in one column or one row, with an optional column or row of category names.

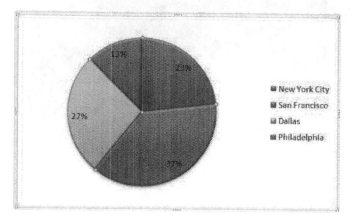

You can consider using a pie chart when:

- You have only a few numbers to chart (you should not have more than seven categories).
- You have only one data series to plot
- You don't have any negative or zero values
- Your data series does not include many low numbers (they will be too small to compare)
- You want to show how each value in your series contributes to the whole

Once your pie chart is created, you can then rotate the slices for different perspectives or pull individual slices out of the chart to draw attention to them. Use the Layout, Data Labels or More Data Labels options to specify the labeling of the pie slices.

✓ Create a Pie Chart

1. Make sure the **Lesson8.xlsx** file is active. Click the **Sheet 2** tab on the bottom of the worksheet.
2. Select the cell range **A4:B7**.
3. Click the **Insert** tab on the Ribbon.
4. Click the **Pie** button on the Charts group and choose the first selection under the **3-D Pie category** as shown.

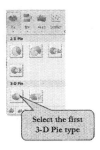

Select the first
3-D Pie type

5. Click the **Layout** tab on the Ribbon.
6. Click the **Data Labels** button on the Labels group and click **More Data Label Options** from the menu.
7. Click **Label Options** in the left pane.
8. Click on the **Percentage** checkbox.

Click the
Percentage box
to check it

9. Click to uncheck the **Value** checkbox.
10. Click the **Center** radio button under the Label Position category.
11. Click **Close**.
12. Click on the **Pie Slice** for **San Francisco** (the red-colored slice).
13. Click and drag downward about ½-inch.

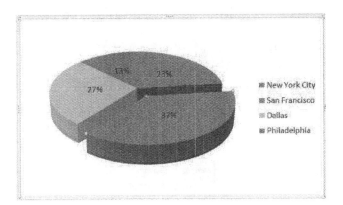

14. Click on the **Chart Title** button on the Labels group and click **Above Chart** from the menu.
15. Select the text in the Chart Title text box and type: **Yearly Sales by Store** in the **Chart Title**.
16. Click in the white chart area and **drag** until the top left corner of the chart is in cell **A10**.
17. Click the **Save** button.

8.12 Changing a Chart's Source Data

As you add additional columns or rows of information to your worksheet or remove data that is no longer relevant, you will need to modify the **source data** for your chart. The source data consists of the cell references of the underlying data upon which a chart is based.

To change the source data of a chart, activate the chart, click the **Select Data** button on the Data group of the Design Ribbon, click the collapse dialog box button and then highlight the new range of data to be included in the chart.

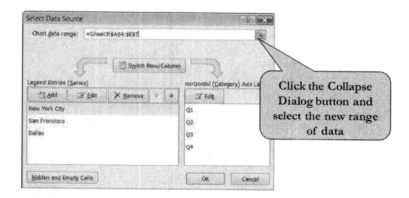

Click the Collapse Dialog button and select the new range of data

You can also delete a data series by selecting the data series you want to remove and clicking the Remove button. To reorder your data series, click the data series you want to move and click the **Move Up** or **Move Down** arrows.

✓ Change the Source Data of a Chart

1. Make sure the **Lesson8.xlsx** file is active. Click the **Sheet 3** tab on the bottom of the worksheet.
2. Click the **Chart area**.
3. Click the **Design** tab on the Ribbon.
4. Click the **Select Data button** on the Data group.

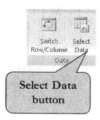

Select Data button

5. Click the **Collapse Dialog** button next to the Chart Data Range text box.
6. Select the cell range **A4:E8**.

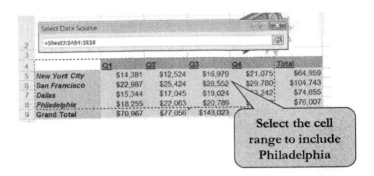

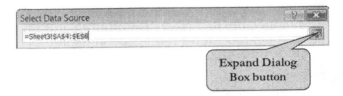

> Select the cell range to include Philadelphia

7. Click the **Expand Dialog Box** button.

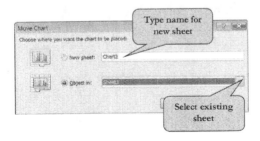

> Expand Dialog Box button

8. Click **OK**. Notice that Philadelphia is now included in your chart.
9. **Save** the worksheet.

8.13 Moving a Chart to a Different Worksheet

By default, all new charts are created in the active worksheet as embedded objects. To move a chart to a new worksheet or to a different worksheet, click the **Move Chart** button on the Location group of the Design Ribbon. The Move Sheet dialog box will display, allowing you to select an existing worksheet to move your chart to or specify the name for a new worksheet.

> Type name for new sheet

> Select existing sheet

✓ Move a Chart to a Different Worksheet

1. Make sure the **Lesson8.xlsx** file is active. Click the Chart to activate it.
2. Click the **Move Chart** button on the Location group on the right side of the Ribbon.

3. Click the **New Sheet** radio button.
4. Type: **Sales Chart**.

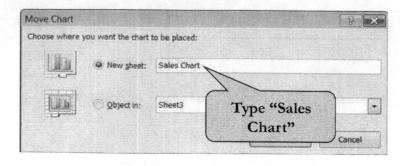

5. Click **OK**.
6. Click the **Sales Chart** tab on the bottom of the screen and observe the chart. Notice that the chart takes up the entire worksheet window.
7. Click the **Save button**.

8.14 Saving a Chart Template

I f you have spent some time extensively customizing a chart, you can save its formatting as a chart template. Saving a chart as a template will save any customization you have made to a chart and will be available for use in other workbooks. This is especially handy for companies who like to maintain a collection of standard charts to maintain consistency in their reporting.

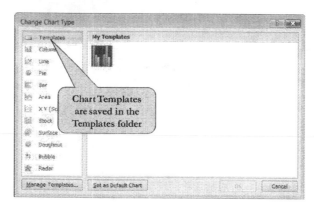

All chart templates that you save will appear in the Templates category of the Insert Chart dialog box. This means that you can create new charts based on your template or apply the template to an existing chart. If need to copy your templates to another computer, click the **Manage Templates** button on the Insert Chart dialog box to open an Explorer window. From there, you can copy and paste your templates to another folder or disk drive.

✓ Save a Chart as a Template

1. Make sure the **Lesson8.xlsx** file is active. Click the **Sheet 1** tab on the bottom of the worksheet.
2. Select the **Chart area**.
3. Click the **Design** tab on the Ribbon.
4. Click the **Save as Template button** on the Type group.

Save As
Template button

5. In the **File Name** box, type: **Sales 3-D Chart**.

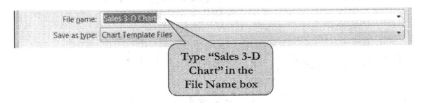

Type "Sales 3-D
Chart" in the
File Name box

6. Click **Save**.
7. Click the **Sales Chart** worksheet tab on the bottom of the worksheet.
8. Click the chart area to select the chart
9. Click the **Design** tab on the Ribbon.
10. Click the **Change Chart Type** button on the Type group.
11. Click **Templates** in the left pane. This displays all chart templates that have been saved.
12. Click the thumbnail for the **Sales 3-D Chart** template and then click **OK.**
13. Click the **Microsoft Office button** and select **Close** from the menu. Click **Yes** when asked to save your changes

Excel Quiz

1. Name four parts of the Excel window.
    cell name box, Ribbon, columns, Rows

2. What are three views available in Excel?
    A. Page Layout, Outline and Online
    B. Normal, Tabloid and Page Layout
    C. Normal, Page Layout and Page Break Preview
    D. Spreadsheet View, Normal and Page Layout

3. What are two ways to edit the contents of a cell?
    *Activate the cell and type over contents
    activate cell + double click the formula bar*

4. What are two methods for copying and pasting text?
    *Ctrl + C (copy) Ctrl + V (paste)
    right click copy right click paste*

5. How can you add an item from the Office Clipboard to your worksheet?
    Open Clipboard select material to paste

6. Name three formatting effects that you can apply from the Font Group on the Home Ribbon.
    Color, size, font

7. What can you find on the Format Cells dialog box? How do you display it?
    *number, alignment, font, border, fill, protection
    Ctrl + Shift + F*

8. How can you combine 4 cells into one larger cell?
    Select the 4 cells + click merge cells on the Alignment box

9. Outline the steps to create a custom footer in your worksheet.

11. Give an example of a relative cell reference. *When formula is copied to a new location*

12. Give an example of a mixed cell reference.

CAP 100: AN INTRODUCTION TO COMPUTER APPLICATIONS

Fundamentals of MS Office 2007

An Introduction to PowerPoint 2007

Table of Contents

Lesson 1 - PowerPoint Basics

1.1 Examining the PowerPoint Environment

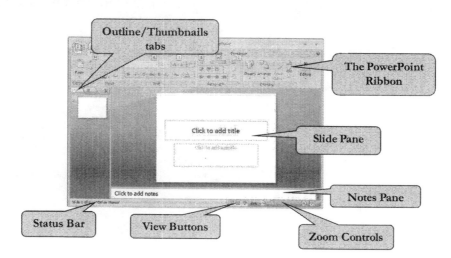

When you first launch PowerPoint, you are presented with a blank presentation consisting of a blank title slide in **Normal** view. This is the main editing view to write and design your presentation. On the left side of the screen is the **Outline/Thumbnails** pane and on the right side is the **Slide Pane**. If you have worked with previous versions of PowerPoint, you will immediately notice that the user interface has been completely redesigned.

The menu and toolbar system have been replaced by the **Ribbon**. The Ribbon is designed to help you quickly find the commands you need to complete a task. On the Ribbon, the menu bar has been replaced by **Command Tabs** that relate to the tasks you wish to accomplish. The default Command Tabs in PowerPoint are: **Home, Insert, Design, Animations, Slide Show, Review** and **View**.

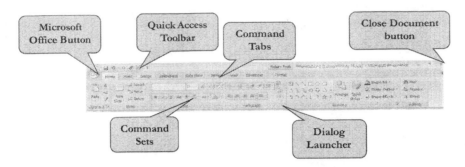

Different command icons, called **Command Sets** appear under each Command Tab. Each command set is grouped by its function. For example, the Insert tab contains commands to add graphics, tables, headers, footers, symbols and text objects to your presentation. **Contextual Commands** only appear when a specific object is selected.

On the bottom of many of the Command Sets is a **Dialog Launcher.** This is used to access a dialog box for that set of commands.

To the right of the **Microsoft Office icon** is the **Quick Access Toolbar.** This toolbar contains, by default, the Save, Undo, and Redo commands. In addition, clicking the drop-down arrow to the right allows you to customize the Quick Access Toolbar to add other tools. You can choose from the list those tools to display on the Quick Access Toolbar or select **More Commands** to add commands.

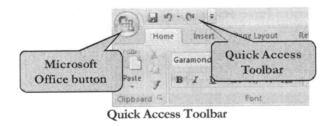

Quick Access Toolbar

You will be working in detail with the various PowerPoint tabs and commands in subsequent lessons.

1.2   Opening an Existing Presentation

If you have worked with previous versions of PowerPoint, you will notice that the **File > Open** command on the menu is no longer available. Instead of the word "File", the **Microsoft Office Button** indicates where the file menu commands are now located. To open an existing presentation, click the Microsoft Office button and then click the **Open** icon to display the Open dialog box. From there, navigate to the folder that contains that PowerPoint presentation you wish to open. If you have recently opened a presentation file, it may be listed in the right pane. Click on the file name in the recent files list to quickly open it.

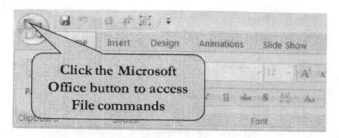

As you will quickly discover, there are several ways to accomplish the same task in Microsoft PowerPoint. Many commands under the File Options menu have an equivalent keyboard command that will accomplish the same thing. For instance, to open an existing document in Microsoft PowerPoint, you can also use the keystroke combination **Ctrl + O** which will bypass the File Options menu and directly display the Open dialog box. To display the File Options menu, you can press the **Alt + F** keystroke combination rather than clicking the Microsoft Office button.

✓ Open an Existing Presentation

1. Click the **Microsoft Office Button** on the top left of your screen. This displays the **File Options** menu.
2. Click **Open** in the left pane to display the Open dialog box.
3. Locate your copy of the Course Docs folder and open it.
4. **Open** the Lesson1.ppt file found in the 'PowerPoint Tutorials' folder.

1.3 Exploring PowerPoint's Views

PowerPoint has three basic views: Normal, Slide Sorter View and Slide Show View. **Normal view** is the main editing view – this is where you will do most of your work such as creating, formatting and modifying your presentation. Normal view has three working areas:

- On the left, there are two tabs that alternate between a display of your slides as an outline (**Outline** tab) and a display of your slides as thumbnails (**Slides** tab).

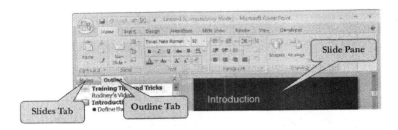

- On the right, there is the **Slide pane**, which displays a large view of the current slide as it will be printed.

- On the bottom of the screen is the **Notes pane** where you can add notes that relate to each slide's content. These can be printed out and handed to your audience as a reference.

In **Slide Sorter view**, all of the slides in your presentation are displayed in thumbnail format, providing you an overall picture of your presentation. Slide Sorter view makes it easy to reorder, add, or delete slides as well as preview your transition and animation effects.

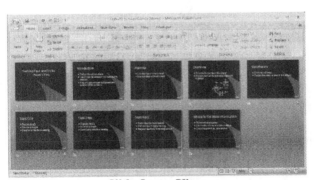

Slide Sorter View

In **Slide Show view**, the presentation takes up the full computer screen, like an actual slide show presentation. In this full-screen view, you see your presentation the way your audience will. You can see how your graphics, timings, movies, animation and transition effects will look in the actual show. Clicking with your mouse or pressing the space bar will advance from one slide to the next. Pressing the **Esc** key will return you to Normal view.

To switch among views, click the appropriate view button on the bottom right of the screen.

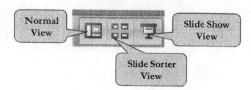

The View Buttons

✓ **Switch among Views**

1. Make sure the **Lesson1.ppt** file is active. Click the **Slide Sorter** view button (the middle button on the bottom right of your screen). PowerPoint switches to Slide Sorter view where the slides are displayed as thumbnails.
2. **Double-click** on **Slide 8**. This displays Slide 8 in Normal view.
3. Click the **Slide Sorter** view button.
4. **Double-click** on **Slide 1** to return to the first slide in Normal view.
5. Click the **Slide Show** button (the third button on the bottom right of your screen) to enter full-screen Slide Show view.
6. Click your left mouse button several times to easily advance from one slide to the next.
7. Press the **Esc** key to return to Normal view.

1.4 Creating a Blank Presentation

We have already seen that when you first launch Microsoft PowerPoint, a new blank presentation consisting of a single title slide is created. This blank presentation consists of a simple layout with minimal formatting, no design styles and two text boxes for you to enter a Title and a Subtitle. To change the layout of your blank presentation, click the **Layout button** in the Slides group on the Home Ribbon and choose the layout you want.

You can also create a new presentation from within another presentation. The new document command is located under the **File Options** menu. You can also use the keyboard shortcut **Ctrl + N** to bypass the File Options menu.

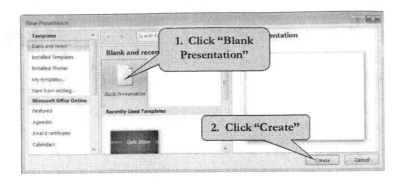

Layouts refer to the way objects are arranged on a slide. Layouts consist of placeholders that contain slide content such as titles, bulleted lists, tables, charts, and pictures. Each time you add a new slide, you can chose a different layout for that slide from the **Layout gallery**. Of course, if you prefer to do things manually, you can choose a blank layout.

✓ Apply a Layout to a Slide

1. Open a new presentation and click the **Slides** tab
2. Select the first slide.
3. Click the **Home tab** on the Ribbon.
4. Click the **Layout button** in the **Slides group**.
5. Click the **Title and Content** layout.

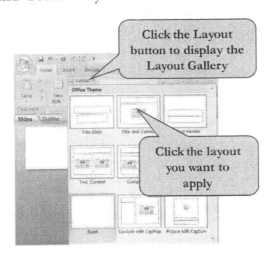

1.5 Creating a Presentation Using Templates

We have seen how to create a basic, blank presentation. An easier way to create a presentation in PowerPoint is by using Templates. Templates provide a preset design as well as ready-to-use slides with sample content. You can use the installed templates that came with PowerPoint or download hundreds of additional templates from Microsoft Office Online.

Create a Presentation using a Template

1. Click the **Microsoft Office Button** and then click **New** from the menu. This displays the **New Presentation** pane.
2. Under the **Templates** area in the left pane, click **Installed Templates**. This displays a list of templates that are installed on your computer.

3. Click the **Introducing PowerPoint 2007** template in the center pane.
4. Click **Create**.

1.6 Navigating a Presentation

While in Normal view, there are several ways to move from slide to slide. You can quickly move from one slide to the next by using PowerPoint's vertical **Scroll Bar**. Clicking and dragging the vertical scroll bar will quickly you from one slide to the next, dispaling a small information box as you drag what informs you of which slide would be active should you release the mouse button.

Above the scroll box is the **Scroll Up button** which when clicked with your mouse, moves you upwards one position in your presentation. Likewise, the **Scroll Down button** moves you downwards in your presentation one slide at a time.

On the bottom of your scroll bar are the **Previous Slide** and **Next Slide** buttons which move you back one slide or forwards one slide in your presentation.

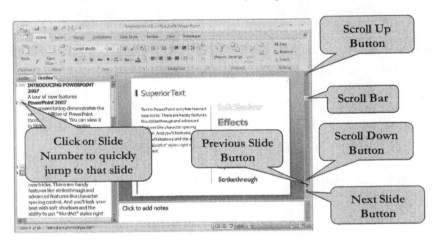

Additionally, there are some **keyboard shortcuts** that allow you to navigate your presentation. These are:

Page Up	Moves to the previous slide
Page Down	Moves to next slide
Ctrl + Home	Moves to the first slide in the presentation
Ctrl + End	Moves to the last slide in the presentation

1.7 Adding Slides to a Presentation

When inserting a new slide in your presentation, that slide will immediately follow the active slide in your presentation. You can add a new slide to your presentation in either Normal View or Slide Sorter View by clicking the arrow on the **New Slide Button** under the **Slides** group on the Home Ribbon and choosing the desired slide layout from the gallery. If you wish to insert a new slide with the same layout as the active slide, click the **New Slide Button** (above the words "New Slide").

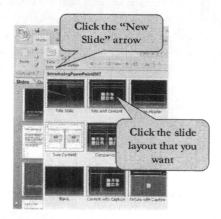

With the exception of the blank layout, all new slides contain **placeholders**. Placeholders are boxes with dotted or hatch-marked borders that hold titles, body text and objects such as charts, tables and graphics.

✓ **Add a New Slide to your Presentation**

1. Make sure the **Lesson1.ppt** file is active. Click the **Slides Tab** on the left side of the screen. This displays the slides in thumbnail view.
2. Click on **Slide 5**.
3. Click the **New Slide arrow** as shown and click the **Title and Content** layout. A new slide is inserted with 2 placeholders – a title placeholder and a content placeholder.

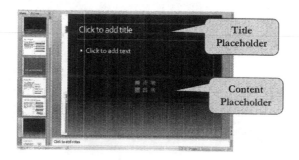

1.8   Deleting Slides

L ike adding slides, you can delete slides from your presentation in both Normal view and Slide Sorter view. To delete a slide, select the slide you want to delete and then press the **Delete** key, or click the **Delete button** on the Slides group on the Home Ribbon.

If you wish to delete more than one slide at a time, select the first slide to be deleted in either the Outline Pane or the Slides Pane, hold down the **Shift** key, select the last slide to be deleted, and then press the delete key. All slides between and including the first and last slide will be deleted. To select non-adjacent slides, hold down the **Ctrl** key and then select the slides to be deleted. Press the Delete key.

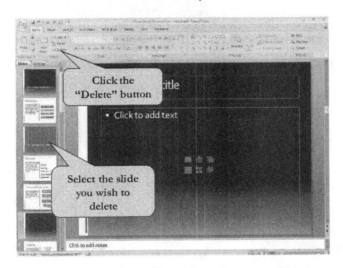

✓ Delete Slides from your Presentation

1. Make sure the **Lesson1.ppt** file is active. In the **Slides Pane**, click on **Slide 9**.
2. Press the **Delete** key.
3. In the **Slides Pane**, click on **Slide 4**.
4. Hold down the **Ctrl** key and click on **Slide 6**. This selects Slide 6 in addition to Slide 4. Since they are non-adjacent slides, use the Ctrl key to select them
5. Click the **Delete** button on the Slides group.

Tip:	You can also **right-click** the slide you wish to delete and choose **Delete** from the menu.

1.9 Hiding Slides

Rather than deleting slides from your presentation, you can simply **hide slides**. Hidden slides will still appear in Normal and Slide Sorter view but will not appear in Slide Show view (when running a slide show). This is especially userful when tailoring your presentation to different audiences.

Right-click the slide and choose "Hide Slide"

When a slide is hidden, the hidden icon is displayed next to the slide with the slide number inside.

✓ Hide a Slide

1. Make sure the **Lesson1.ppt** file is active. In the **Slides Pane**, **right-click** on **Slide 1**.
2. Select **Hide Slide** from the menu.
3. Click the **Slide Show tab** on the Ribbon.
4. Click the **From Beginning** button on the Start Slide Show group as shown. Notice that the presentation begins with slide 2.

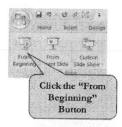

Click the "From Beginning" Button

5. Press the **Esc** key to return to normal mode.
6. In the **Slides Pane**, click on **Slide 1.**
7. Click the **Hide Slide** button on the Ribbon. This reveals slide 1.

> **Tip:** To display a hidden slide when presenting a slide show, right-click the active slide in your show, point to **Go to Slide** and then click the slide you wish to display.

1.10   Applying a Theme to a Presentation

Themes are a quick way to apply preconfigured formatting to your presentation. Themes consist of theme colors, theme fonts and theme effects that give your presentation a professional and polished look. You can add themes from the **Design tab** on the Ribbon. PowerPoint comes with 20 installed themes that you can use. You can download additional themes from Microsoft Office Online.

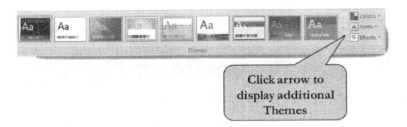

> Click arrow to display additional Themes

As you move your mouse pointer over each theme in the gallery, your presentation changes to reflect what it would like like if you apply the theme. This is an example of Microsoft Office's new **Live Preview** feature.

You can apply a theme to your entire presentation or to selected slides.

✓ To Apply a Theme to Selected Slides

1.   Make sure the **Lesson1.ppt** file is active. Click the **Design tab** on the Ribbon.
2.   Move your mouse pointer over the **6th theme from the left** (the Concourse theme) as shown. This displays a preview of the Concourse theme.

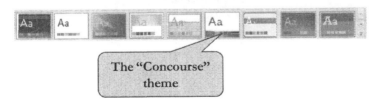

> The "Concourse" theme

3.   Click the Concourse theme thumbnail. This applies the Concourse theme to your entire presentation.
4.   Make slide 2 the active slide.
5.   Hold down the **Ctrl** key and then select **Slide 4**. This selects slides 2 and 4. Holding down the Ctrl key allows you to select non-adjacent slides.

6. Right-click on the **third theme from the left** (the Apex theme) and choose **Apply to Selected Slides** from the menu.
7. Press the **Alt + F** keystroke combination to display the File Options menu.
8. Click **Save As**.
9. In the **File Name** text box, type: **MyNewDesign**
10. Click the **Save** button.

> **Tip:** To set a theme as the default theme for all new PowerPoint documents, right-click the theme thumbnail and choose **Set as Default Theme**.

1.11 Setting PowerPoint Options

In previous versions of PowerPoint, you could set preferences for specific program settings from the Options dialog box. The Options command has been moved to the **PowerPoint Options** button on the File Options menu which displays when you click the **Microsoft Office Button**.

From the PowerPoint Options dialog box, you can specify such options as setting the color scheme for the PowerPoint application, specifying a default location to save files, setting the default file format, and much more. You may wish to spend some time browsing through the PowerPoint Options dialog box and set any preferences that may help you work with less effort.

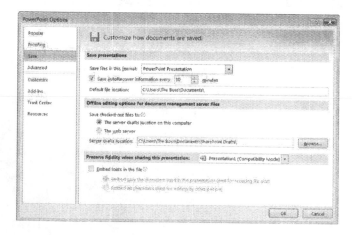

✓ Set PowerPoint Options

1. Make sure the **Lesson1.ppt** file is active. Click the **Microsoft Office Button** to display the File Options menu.
2. Click the **PowerPoint Options** button.

3. Click the **Save** category in the left pane.
4. Click the **Save files in this Format** drop-down arrow and choose **PowerPoint Presentation 97-2003**. This sets the default file format to PowerPoint 97-2003, allowing users of previous version of PowerPoint to be able to access your files.

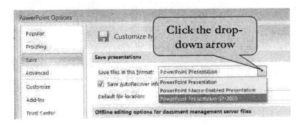

5. Click **OK.**

Lesson 2 - Inserting and Modifying Text

2.1 Creating Headers and Footers

Headers and footers are text displayed on the top or bottom of every page of your slides, notes or handouts. Headers and footers can consist of specific text, such as a company logo, the slide or page number, or a date. Headers will appear at the top of every printed page while footers will appear at the bottom of every printed page.

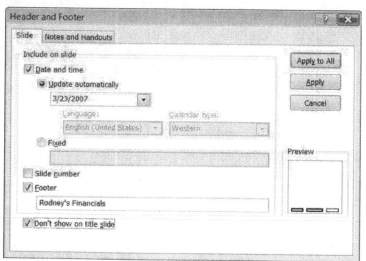

Header and Footer dialog box

Slides can contain only footers whereas Notes and Handouts can contain both headers and footers. Headers and footers can be applied to a single selected slide or to all of slides in your presentation.

By **default**, Notes and Handouts include page numbers, but you have the ability to turn these off. You might choose to include no headers and footers on your slides but instead to reserve them for notes and handouts for that presentation.

✓ Add a Footer to Slides

1. Open the **Lesson2.ppt** presentation found in **your** Course Docs folder..
2. Click the **Insert** tab on the Ribbon.
3. Click the **Header and Footer** button in the Text group on the Ribbon. This displays the Header and Footer dialog box.
4. Click the **Date and Time** checkbox.

5. Click the **Update Automatically** radio button. The current date and time will be inserted and updated automatically each time the presentation is opened.
6. Click the **Slide Number** check box.
7. Click the **Footer** check box and type: **Rodney's Financials** in the Footer text box.

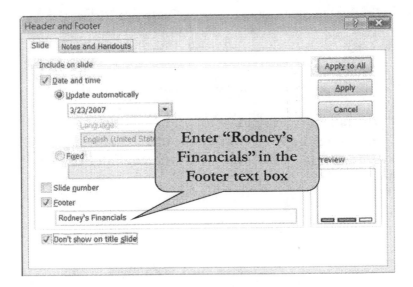

8. Click the **Don't Show on Title Slide** check box. This omits the footer information from the first slide in the presentation.
9. Click **Apply to All**. This applies the footer settings to all other slides in the presentation and closes the Header and Footer dialog box.
10. Click the **Next Slide** button and observe the slide footer. The footer information that you specified is inserted on the bottom of each slide.

Add a Header to Notes and Handouts

1. Make sure the **Lesson2.ppt** presentation is active. Click the **Header and Footer** button in the Text group on the Ribbon. This displays the Header and Footer dialog box.
2. Click the **Notes and Handouts** tab.
3. Click the **Date and Time** checkbox. This includes the Date and Time in the footer.
4. Click the **Fixed** radio button and type: **1/15/2007** in the Date/Time text box. A permanent date of 1/15/2007 will be displayed in the footer.

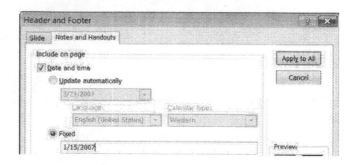

5. Click the **Header** checkbox and then type: **Rodney's Video, Inc.** in the Header Text Box. Header text will appear at the top of each page.
6. Include the Page Number in the footer.
7. Click the **Footer** check box and then type: **Rodney's Financials**
8. Click **Apply to All**. This applies the footer settings to all other slides in the presentation.
9. Click the **View tab** on the Ribbon.
10. Click the **Notes Page** button on the Presentation Views group on the Ribbon and observe the header and footer. Notice the header information is inserted on the top of each notes page.

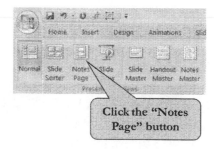

Click the "Notes Page" button

11. Click the **Normal** button on the Presentation Views group on the Ribbon.

2.2 Entering Text onto Slides

In order to enter text onto your slides, you must enter it into a **placeholder** (the containers with dotted lines that are part of slide layouts). Placeholders can hold text such as title text, bulleted lists, and numbered lists as well as objects such as ClipArt and charts. To enter text into a placeholder, click inside of the placeholder object and then begin typing. When working with bulleted lists, press the **Enter** key to automatically insert a new bullet on the new line. The text you type into placeholders can be edited directly on the slide or from the **Outline Pane**.

✓ Enter Text onto Slides

1. Make sure the **Lesson2.ppt** file is active. Select the first slide of the presentation.
2. Click inside the placeholder that contains the text: **Rodney Larson** as shown.
   An insertion point appears inside of the placeholder indicating that you can begin entering text.

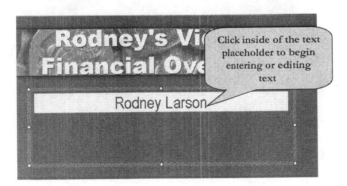

3. Click to the right of the **n** in **Larson**.
4. Press the **Enter** key to insert a new line.
5. Type: **President**
6. Click anywhere outside of the placeholder. This deactivates the placeholder.
7. Press **Ctrl + M** to insert a new blank slide after Slide 1.
8. Click in the **Title Placeholder** and type: **Store Managers**.
9. Click in the **Bulleted List Placeholder** and type: **Jon Harris**.
10. Press **Enter**. A new bulleted line is inserted.
11. Type **Ann Harwood**.
12. Insert a new bulleted line.
13. Type **Jodi Barr** and then click anywhere outside of the placeholder. This enters the third store manager then deselects the placeholder.

2.3   Using the Notes Pane

When preparing a presentation, you can use the **Notes Pane** to provide anecdotes, additional details relating to a slide, or any other information that you want to mention in your presentation but do not want to include on your slides. The Notes Pane is displayed in normal view and you type text directly into the notes pane box. Notes are not displayed to the audience when you are running a slide show. When printing your presentation, you have the option of printing your **Notes Pages** as well. These can serve as handy cue cards when delivering your presentation.

✓ Enter Text into the Notes Pane

1.   Make sure the **Lesson2.ppt** file is active. Select **Slide 6** in the **Slides Pane**.
2.   Click in the **Notes Pane** for Slide 6.
3.   Type: **Dallas Store was closed for 1 month for renovations**.
4.   **Save** the active presentation.
5.   Click the **Notes Page** button on the Presentation Views group on the View Ribbon and observe the Notes page.
6.   Click the **Normal** button on the Presentation Views group on the Insert Ribbon.

2.4   Formatting Text

You can change the appearance of the text in your slides by applying various types of **formatting**. For instance, you can modify the typeface (or font) of your text, change the size of your text, or emphasize text by applying bold, italics or underlining. When typing text in your document, each new character you type takes on the formatting of the previous character unless you apply new formatting. When creating a new paragraph (by pressing Enter), the first character takes on the formatting of the paragraph mark.

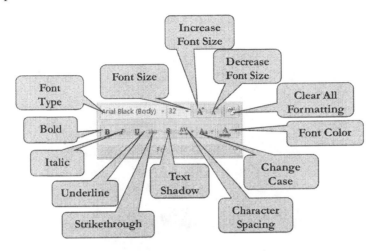

Common Formatting Options on the Font Group

The quickest and easiest way to apply and modify text formatting is to use the Formatting Tools on the Home tab under the **Font group**. To change text emphasis, select the text you wish to format then click on the appropriate icon (Bold, Italics or Underline). To change the font or font size, select the text then choose the desired option from the font or font size drop-down list. For an explanation of what a tool does, move your mouse pointer over a tool to display an informational box. The box will also display the **keyboard shortcut** for the command, if any.

New in PowerPoint 2007 is the **Mini-Toolbar**. The Mini-Toolbar displays whenever you select text or right-click on selected text and provides quick access to common formatting commands such as bold, italic, font color, font type, font size, fill color, increase indent, decrease indent and increase/decrease font size. If you wish to turn off this feature, you can do so from the PowerPoint Options dialog box.

Mini-toolbar displays when you select text

Tip:	You can also apply formatting from the **Font Dialog Box**, which allows you to apply multiple formats (bold, italics, font size, font type, font color, etc.) to selected text at once. To apply multiple formatting to selected text, click the **Font Dialog Box Launcher** on the lower-right corner of the Font command set then make your desired selections.

✓ Use Formatting Tools

1. Make sure the **Lesson2.ppt** file is active. Select **Slide 2**. Enter **Rodney Larson, President** as the fourth bulleted item

2. Click inside the bulleted list placeholder and then **position your mouse pointer** before the word **Jon**.

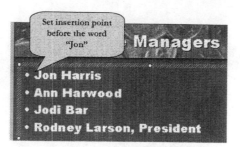

3. Click with your left mouse button and drag downwards until **all four lines** are **selected**.

4. Click on the arrow next to the **Font** drop-down list on the Home Ribbon. This displays a list of available typefaces

5. Scroll down and **click on Times New Roman.**

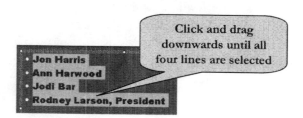

6. Click the **Bold** icon on the Ribbon.

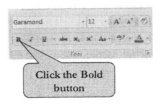

Click the Bold
button

7. Click the **Font Size** drop-down list on the Ribbon and select **44**.

8. Click the **arrow** to the right of the **Font Color button** on the Ribbon. This
   displays the Color Palette.

Click the Font
Color arrow

9. Click on the **Yellow** color button under the Standard Colors category. This
   selects Yellow for the font color of the selected text and closes the Colors Palette.

10. **Save** the active presentation.

2.5 Importing Text from Word

Many people create their presentation outlines in a word processing program
such as Microsoft Word and later wish to generate a PowerPoint
Presentation based upon their outlines. PowerPoint makes importing
documents easy with its **Insert Slides from Outline** feature. This allows
you to import a document into PowerPoint from another file format such as text, rich
text format, or Microsoft Word. The source document should be in outline format with
first level headings indented under top level headings. Top level headings will be treated
as the Slide's title and first level will be imported as bulleted points under the Top Level
Heading. The inserted slides will be placed after the active slide in your presentation.

✓ Import an Outline from World

1. Make sure the **Lesson2.ppt** file is active. Select **Slide 6**. The inserted slides will
   be placed after this slide.

2. Click the arrow next to **New Slide** on the Slides Group on the Home Ribbon.

3. Click **Slides from Outline** from the menu. This displays the Insert Outline dialog box.

7. Click on the **Sales by Store.doc** file in your Course Docs folder.

8. Select **Insert** and observe the new slide.

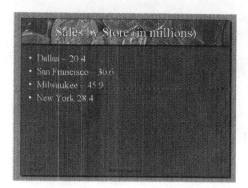

9. Press the **Page Down** key to move to the next slide outline that you imported.

2.6   Using Bulleted Lists

Bulleted Lists are the foundations of conventional presentations. By default, the text placeholder in PowerPoint is formatted to be a bulleted list using the traditoinal ● character as the bullet. Bulleted lists present key ideas in a list format but do not necessarily suggest a particular sequence. To create a bulleted list, click on the **Bullets** button on the Home Ribbon. Click the bullets button again when you are finished with your list. To specify the type of bullet, click the arrow next to the Bullets icon and choose the desired bullet type from the gallery.

For more bullet options, such as setting the type of bullet, indentation, etc., click the arrow next to the Bullets button. To Modify bullet indentation or to create a new bullet type, click **Bullets and Numbering** on the menu, click the Bulleted tab and make your selections.

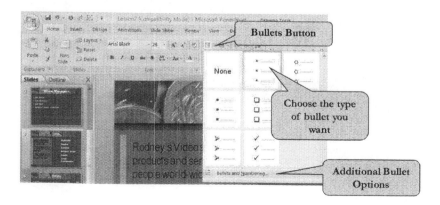

✓ Create a Bulleted List

1. Make sure the **Lesson2.ppt** file is active. Make Slide 3 the active slide.

2. Select the border of the placeholder that contains the bulleted list.

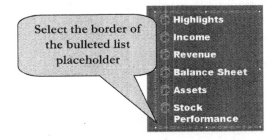

3. Click the drop-down arrow next to the Bullets icon. This displays the Bullets gallery.

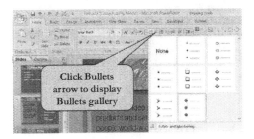

4. Click the second bullet option in the first row.

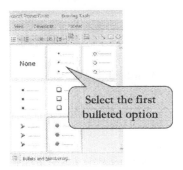

5. Click anywhere outside of the placeholder to deselect it.

2.7 Creating a Numbered List

If your list of items needs to follow a particular order, such as step-by-step instructions for accomplishing a task, you will want to use a **Numbered List**. With a numbered list, each item in your list is preceeded by a sequential number. To turn on numbering, click the **Numbering** icon on the Home Ribbon.

For more numbering options such as setting the number format, indentation, and starting number, click the arrow next to the Numbering button and choose the number format you want. For additoinal options, click **Bullets and Numbering** on the menu, click the Numbered tab and make your selections.

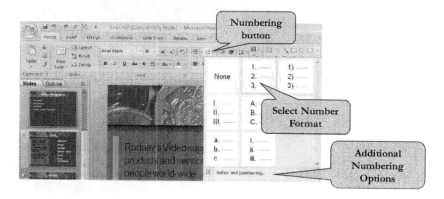

✓ Create a Numbered List

1. Make sure the **Lesson2.ppt** file is active. Select **Slide 3**.
2. Select the border of the placeholder that contains the bulleted list. You will change the bulleted list to a numbered list.
3. Click the **Numbering button** on the Ribbon. This applies the default numbering format to the selected text.
4. **Save** the active presentation.

2.8 Setting Paragraph Alignment

Alignment refers to the arrangement of text in relation to the left and right edges of the text placeholder. For example, a paragraph that is left-aligned is flush with the left placeholder edge. There are four types of alignment that you can apply to a paragraph:

- **Align Left** – text is flush with the left placeholder edge

- **Align Right** – text is flush with the right placeholder edge

- **Center** – text is positioned with an even space from the left and right placeholder edges

- **Justify** – both edges of the paragraph are flush with the left and right placeholder edges (extra spaces are added between words to create this effect).

To change the alignment of a paragraph, click anywhere within the paragraph and click the desired alignment button on the Home Ribbon, as shown.

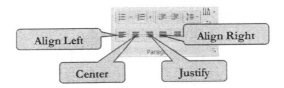

Alignment buttons on the Home Ribbon

You can also vertically align text from the top and bottom edges of the text placeholder. Click the **Align Text** button in the Paragraph group on the Home Ribbon and choose **Top, Bottom** or **Middle**. For additional alignment options, click **More Options** and make your desired selections from the Format Text Effects dialog box.

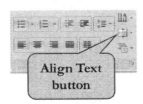

✓ Align Text from the Left and Right Edges of the Placeholder

1. Make sure the **Lesson2.ppt** file is active. Select **Slide 8**.
2. Select the border of the placeholder that contains the salesperson and store information.
3. Click the **Center alignment button** on the Home Ribbon. This applies center alignment to all items within the placeholder.
4. Click the **Align Text** button and choose **Middle** from the gallery to vertically center the text within the placeholder.

2.9 Adding Columns

New in PowerPoint 2007 is the ability to create columns within a text box. This is especially handy if you have a long list of items that you wish to transform into two, three or more columns. After you insert your columns, you can then modify the spacing between them. The columns button is located on the Paragraph group of the Home Ribbon.

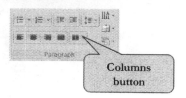

✓ Create and Modify Text Columns

1. Make sure the **Lesson2.ppt** file is active. Select **Slide 3**. This **Makes Slide 3** the active slide.
2. Click inside the placeholder that contains the three paragraphs (beginning with "Rodney's Video supplies…).
3. Click the **Columns button** on the Ribbon and choose **Two Columns**. This transforms the text into two columns.

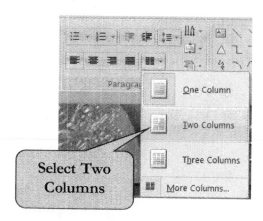

4. With the text box still selected, click the **Columns button** again and select **More Columns** from the menu.
5. In the **Spacing box**, type: **1** and then click **OK**.
6. Save and close the presentation

Lesson 3 - Working with Graphics

3.1 Adding Clip Art

Microsoft Office comes with a collection of images called **Clip Art** that you can add to your PowerPoint presentations as well as other Microsoft Office documents to make your documents more visually striking. To insert and search for clip art, click the **Clip Art** button on the Illustrations group of the **Insert tab** on the Ribbon to display the **Clip Art Task Pane**. To browse clip art, enter a **keyword** in the **Search for:** text box.

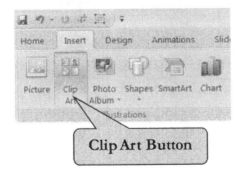

Clip Art Button

You can also insert clip art using the **Microsoft Clip Organizer** (the **"Organize Clips"** link at the bottom of the Clip Art Task Pane). Here, you can browse through clip collections, add clip art or catalog your clips.

✓ Insert Clip Art

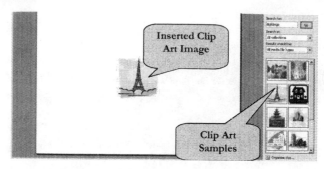

1. Open **Lesson3a.ppt** found in your copy of the Course Docs folder.
2. Click the **Insert tab** on the Ribbon.
3. Click the **Clip Art button** on the Illustrations group to display the Clip Art Task Pane.
4. In the **Search for:** text box, type in: **Computers** as shown and then click the **Go** button. This returns samples of a clip art with the keyword computers.

5. Click the sample in the **third row, first column** to insert the Clip Art image into the active slide.
6. Double-click the word **Computers** in the Search for: box. You are going to perform a new clip art search.
7. In the **Search for:** text box, type: **Buildings** and then click the **Go** button. This returns samples of a clip art with the keyword buildings.
8. Click on the image of the **Eiffel Tower** (2ⁿᵈ row, 1ˢᵗ column). Since the previous image was still selected, the Eiffel Tower image replaced the selected Computer image.
9. Close the Clip Art task pane.

3.2 Adding Pictures

In addition to Clip Art, you can insert graphical images into your presentations from your computer or network drive. These can be images that you have created in another program, images that you have uploaded from a digital camera, or images that have been purchased. PowerPoint supports a wide variety of graphical formats such as .jpg, .gif, .bmp, etc. Adding images to your slides can really add an extra touch to your presentations.

✓ Insert a Picture

1. Make sure the **Lesson3a.ppt** file is active. Click the **Home** tab on the Ribbon.
2. Click the **New Slide arrow** on the Ribbon. This displays the layout gallery.
3. Click the **Blank** Layout in the layout gallery.

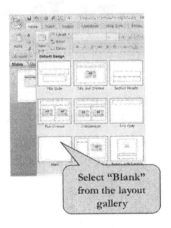

Select "Blank" from the layout gallery

4. Click the **Insert tab** on the Ribbon.
5. Click the **Picture button** on the Ribbon to display the Insert Picture dialog box.
6. Select the file named: **BROKE** from your Course Docs folder.

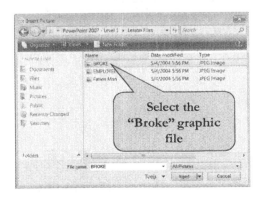

Select the "Broke" graphic file

---

7. Click **Insert**. Since the picture came in larger than desired, its height will be modified

8. Click in the **Shape Height** box on the Size group on the Ribbon and type in: **4.5**. Press **Enter**.

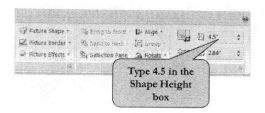

Type 4.5 in the Shape Height box

9. Click on the picture and drag about one inch down and about three inches to the right until the picture is on the right side of your screen.

10. **Save** the active presentation.

3.3   Using Drawing Tools

PowerPoint contains many powerful drawing tools that allow you to add lines, arrows, shapes, text boxes, and more to your slides. These tools are located on the **Drawing group** under the Home Ribbon. Move your mouse pointer over any drawing icon to display an informational box explaining what the drawing tool is.

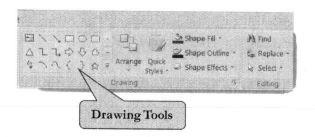

Drawing Tools

One of the most common tools you will use is the **text box**. Text boxes allow you to place text anywhere on your slide, outside of any existing placeholders. For example, you can add a caption to a picture by creating a text box and situating it near the picture. Using text boxes as well as the other drawing tools can help you convey your message more easily and effectively.

Add a Drawing Object to Your Slide

1. Make sure the **Lesson3a.ppt** file is active. Click the **Home tab** on the Ribbon.

2.   Click the **Text Box** drawing tool. You are now ready to draw an object on your slide.

3.   Move the mouse pointer **about 1 inch from the left margin,** and about ¾ **of the way down the page.** (the area where you will begin drawing the text box).

4.   Click and drag downward and to the right until your text box is about 1 inch high and 4 inches long. **Release** the mouse button.

5.   Click inside the text box and then type: **Don't Let This Be You!**
6.   Click anywhere outside of the text box to deselect it.
7.   Click the **Arrow** drawing tool   .
8.   Move your mouse pointer to the right of the word **You!**
9.   **Click and drag** towards the paintbrush in the picture until your arrow is about **3 inches long. Release** your mouse button. This creates an arrow pointing from the text box to the paintbrush the man is holding in the picture.

10.   **Save** the active presentation.

3.4 Formatting Drawing Objects

C hances are that after drawing your object, you will want to apply formatting to it so that it blends in with the rest of your presentation or slide background. The Drawing Group on the Home Ribbon contains several tools which allow you to modify such settings as line color, width and style, fill color, etc. .

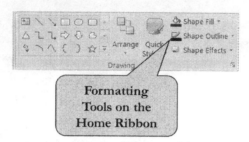

Formatting
Tools on the
Home Ribbon

When you click an object, the **Drawing Tools tab** appears on the top of your screen. Under this tab, you can find the same object formatting tools as under the Drawing Group on the Home Ribbon as well as additional formatting tools including various object styles that you can apply to a drawing object.

✓ Apply Formatting to Drawing Objects

1. Make sure the **Lesson3a.ppt** file is active. Click the **arrow** object that you drew in the last lesson.
2. Click the **Quick Styles** button on the Drawing Group. This displays a gallery of quick formatting that you can apply to the selected object.
3. Move your mouse pointer over the **Moderate Line – Accent 2 style**, in the second row, third column.

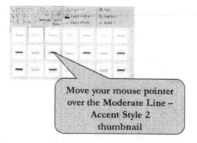

Move your mouse pointer
over the Moderate Line –
Accent Style 2
thumbnail

4. Click the **Moderate Line – Accent 2 style** in the gallery.
5. With the arrow still selected, click the **Shape Outline** button. This displays various shape outline options.

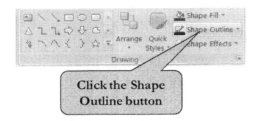

Click the Shape Outline button

6. Click the **black color swatch** in the color palette.
7. Click the **Shape Outline** button again and point to **Weight** to display a gallery of various line thickness formatting that you can apply.
8. Click on ¾ **pt** in the gallery.
9. **Save** the changes.

> **Tip:** You can see a preview of most formatting and styles by moving your mouse pointer over any gallery thumbnail or color swatch button. The effect will be temporarily applied to the selected object. This is an example of PowerPoint's Live Preview feature.

3.5 Formatting Text Boxes

One of the most commonly used drawing objects is the **text box**. Text boxes allow you to add additional information to any location on any slide. In order to change the formatting of a text box, you must first **select** it by directly clicking on the dashed border that surrounds it. It is easiest to first **click inside** of the text box to activate it, and then click on the text box **border**.

The formatting options for text boxes are numerous. Some options are:

- Changing the font size and font type (typeface) of the text
- Change the alignment (left, center or right) of the text
- Add bold, italics or underline to the text
- Change the line spacing
- Add a fill color to the text box
- Change the font color of the text
- Add a border and/or a border color to the text box
- Set the border style (line thickness and line type)

You can apply some formatting such as font size and typeface, bold, italics, underline and text alignment by selecting the text box and then selecting the appropriate formatting command button on the Font of the Home Ribbon. For object formatting, choose the desired tool from the Drawing Group on the Ribbon.

✔ Apply Formatting to Text Boxes

1. Make sure the **Lesson3a.ppt** file is active. Click **inside** the text box..
2. Click on the **dashed border** of the text box to select it.

Click on the text box border to select it

Don't Let This Be You!

3. From the **Font** drop-down list on the Font group, select **Times New Roman**.
4. Click on the **Font Size** arrow and select **24** from the list.
5. Apply **Bold** formatting to the text.
6. Apply **Italics** to the text.
7. Click the **Shape Outline** button on the Drawing group on the Ribbon. This displays the color palette and line options.
8. Click the **Black** color swatch on the color palette to apply an automatic black border to the text box.
9. Click the **Shape Outline** button again on the Drawing group on the Ribbon.
10. Point to **Weight** button on the menu and choose **2 ¼ pt**

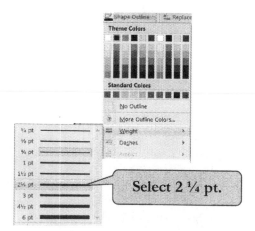

Select 2 ¼ pt.

11. **Save** the active presentation.

3.6 Using the Format Shape Dialog Box

Another way to format a shape is from the **Format Shape dialog box**. From there, you can set such options as line color and style, fill, shadow, adding 3-D effects, rotating objects and more. The available options will depend on the type of object.

Format Shape dialog box

To display the Format Shape dialog box, right-click the object and choose **Format Shape** or **Format Picture** from the menu.

✓ To Use the Format Shape dialog box

1. Make sure the **Lesson3a.ppt** file is active. **Right-click** the border of the text box to display the pop-up menu.
2. Choose **Format Shape** from the menu.

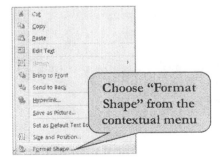

Choose "Format Shape" from the contextual menu

3. Click the **Fill** category in the left pane.

---

4. Click the **Gradient Fill** radio button in the right pane.
5. Click the **Preset Colors** button and choose **Fog** (the last thumbnail in the second row) as shown.

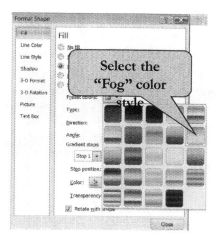

6. **Close** the Format Shape dialog box.
7. Click the **Microsoft Office** button and choose **Close** from the menu. Click **Yes** when asked to save your changes.

3.7 Resizing and Moving Objects

After you've drawn or inserted objects in your presentation, very often you will want to move them to another location on your slide or change their width, length or height. In order to move or resize any object, you first must select the object. When you select an obejct, **sizing handles** appear on the object's border. Sizing handles allow you to change the size of the selected object.

To increase the length of a text box, click the left or right middle sizing handle (your mouse pointer will turn into a double arrow as you position it over a sizing handle) and then drag inwards to decrease the length or outwards to increase the length. Holding down the **Shift** key while resizing allows you to maintain the objects proportions.

To move an object, position your mouse pointer over the border of an object or directly over a graphic until your mouse pointer transforms into a 4-way arrow. Then, click and drag to a new location.

✓ Resize and Move an Object

1. Open the **Lesson3b.ppt** found in your Course Docs folder.
2. Click on the **Slides tab.**
3. In the Slides Pane, select **Slide 7.**
4. Click **inside** of the text box with the text: **Know your competitors!**
5. Move your mouse pointer over the **dashed border** until the pointer transforms into a 4-way arrow.
6. Click and drag the text box to the **bottom center** of the screen.
7. Click on the **lighthouse graphic** in the top right hand corner of your screen.
8. Move your mouse pointer over the **lower left sizing handle** until the pointer transforms into a double white arrow.

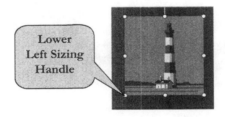

9. Click and drag **inward** until the picture is about 1 in. tall and 1 in. wide. Release the mouse button. Using the sizing handles on the corners allows you to both change the height and width of an object at the same time.
10. Click on the white line directly below the text placeholder.

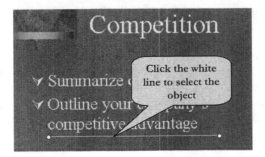

11. Move your mouse pointer over the line until the pointer transforms into a 4-way black arrow.

12. Click and drag until the line is **directly above the text box** on the bottom of the screen. Line up the left edge of the line with the left edge of the text box, as shown, and then release the mouse button. This moves the white line to the bottom of the screen, directly above the text box.

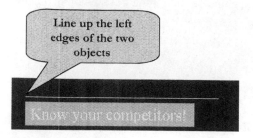

13. With the line still selected, move your mouse pointer over the **right sizing handle** until your mouse pointer transforms into a double arrow.

14. Click and **drag to the left** until the line is the same width as the text box. Release the mouse button. This resizes the line so that it is the same width as the text box.

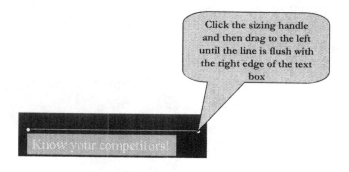

15. **Save** the active presentation.

3.8   Grouping Objects

Grouping allows you to combine objects so you can work with them as though they were a single unit. Once objects are grouped, you can apply the same formatting to every object in the group with a single setting or move every object in your group to a new location at once, rather than selecting each item individually and moving them one by one. Additionally, you can resize or scale all objects in your group as a single unit.

To select more than one object, select the first object, hold down the **Shift** key, and then select any additional objects. You can also select several objects by clicking on the slide with your mouse and then dragging around the objects you want to select. As you drag, a dotted line appears on your screen indicating the boundary of the selection.

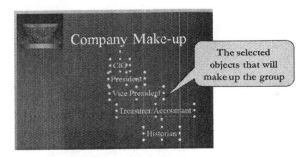

Once your objects are grouped, you can manipulate the group by selecting the placeholder surrounding the group. This will select the entire group. A grouped object has one set of resizing handles for the entire group and one rotating handle. You will learn more about rotating objects in a later section.

> **Tip:** Even though your objects are grouped as a single unit, you can still edit the text in individual text boxes.

✔ Group Objects

1. Make sure the **Lesson3b.ppt** file is active. Select **Slide 12** in your presentation.
2. Click inside the **CIO** text box.
3. Click the border of the text box.
4. Hold down your **Shift** key and then click the **President** text box, the **Vice-President** text box, the **Treasurer/Accountant** text box, and then the **Historian** text box.. This selects all five text boxes.
5. **Right-click** on any **border** of the selected objects.
6. Point to **Group** and then click on **Group** in the submenu. This groups the selected objects together so they can be worked with as a single unit.

Once your objects are grouped, you can **Ungroup** them by selecting **Group** and then pointing to **Ungroup** from the menu or from the Format tab. The objects will once again become individual units.

✓ Ungroup Objects

1.   Make sure the **Lesson3b.ppt** file is active. Select the group on Slide 12 by clicking any of the objects within the group.
2.   **Right-click** on any **border** of the selected objects.
3.   Point to **Group** and then click on **Ungroup** in the submenu.

3.9   Aligning Objects

A nother feature on the **Format** tab under the **Drawing Tools** group is the **Align** command. This feature allows you to align your objects relative to one another. For instance, you can use the Align command to ensure that the left edges of all of your text boxes begin in the same position on your slide. You can also align objects by their right, top, bottom and middle edges or even center them relative to each other.

To ensure that objects are arranged in equal distances from each other, use the **Distribute Horizontally** or **Distribute Vertically** commands.

✓ Align Objects

1.   Make sure the **Lesson3b.ppt** file is active. With your mouse, draw a square around the five text boxes on your screen, beginning with CIO. Release the mouse button. This selects all 5 of the text boxes containing the management titles.

2.   Click the **Format tab** under the **Drawing Tools** tab.
3.   Click the **Align** button on the Arrange group and choose **Align Left** from the drop-down menu. This aligns the selected texts boxes to the left edge of the leftmost text box.
4.   Click the **Align** button on the Arrange group and choose **Distribute Vertically** from the drop-down menu to arrange the selected text box so that the vertical distance between them is the same.
5.   Click the **Save** button on the Quick Access toolbar to save any changes.

3.10 Rotating Objects

G raphical objects in PowerPoint can be **rotated**. Using the **Rotate** feature on the Arrange group of the Format tab, you can rotate an object in 90 degree increments or you can use the **freeform rotate tool** to rotate an object by any increment that you wish. When you select a graphical object, a green rotate handle appears, allowing you to rotate the object freeform style to any orientation you wish.

You can also rotate objects from the 3-D rotation category in the Format Shape dialog box.

✓ **To Rotate an Object**

1. Make sure the **Lesson3b.ppt** file is active. Select **Slide 9** in the slides pane.
2. Click on the **arrow** object as shown. Notice the green rotate handle.

3. Position your mouse pointer over the green rotate handle until the freeform
   rotate tool ⟳ appears .
4. Hold down your left mouse button and drag to the **left** until the arrow is pointing
   directly upwards. This rotates the object 90 degrees to the left.
5. Release the mouse button. The object is now in its new position.
6. From the **Slides Pane**, select **Slide 5**.
7. Select the **Film** graphic on the bottom of the screen. The green rotate handle
   appears.
8. Click the **Format tab** under the **Drawing Tools** tab.
9. Click the **Rotate button** on the Arrange group and click **Rotate Right 90°** from
   the drop-down menu.
10. Click and drag the object to the right about 1-inch.

> **Tip:** You can also rotate objects from the Format Shape dialog box. Click the 3-D
> Rotation category in the left pane and enter the degrees in the Z: box (or click
> the Clockwise or Counter-clockwise button until the desired rotation
> increment is attained).

3.11 Layering Objects

As you add objects to your slides, you may find that one object overlaps another
or causes another object to disappear completely. For instance, you may add a
Clip Art graphic to your slide and then want to draw a rectangle around the
graphic.   However, when you draw the rectangle, you find that the graphic has
disappeared from the screen.

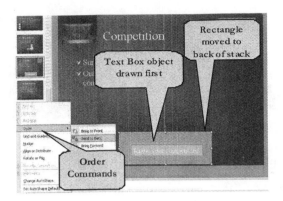

PowerPoint **layers** objects in a stack, that is to say, the first object drawn or inserted is on the bottom, the next obejct appears on top of the previous object, and so on. You can change the position of an object in the stack by using one of the **Order** commands. There are four order commands:

- **Bring to Front** – moves the selected object to the very top of the stack
- **Send to Back** – moves the selected obejct to the very back of the stack
- **Bring Forward** – moves the selected object one position up in the stack
- **Send Backward** – moves the seleted object one position back in the stack

In the example above, if you selected the rectangle and chose the **Send to Back'** command, the clip art image would now be visible as the rectangle has now moved to the back of the layered stack.

✓ Change the Layering Order of Objects

1. Make sure the **Lesson3b.ppt** file is active. Select **Slide 7** in the slides pane.
2. Click the rectangle tool on the Ribbon as shown.

3. Position your mouse pointer above and to the left of the text box that contains the text: **Know your competitors!**
4. Click your left mouse button and then draw a rectangle so that it completely surrounds the text box. Release the mouse button. Notice that the rectangle is now layered on top of the text box.

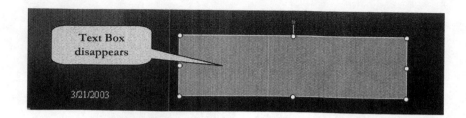

5.   With the rectangle still selected, click the **Format tab** under the Drawing tools tab and click the **Send to Back** button on the Arrange group. This sends the rectangle to the back of the stack. The text box is now visible.

6.   **Save** the active presentation.

3.12 Using Shapes

Another nifty feature you can find on the Insert Tab is **Shapes.** Shapes consist of a group of ready-made drawing objects that you can add to your presentation. These include such shapes as rectangles, circles, cubes, lines and connectors, block arrows, callouts, stars and banners and the list goes on. The AutoShapes are grouped for you by the following categories:

- Recently Used Shapes
- Lines
- Rectangles
- Basic Shapes
- Block Arrows
- Equation Shapes
- Flowchart
- Stars and Banners
- Callouts
- Action Buttons

As with other drawing objects, select the AutoShape you want from the Ribbon and then draw the shape on your slide until it is the desired size. You can add text to Shapes which then becomes part of the object. That is to say, if you rotate or move the AutoShape, the text rotates or moves with it.

✓ Add a Shape

1. Make sure the **Lesson3b.ppt** file is active. Select **Slide 3** in the slides pane.
2. Click the **Insert tab** on the Ribbon.
3. Click the **Shapes** button on the Illustrations group. This displays the Shapes gallery.
4. Under the **Basic Shapes** category, click on the **Heart Shape** (third row, seventh column) as shown.

5. Click on the slide to the right of **The Team** and then draw the AutoShape until it is about ½ high. **Release** the mouse button.

6. Click on the Shape.
7. Click the **Format** tab under the **Drawing Tools** tab on the Ribbon.
8. Click the **Shape Fill** button on the Shape Styles group and then choose **Red** from the color palette.

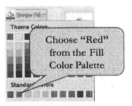

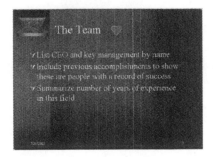

> **Tip:** The Shapes under the Shapes button on the Insert Ribbon and those under the Drawing group of the Home Ribbon are the same.

3.13 Inserting WordArt

WordArt is a gallery of text styles and effects. With WordArt, you can add spectacular effects to the text of your slides – you can shadow it, bevel it, mirror it, and make it glow. In addition, PowerPoint 2007 allows you convert existing text into WordArt format. As with text boxes, you can apply formatting to WordArt shape as well as change the text itself.

The WordArt button is located on the **Insert Ribbon** on the **Text group** and will launch the **WordArt Gallery** when clicked. From the Gallery, select the **style** of WordArt you wish to add and then type the text for your WordArt object.

From the **Format tab** that displays when the WordArt object is selected, you can apply a variety of text effects by clicking the **Text Effects** button on the WordArt styles group.

 **Insert WordArt**

1. Make sure the **Lesson3b.ppt** file is active. Select **Slide 11** in the slides pane.
2. Click the **Insert tab** on the Ribbon.
3. Click the **WordArt** button on the Text group. This displays the WordArt Gallery.

4. Select the WordArt Style in the **third column, last row**.

5. Type: **Risk leads to Rewards**.

6. With the object selected, move your mouse pointer over the object until the pointer transforms into a 4-way arrow.
7. Click and drag the WordArt object to the bottom center of the slide.
8. Click the **Home** tab on the **Ribbon**.
9. With the WordArt object still selected, click the **Font Size** drop-down list and choose **44**.
10. With the object still selected, click the **Format tab** under the Drawing Tools tab.
11. Click the **Text Effects** button on the WordArt Styles group.

Displays the Text Effects gallery.

12. Point to **Glow** and select the Glow style in the last row, first column.

13. Click the **Text Effects** button on the WordArt Styles group again and point to **Transform**.
14. Click the **Arch Up** transform style, the first style under the **Follow Path** category as shown.

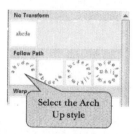

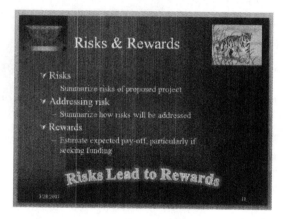

3.14 Inserting SmartArt

SmartArt is a new feature in Microsoft Office 2007 that allows you to insert grapical objects such as diagrams, organiazation charts, flow charts, graphical lists, matrix, and much more. With the wide-range of formatting tools available such as colors, bevels, shadeows, etc., you can easily create an extremely impressive presentation.

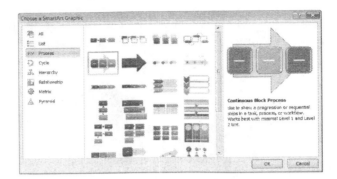

After you have inserted a SmartArt object, you can manipulate and format the object in many ways from the **Design tab** on the Ribbon. Options include appying a quick style to a SmartArt graphic, changing its orientation, changing its layout, and changing its colors, just to name a few.

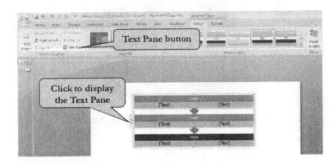

The quickest way to add text is to click directly into a SmartArt object and begin typing. You can also use the **Text Pane** to enter your text. Click the **Text Pane** button on the Design tab on the Create Graphic group or click the control with two arrows along the left side of the object to display the text pane.

PowerPoint 2007 allows you to convert existing text to a SmartArt graphic. To do this, select the text box you want to convert, click the **Convert to SmartArt button** on the Home Ribbon and choose the desired layout from the gallery.

✓ Use SmartArt in a Presentation

1. Make sure the **Lesson3b.ppt** file is active. Click the **Home** tab on the Ribbon.
2. Click the **New Slide** arrow on the Ribbon and choose the **Title Only** layout..
3. Click in the **title box** and type: **Agenda**.
4. Click outside of the placeholder to deselect the title placeholder.
5. Click the **Insert tab** on the Ribbon.
6. Click the **SmartArt button** on the Illustrations group. This displays the SmartArt gallery.
7. Click the **List** category in the left pane.

8. Click the **Trapezoid List** thumbnail in the second column, fifth row. This displays information about the object in the right pane.

9. Click **OK** to insert the SmartArt graphic into the slide.
10. Click in the title Text bullet in the left pane and type: **Process**.

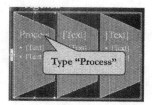

11. Click in the second level bullet text area below Process in the first pane and type: **Benefits**
12. Click in the second level bullet text area below Benefits in the first pane and type: **Results**
13. Click in the title Text bullet in the center pane and type: **Employees**.

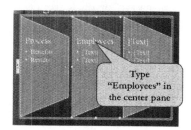

14. Click in the second level bullet text area below Employees in the center pane and type: **Office**
15. Click in the second level bullet text area below Office in the center pane and type: **Union**
16. Press **Enter** to insert a new bulleted item.
17. Click in the second level bullet text area below Union in the center pane and type: **Management**
18. Click the **Design tab** on the Ribbon under the SmartArt Tools tab.
19. Move your mouse pointer over any of the style thumbnails in the SmartArt Styles group to display a preview of the style.

20. Click the **More** button on the **SmartArt Styles** group. This displays the SmartArt Styles gallery.

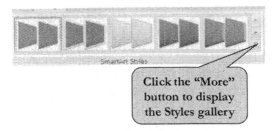

21. Click the last style in the gallery (Birds Eye Scene).

22. Click the **More** button on the **Layouts group** and choose the **Vertical Block List layout,** the last layout in the third row.

23. Make Slide 11 the active slide.
24. Select the text box containing the bulleted items.
25. Click the **Convert to SmartArt Graphic** button on the Paragraph Group as shown.

26. Click **More SmartArt Graphics** on the bottom of the gallery to display the entire SmartArt gallery
27. Click the **List** category in the left pane.
28. Click the **Hierarchy List** thumbnail in the **third column, last row** and then click **OK.**
29. Click the **Change Colors** button on the SmartArt Styles group on the Ribbon (under the Design Tab) to display the Colors gallery.
30. Click the **second thumbnail** under the **Primary Theme Colors** category.
31. Click the **Microsoft Office button** and select **Close** from the File Options menu. Click **Yes** when asked to save your changes.

Lesson 4 - Tables and Charts

4.1 Inserting a Table

Sales by Rep			
	2001	2002	Variance
Darby	$65000	$75000	$10000
Sanford	$80000	$60000	($29000)
Clarke	$55000	$70000	$15000
Morgan	95000	130000	$35000

Tables are an excellent way to present data. Similar to spreadsheets, tables are organized in rows and columns. An intersection of rows and columns is called a cell. You decide how many rows and columns you want to appear in your table. Pressing the **Tab** key moves your cursor from one cell to another when entering data. Once you insert a table, you can add more rows or columns later if need be. Like other objects in PowerPoint, you can apply a wide array of formats to your table such as borders, cell shading and cell fill.

✓ **To Insert a Table on a New Slide**

1. Open the **Lesson4a.ppt** presentation found in your Course Docs folder
2. Click the **Layout button** on the Slides group of the Home Ribbon and choose **Title and Content** from the gallery.
3. Click the **Insert Table** icon in the Content placeholder. This displays the Insert Table dialog box.

4. **Type 4** in the Number of columns box as shown.

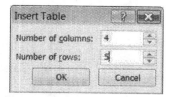

5. **Type 5** in the Number of rows box.
6. Click **OK** to close the Insert Table dialog box and create the table.
7. Click in the **Title Placeholder** and type: **Sales by Rep**
8. Enter the table data as follows:

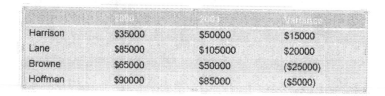

	2000	2001	Variance
Harrison	$35000	$50000	$15000
Lane	$85000	$105000	$20000
Browne	$65000	$50000	($25000)
Hoffman	$90000	$85000	($5000)

9. Save the presentation.

4.2 Applying Quick Styles to a Table

PowerPoint includes several **quick styles** that you can add to your table. These table formats include preset colors and borders styles. Under the Design tab under the Tables tab, you will see several Table Style thumbnails displayed on the Ribbon. Move your mouse pointer over any of these styles to see a preview of the selected style. Click the **Scroll Up** or **Scroll Down arrow** to scroll the style list. To view the entire Table Styles gallery, click the **More Styles** button.

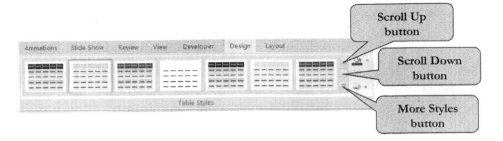

✓ To Apply a Quick Style to a Table

1. Make sure the **Lesson4a.ppt** file is active. Click anywhere inside of the table to select it.
2. Click the **Design tab** on the Ribbon.
3. Move your mouse pointer over the third Table Styles thumbnail from the left in the Table Styles group. This displays a preview of the Table Style.

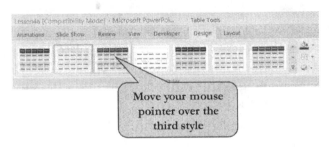

4. Click the **Scroll Down** arrow on the Table Styles group to display the next row of thumbnails.
5. Click the third Table Styles thumbnail from the left in the Table Styles group.
6. Click the Microsoft Office button and select **Close** from the menu. Save your changes.

4.3   Inserting/Deleting Rows & Columns

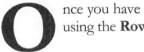nce you have created your table, you can add or remove rows and columns by using the **Row and Column** tools on the **Layout** Ribbon.

Rows & Columns group

To add or delete columns and rows, click in the area of the table where you want to add or delete a row or column, and then choose from the following options on the Table submenu of the Tables and Borders toolbar:

- Insert Left (inserts columns to the left of the selected column)
- Insert Right (inserts columns to the right of the selected column)
- Insert Above (inserts rows above the selected row)
- Insert Below (inserts rows below the selected row)
- Delete (choose rows or columns)

You can also **right-click** in any table cell, point to insert, and then choose the desired command from the menu. To delete a row or a column, right-click and choose either **Delete Rows** or **Delete Columns**.

 Add/Delete Columns or Rows

1. Open the presentation file **Lesson4b.ppt** found in your Course Docs folder
2. Click in the row containing the name **Sanford**.
3. Click the **Layout** tab on the Ribbon.
4. Click the **Insert Above** button on the Rows & Columns group.

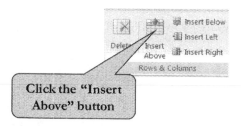

Click the "Insert Above" button

5. Click in the row containing the name **Morgan**.
6. Click the **Layout** tab on the Ribbon.
7. Click **Delete** button on the Rows and Columns group and click **Delete Rows** from the drop-down menu.
7. Select the cell with the text **2001**.
8. Click the **Insert Left** button on the Ribbon. This inserts a new blank column to the left of the selected column.

4.4 Adjusting the Width/Height of Rows & Columns

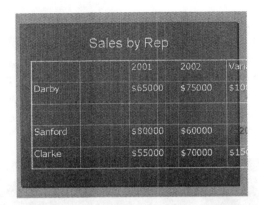

Notice that when you inserted a new column, part of the title text in your last column wrapped to the next. To adjust the width of a column or the height of a row, click on the right border line of the column or the bottom border line of the row (your pointer will become two arrows) and then drag in the direction of the width or height you want to change. You can also double-click on either a row or column border to automatically "AutoFit" the column or row to accommodate the widest column entry or the tallest row entry.

✓ Adjust Column Width and Row Height

1. Make sure the **Lesson4b.ppt** file is active. Move your mouse pointer over the right border of the 1st column, as shown, until the pointer transforms into a double vertical line with an arrow pointing through the center. When the mouse pointer changes, you are now ready to begin sizing the column.

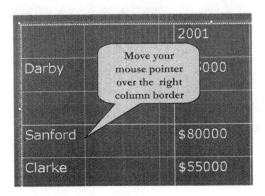

2. Click and drag to the left until the column border is just to the right of the **"d"** in **Sanford**. This reduces the width of the column to accommodate the widest entry.

3. Move your mouse pointer over the right border of the **blank column** until the pointer transforms into a double vertical line with a horizontal arrow pointing through the center.

4. Click and drag to the left about **½ inch.**

5. **Double-click** on the right border of the column that contains the word **2001**. This Autofits the column to accommodate the widest entry.

6. **Double-click** on the right border of the column that contains the word **2002.**

7. Move your mouse pointer over the sizing control in the middle of the left border as shown (your mouse pointer will transform into a double arrow) Dragging on the center sizing control allows you to increase the size of the table.

8. Click and drag to the right about 1/2 –inch.

9. **Double-click** on the right border of the first column of the table.

10. Click the **Save** button on the Quick Access toolbar.

4.5   Formatting Table Borders

The **Draw Borders** group, which can be found under the **Design tab**, allows you to change the borders of both the inside and outside lines of your table or remove the borders completely. Options include the border type, the border thickness (weight) and pen color.

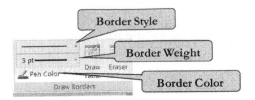

Once you have set the border formatting that you want, click the **Borders button** on the Table Styles group to apply the formatting to the borders.

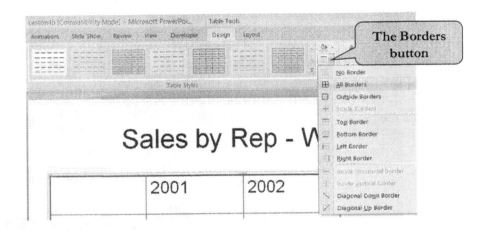

✓ Format Table Borders

1. Make sure the **Lesson4b.ppt** file is active. In the **Slides Pane**, select Slide 2.
2. Click on the placeholder border of the table. This selects the entire table.
3. Click the **Design tab** on the Ribbon to display table design tools and commands.
4. Click the **Pen Weight** drop-down list and then select **3 pt** as shown.

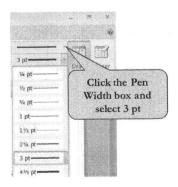

5. Click the **Pen Color** drop-down list and then click the **Dark Blue** color swatch under the Standard Colors category (second to the last color).
6. Click the **Borders button** under the **Table Styles** group and select **All Borders** from the list.

7. Click the **Borders button** under the **Table Styles** group and select **Bottom Border** from the list. This removes the Border Style from the bottom border.
8. Click the **Pen Color** drop-down list and then click the **Red** color swatch under the Standard Colors category. This sets Red as the border color.
9. Click the **Borders button** under the **Table Styles** group and select **Bottom Border** from the list.
10. Click the **Borders button** again and select **Top Border** from the list.
11. **Save** the active presentation.

4.6   Applying Cell Shading to a Table

You can apply colors to individual cells or to an entire table. To accomplish this, select the **Shape Fill button** on the Home Ribbon or the **Shading button** on the **Design tab**. You can also right-click the table, choose Format Shape and select any fill color options.

By selecting **Shape Fill** formatting, you can also add such effects as gradient, texture and various patterns to your cells. You could even add a background picture to your cells.

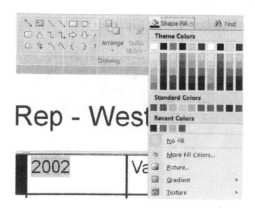

✓ Apply Shading to Cells

1. Make sure the **Lesson4b.ppt** file is active. Click in the blank cell in the first row and drag across until the entire first row of the table is selected. This is the range to which you will apply shading.
2. On the **Tables Styles** group under the Design tab, click the arrow next to the **Shading** button. This displays the Fill Color drop-down list.

3. Click **More Fill Colors** from the menu. This displays the **Colors** dialog box.
4. Click the **Standard** tab to switch to the standard colors palette.
5. Click a **Light Gray** color in the Palette as shown.

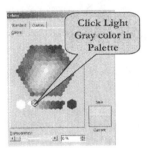

6. Click **OK**.
7. Click anywhere in the table to deselect the first row.
8. **Save** the active presentation.

4.7   Inserting a Chart

Charts are an ideal way to graphically present your numerical data. If you have Excel 2007 installed on your computer, you can add a chart to your slides to provide a visual element for your numeric data. Click the **Chart** on the **Insert Ribbon**, choose the type of Chart you want, and then click OK. An Excel spreadsheet with sample data will display in a separate pane. You can then replace the sample data with your own data.

Some available chart types are:

- Pie Chart
- Line Chart
- Bar Chart
- Area Chart
- Column Chart
- Doughnut Chart

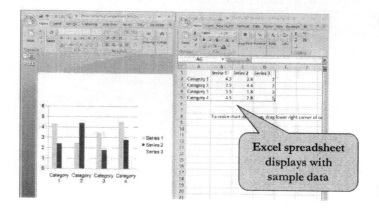

Excel spreadsheet displays with sample data

✓ Insert a Chart on a Slide

1. Make sure the **Lesson4b.ppt** file is active. Click the **Home tab** on the Ribbon.
2. Click the **New Slide arrow** on the Slides group of the Home Ribbon and choose **Title and Content** from the gallery.
3. Click the **Insert Chart** icon in the Content placeholder.

4. Click the **Column category** in the left pane. This displays available chart types in the Column category.
5. Click the **Clustered Bar** chart type in the right pane (first row, first column).

Select the Clustered Bar chart type

6. Click **OK**. This launches the Excel application and displays a worksheet with Sample Data.
7. In the Excel worksheet, click inside of the cell containing the word **Series 1**.
8. Type: **Harrison** and then press **Tab**.

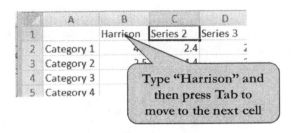

Type "Harrison" and then press Tab to move to the next cell

9. Type: **Browne** and then press **Tab**.
10. Type: **Lane**.
11. Click in cell **E1**.
12. Type: **Hoffman**.
13. Click in the cell with the words **Category 1** (cell A2) and type: **1ˢᵗ Qtr**. Press **Tab**. This enters data into Cell A2 and moves to cell B2.
14. Type: **35000** and then press **Tab**.
15. Type: **85000** and then press **Tab**
16. Type: **65000** and then press **Tab**
17. Type: **90000**.
18. Click in the cell with the words **Category 2** (cell A3) and type: **2ⁿᵈ Qtr**. Press **Tab**.
19. Type: **50000** and then press **Tab**.
20. Type: **105000** and then press **Tab**.
21. Type: **40000** and then press **Tab**.
22. Type: **85000**.
23. Click on the **Lower-right corner** of the blue border surrounding the data and drag upwards until the last two rows are hidden by a gray band. This moves the data selection border up, to exclude the last two rows of sample data.

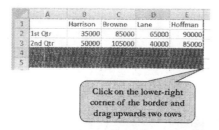

Click on the lower-right corner of the border and drag upwards two rows

24. Click the **Close Button** on the **Excel window**. This closes the Excel spreadsheet and updates the chart to reflect the new data.

4.8   Formatting a Chart

After creating your chart, three Ribbons appear when the chart is selected: **Design, Layout** and **Format**. These enable you to format your chart, apply various styles, and change the chart layout.

From the **Design Ribbon**, you can apply various chart layouts and chart styles as well as change the chart type and modify the existing chart data. The **Layout Ribbon** allows you to modify and add chart elements such as the chart labels, axes, and plot areas. You are already familiar with many of the features on the **Format Ribbon**. From here, you can change the shape borders, modify the colors and patterns of the graphical data series, and modify Shape Styles. To modify specific chart selections such as a data series or axis options, click the chart element and click the **Format Selection** button on the Format Ribbon to display the appropriate dialog box.

Additionally, you can format the text on your chart (font, color, alignment) just as you would any other text contained in a placeholder from the Home Ribbon.

✓ Format a Chart

1. Make sure the **Lesson4b.ppt** file is active. Click on the border of the chart. This selects the chart and displays the Design, Layout and Format Ribbons.
2. Click the **Layout tab** under Chart Tools.
3. Click the **Chart Title** button on the Ribbon and choose **Above Chart** from the menu.

Click the Chart Title button and choose "Above Chart"

4. Select the text in the **Chart Title** box, type: **Sales by Rep**
5. Click the **Axis Titles** button on the Ribbon, point to **Primary Horizontal Axis Title** and choose **Title Below Axis** from the menu.
6. Select the text in the **X-Axis Title** box, type: **Year.**
7. Click the **Axis Titles** button on the Ribbon, point to **Primary Vertical Axis Title** and choose **Horizontal Title** from the menu. This inserts a horizontal text box to the left of the Value Z axis.
8. Select the text in the **Value axis box**, type: **Sales**.
9. **Right-click** any of the values on the Value Axis (the vertical axis on the left) and select **12** from the Font Size drop-down list on the Mini-Toolbar.

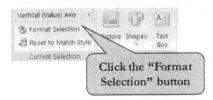

Select "12" from the Font Size list on the Mini-toolbar

10. **Click** any of the values on the Value Axis and click the **Format Selection** button under the Current Selection group. This displays the Format Axis dialog box.

Click the "Format Selection" button

11. Click the **Number** category in the left pane. This displays number formatting options.
12. In the **Category** box in the right pane, select **Currency**.

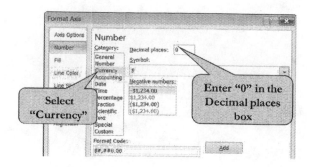

Select "Currency"

Enter "0" in the Decimal places box

13. In the **Decimal places** box, type: **0**. Click **Close** to set the number formatting to no decimal places.
14. With the value series still selected, click the **Home tab** on the Ribbon.
15. Click the **Font Color arrow** on the Font group and click the **Red** color swatch in the palette.
16. Click on the either of the values (1ˢᵗ Qtr or 2ⁿᵈ Qtr) on the Category-X axis.
17. Click the **Font Color arrow** on the Font group and click the **Red** color swatch in the palette.
18. Click the **Font Size arrow** on the Font group and click **12**.
19. Click on either of the **white bars** for **Lane**.

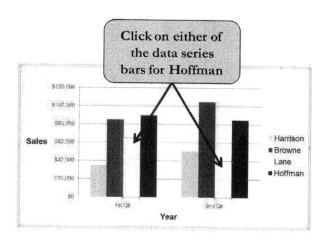

Click on either of the data series bars for Hoffman

20. Click the **Shape Fill** button on the Drawing group and click the **yellow** color swatch under the Standard Colors category.
Changes the bar color for Hoffman to yellow.
21. Click the **Design** tab under **Chart Tools** on the Ribbon.
Switches to chart design options.
22. On the **Chart Layouts** group, click the **third thumbnail** as shown.

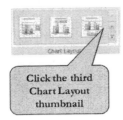

Click the third
Chart Layout
thumbnail

23.   Click the **More** button to display the Chart Styles gallery.

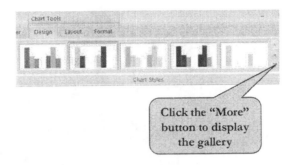

Click the "More"
button to display
the gallery

24.   Click the **last style** in the **last row** .
25.   **Save** the active presentation.

4.9   Changing the Chart Type

PowerPoint offers several chart types to aid you in communicating different types of information. To change the chart type, click the **Change Chart Type** button on the Type group under the **Design tab** under Chart Tools to display the Chart Type dialog box. From there, you can choose from a wide array of chart types.

✓ Change the Chart Type:

1.   Make sure the **Lesson4b.ppt** file is active. Click anywhere on the chart.
2.   Click the **Design tab** on the Ribbon to switch to chart design tools and commands.
3.   Click the **Change Chart Type** button on the Type group as shown.

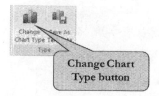

Change Chart Type button

4. Click **Line** in the left pane. This displays chart types in the Line category.
5. Click the **fourth** chart type from the left in the right pane in the Line category **(Line with markers)**

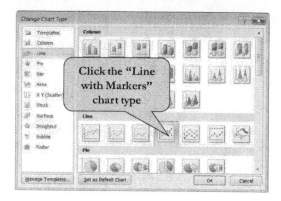

Click the "Line with Markers" chart type

6. Click **OK** to close the Chart Type dialog box and apply the new chart type.
7. Click the **Change Chart Type** button on the Type group.
8. Click **Bar** in the left pane to display chart types in the Bar category.
9. Click the **first** chart type from the left in the right pane in the Bar category **(Clustered Bar)**
10. Click **OK.**
11. Click the **Format** tab on the Ribbon to switch to chart formatting tools and commands.
12. Click the **bottom bar** in the chart area (Harrison) under 2nd Qtr.

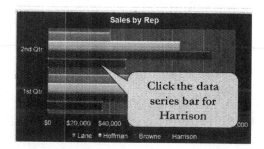

Click the data series bar for Harrison

13. Click the **Shape Fill** button and click the **Purple** color swatch under the Standard Colors category to change the data series bars for Harrison to purple.
14. **Save** the active presentation.

4.10 Inserting an Organization Chart

Microsoft Office provides the ability to insert **diagram objects** into your presentations. One of these diagram objects is the **Organization Chart** which allows you to illustrate hierarchical relationships such as the structure of a business (i.e. names, titles and departments of managers).

The organization chart is the 1st object located in the **Hierarchy category** of the **SmartArt gallery**.

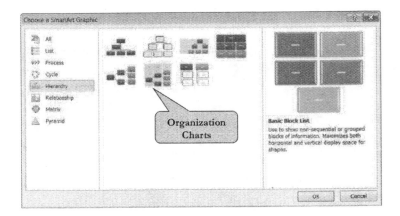

✓ Insert an Organization Chart:

1. Make sure the **Lesson4b.ppt** file is active. Click the **Home tab** on the Ribbon.
2. Click the **New Slide arrow** and select **Blank** from the layout gallery.
3. Click the **Insert tab** on the Ribbon.
4. Click the **SmartArt** button on the Illustrations group.
5. In the left pane, click **Hierarchy**. This displays available Organization Chart shapes.
6. Click on the **Organization Chart** diagram object (1st row, 1st column).
7. Click **OK** to insert the Organization Chart onto your slide.

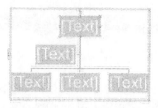

8. Click in the topmost box and then type: **Rodney Davis.**
9. Press **Enter**.
10. Type: **Owner**.

Enter the second line of text in the topmost row.

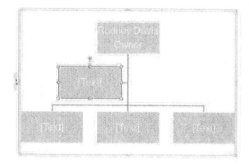

11. Click the **border** of the **leftmost shape** on the second row and press the **Delete** key
12. Click in the **leftmost shape** on the second row and type the following two lines:
    Diane Harrison
    Regional Mgr.
13. Click in the **middle shape** on the second row and type the following two lines:
    Richard Lane
    District Mgr.
14. Click in the **rightmost** shape on the second row and type the following two lines:
    Debra Browne
    Area Mgr.

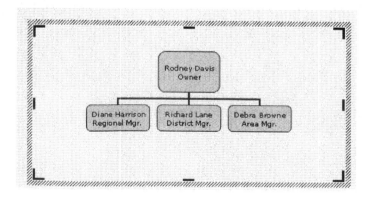

15. Click outside the shape anywhere on the active slide to deselect the Organization Chart object.

4.11 Modifying an Organizational Chart

After you create your Organizational Chart, you can add additional shapes/relationships (or nodes) by clicking on the shape to which you want to add a relationship, clicking the **Add Shapes arrow** on the Create Graphic group, and selecting the position where you wish to insert the new shape. You can also add new shapes from the Text Pane by setting the insertion point in the shape where you want to add a new shape and pressing the Enter key. You can then press the Tab key to indent the shape or the Shift tab to demote the position of the shape.

To **delete** a shape/relationship, select the relationship, and then press the delete key.

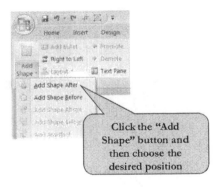

Click the "Add Shape" button and then choose the desired position

Like the other graphical object with which you have been working, you can format your Organization Chart by adding special effects such as glow, 3-D rotation and bevel as well as changing the layout or applying SmartArt Styles to the object.

✓ To Format an Organization Chart

1. Make sure the **Lesson4b.ppt** file is active. Click the shape containing the text: **Rodney Davis.**

2. Click the **Design tab** under SmartArt Tools on the Ribbon.
3. Click the **arrow** under the **Add Shape** button on the Create Graphic group to display a menu of available shape positions.
4. Choose **Add Assistant** from the menu.
5. Click inside the new object and type the following two lines of text:
   Paul Hoffman
   Assistant Mgr.
6. Click outside the shape to deselect the new shape.
7. Click the shape containing the text: **Debra Browne.**
8. Click the **arrow** under the **Add Shape** button on the Create Graphic group to display a menu of available shape positions.
9. Choose **Add Shape After** from the menu.
10. Click inside the new object and type:
    Stan Darby
    Area Mgr.
11. Click the **More** button on the **SmartArt Styles** group to display the SmartArt Styles gallery.
12. Click the **first style (polished)** under the 3-D category.
13. Click the **Microsoft Office** button and choose **Close** from the menu. Click **Yes** when asked to save your changes.

Lesson 5 - Presentation Output

5.1 Previewing a Presentation

Previewing your presentation before printing allows you to get an idea how your presentation output will appear. Additionally, you can change printing options such as setting page orientation (portrait or landscape), including a header or a footer on your output (date, time, page numbers), previewing Notes and Handouts, viewing your output in grayscale, and more. Many additional printing options are found under the **Options** button on the **Print Preview Ribbon**.

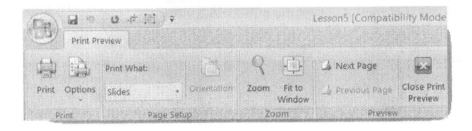

Print Preview Toolbar

✓ **Preview a Presentation**

1. Open **Lesson5.ppt** in your Course Docs folder
2. Click the **Microsoft Office Button**, point to **Print** and then click **Print Preview**.
3. Click the **Next Page** button on the Preview group.

4. Click the drop-down arrow next to **Print What** and then select **Notes Pages**
5. Click the **Print** button. This displays additional printing options.
6. Click **Cancel** to close the Print dialog box.
7. Click the **Close Print Preview** button to return to Normal View.

5.2   Page Setup

You can change the settings for the printed output of your presentation from the **Page Setup** dialog box. Settings you can modify include:

- Page Orientation for Slides and Notes/Handouts/Outline
- Paper Type (on-screen, letter, ledger, etc.)
- Page Margins (Width & Height)
- Page Numbering

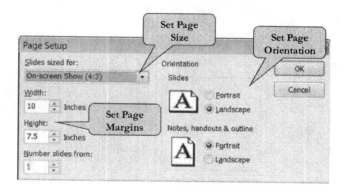

Page Orientation can be set to **Portrait** (taller than wider) or **Landscape** (wider than taller). You can set a different orientation for your slides than for your notes, handouts, and outline. The default orientation for slides is landscape whereas the default orientation for your notes, handouts and outline is portrait.

✓ Modify Page Setup

1. Make sure the **Lesson5.ppt** file is active. Click the **Design tab** on the Ribbon to display Design commands and tools
2. Click the **Page Setup** button on the Page Setup group.
3. From the **Slides Sized for** drop-down list, choose **Letter Paper**.

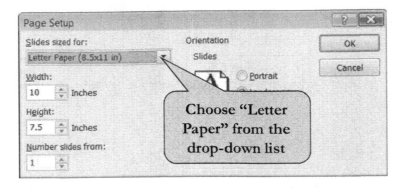

4. In the **Height** drop-down box, type: **7** This Increases the top and bottom margins by ½ inch.
5. Click **OK** to close the Page Setup dialog box.

5.3 Printing Slides

Before printing your document, you may first want to set some **Printer Options**. For instance, you may need to specify which printer to use, the number of copies to be printed, or even designate PowerPoint to print only a specific range of your document. Printer options you can set will vary, depending on the type of printer you are using.

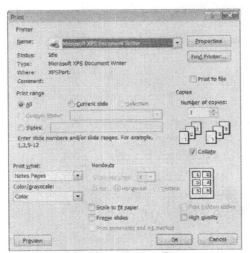

The Print Dialog Box

The **Print** command launches the **Print** dialog box, from which you can then choose additional printing options such as:

- Choosing which printer to use
- Setting the print range
- Choosing to Print in color or in grayscale
- Setting the number of copies to print
- Choosing what to print (Slides, Notes, Handouts or Outline)

✓ # Print Slides

1. Make sure the **Lesson5.ppt** file is active. Click the **Microsoft Office** button and then click **Print**. This displays the Print Dialog box.
2. In the Print Range area, click the radio button next to **Slides**, and then type: **2-4** in the text box. This sets the option to print only slides 2 through 4.

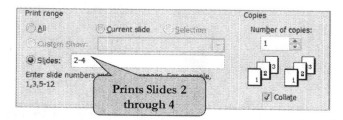

3. Click the **Print What** drop-down arrow and choose **Slides**.
Chooses Slides as the object to print.

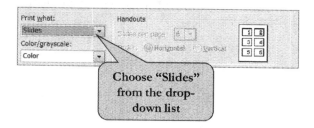

4. Click **Cancel** to close the Print dialog box without printing the presentation.

Tip: To send a document directly to the printer, click the Microsoft Office button, point to Print and then click the Quick Print option in the second pane. The Print dialog box will not open.

5.4   Printing Slide Outlines

From the Print dialog box, you can choose to print only your presentation **Outline.** To select Outline as the object to print, click the **Print What** drop-down arrow and then choose **Outline** from the list. You can additionally choose the slides whose outline you want to print from the Print Range area.

You can manually select the text you wish to print in the **Outline Pane** and then opt to print only what you have selected by choosing **Selection** under the print range area.   In this way, you can print outlines for only the slide text that you have selected.

✓ Print Slide Outlines

1. Make sure the **Lesson5.ppt** file is active. Click the **Microsoft Office** button and then click **Print** from the menu.
2. Click the **Print what** drop-down arrow and choose **Outline View.**

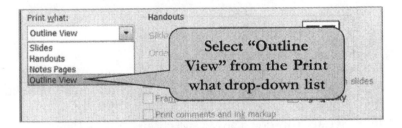

3. Click the radio button next to **Slides** and then type in: **2, 4** in the text box. Entering slide numbers separated by a comma designates that PowerPoint will print out only those individual slide outlines.

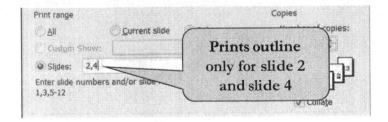

4. Click the **Preview** button in the bottom left corner of the Print dialog box Notice that only the outline of Slide 2 and Slide 4 will be printed.
5. Click the **Close Print Preview** button. PowerPoint returns to presentation view without printing the outlines.

5.5   Printing Speaker Notes

Speaker Notes include a copy of the slide and any notes that you have entered in the Notes area. Each slide along with its notes is printed on a separate page. Speaker notes are quite helpful when delivering your presentation.

To print the notes along with your slides, select **Notes Pages** from the Print What drop-down list in the Print Dialog Box.

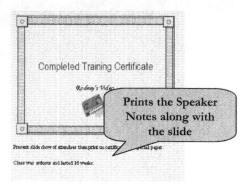

✓ Print Speaker Notes

1.   Make sure the **Lesson5.ppt** file is active. Click the **Microsoft Office** button and then click **Print** from the menu.
2.   Click the **Print what** drop-down arrow and choose **Notes Pages**

3.   Click the **All** button under the **Print Range** area to print the Notes Pages for all of the slides in the presentation.
4.   Click the **Preview** button and observe the Notes Page.

Notes Pages in Preview Mode

5. Click the **Next Page** button.
6. Click the **Close Print Preview** button to return to presentation view without printing the Notes Pages.

5.6   Printing Handouts

Handouts are printed output of your presentation with 1, 2, 3, 4, 6 or 9 slides on each page that your audience can use for future reference.   In the Print dialog box, select the number of slides you want to be included in each page and the order of the slides (horizontal or vertical).

You might want to consider passing out the handouts at the end of your presentation so that the audience is not reading your handouts instead of listening to you!

✔ Print Slide Handouts

1. Make sure the **Lesson5.ppt** file is active. Display the Print Dialog box.
2. Click the **Print what** drop-down list and then choose **Handouts**
3. Click the **Slides per page** drop-down list and select **4** to print 4 slides per page on each slide handout page.
4. Click the radio button next to **Vertical** as shown.

5. Click the **Preview** button.

Slide Handouts in Preview Mode

6. Click the **Close Print Preview** button to return to presentation view without printing the Handouts Pages.
7. Click the **Microsoft Office** button and then click **Close** from the menu. Click **Yes** if asked to save your changes.

Lesson 6 - Animation Techniques

6.1   Applying Animation

An exciting visual effect that you can add to your slides is **Animation**, which allows you to control how your information appears on the slide during a slide show. For instance, you can have your words fly onto the screen one at a time or slowly fade in. With animation, you can control how and when you want an item to appear on your screen. Using animation in your presentation can help you focus on important points and manage the flow of information – as well as add exciting effects to your slide show.

PowerPoint contains several preset visual effects that will help you get started with animation. You can apply an animation scheme to a single object or to a group of selected objects.

Apply an Animation Scheme

1.   Open the **Microsoft PowerPoint** application.
2.   Display the **Open dialog box.**
3.   Click the **My Documents** button on the left side of your screen
4.   **Double-click** the **PowerPoint 2007 – Level 2** folder.
5.   Double-click the **Lesson Files** folder.
6.   Click on the **Lesson6a** file
7.   Click the **Open** button.
8.   In the **Slides Pane** select **Slide 1.**
9.   Click the **Animations tab** on the Ribbon.
10. On Slide 1, click the **Rodney's Video, Inc.** placeholder.
11. Click the **Animate** combo box arrow on the Animations group to display a list of available animation schemes.

Click the
Animate arrow

12. Move your mouse pointer over the **All at once** scheme under the **Fade** category.
13. Click the **All at once** scheme under the **Fly In** category.

14. In the **Slides Pane** select **Slide 2**.
15. Click the placeholder that contains the bulleted list.

Selects the placeholder to which we want to apply animation.

16. Click the **Animate** combo box arrow on the Animations group and click **By 1st Level Paragraph** under the **Wipe** category as shown.

17. Select **Slide 1** in the Slides pane.
18. Press the **F5** key to enter Slide Show view.
19. Click your left mouse button or press the space bar.

20. Click your left mouse button or press the space bar again.
21. Click your left mouse button or press the space bar again **6 more times**.
22. Press the **Esc** key to return to normal view.
23. **Save** the active presentation.

6.2 Using Custom Animation

In addition to the preset animation schemes, you can also apply **Custom Animation** to the placeholders and objects on your slides. Custom Animation allows you to apply a wide range of animation effects to individual objects on your slide. For instance, you can control the direction of the animation, the event that triggers the animation, and the speed of the playback.

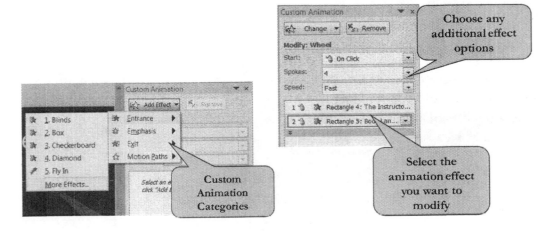

Apply Custom Animation

·

1. In the **Slides Pane** select **Slide 3**.
2. Click the **Custom Animation button** on the Animations group on the Ribbon.
3. Click on the **Title placeholder** on Slide 3.
4. Click the drop-down arrow next to the **Add Effect** button as shown. This displays the four custom animation categories.

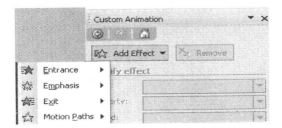

5. Point to **Entrance** from the category menu and then click **Blinds** from the Entrance submenu as shown below.

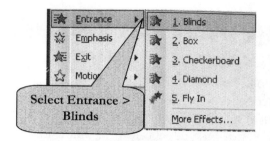

6. Select the placeholder that contains the 5 lines of text.
7. Click the drop-down arrow next to the **Add Effect** button.
8. Point to **Entrance** and then click **More Effects**.
9. Click **Wheel** from the Add Entrance Effect box.
10. Click **OK** to close the Add Entrance Effect dialog box.
11. Make sure that the animation effect preceded by the number **2** is selected in the Custom Animation pane.
12. Click the **Speed** arrow under the Modify area and select **Fast** as shown.

13. Click the **Play** button on the bottom of the **Custom Animation Task Pane**.

6.3   Modifying Effect Options

After you have chosen your custom animation, you can then add additional effects to the animation. For instance, you can dim text after it is animated, animate chart elements, add sound to your animations, and add text by word or by letter, just to name a few.

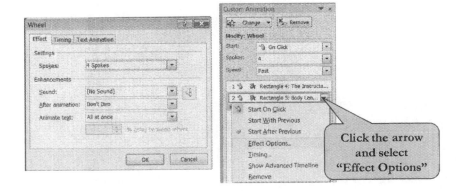

To add effect options, click the object you want to modify in the Animation Order list in the Custom Animation pane. A drop-down arrow will appear next to the object name. Click the arrow and then close **Effect Options** to display the Effect Options dialog box.

Modify Effect Options

1.   Make sure that the animation effect preceded by the number **2** is selected in the Custom Animation pane.
2.   Click the **drop-down arrow on the right** of the effect in the Animation Order list as shown and click **Effect Options**.

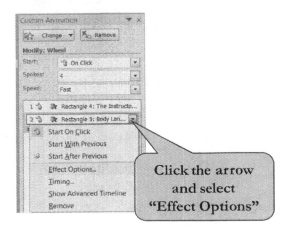

---

3.   Click the **After Animation** drop-down list and click the **gold** color swatch.

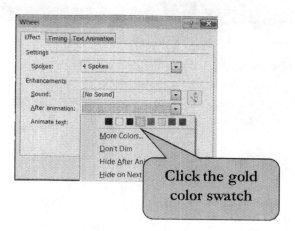

4.   Click **OK**
5.   Click the animation effect preceded by the number **1** in the Custom Animation pane.
6.   Click the **drop-down arrow on the right** of the effect in the Animation Order list and click **Effect Options**.
7.   Click the **Sound** drop-down arrow and select **Applause** from the list.
8.   Click **OK**.
9.   Click the **Play** button on the bottom of the **Custom Animation Task Pane**.
10. Click the **Close button** on the Custom Animation pane.

6.4   Adding Slide Transitions

S lide transitions specify how the display changes when you advance from one slide to the next. For example, you can add an animation effect such as Horizontal Blinds or a Checkerboard pattern. You can also add a preset sound effect to the slide transition or use your own sound file.

To apply transitions to specific slides, select the first slide in the **Slide Pane Window**, hold down the **Ctrl** key, and then select any additional slides. The fastest way to apply transitions to multiple slides is to work in slide sorter view. Click the **Apply to All** button on the Ribbon to apply the transition effect to every slide in your presentation.

Add Slide Transitions

1. Click the **Slide Sorter button** on the bottom right of your screen.
2. Click on **Slide 4**.
3. If necessary, click the **Animations tab** on the Ribbon.
4. Click the **More button** on the Slide Transitions gallery as shown below.

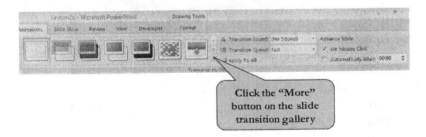

Click the "More" button on the slide transition gallery

5. Scroll down and click the **Checkerboard Across** thumbnail under the **Stripes and Bars** category (3rd thumbnail from the left).

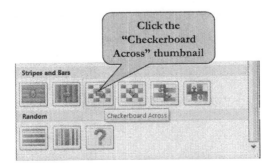

Click the "Checkerboard Across" thumbnail

6. Click the **Transition Speed** drop-down list on the Ribbon and choose **Medium**.

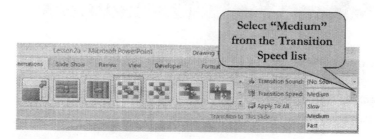

Select "Medium" from the Transition Speed list

7. Click on **Slide 5**.
8. Press and hold down the **Ctrl Key** and select **Slide 6 and Slide 7**.
9. Click the **More button** on the Slide Transitions gallery as shown below.
10. Click **Uncover Left** thumbnail – the **last thumbnail in the 1st row** under the **Wipes** category as shown.

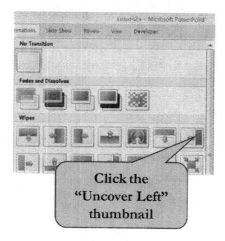

Click the "Uncover Left" thumbnail

11. Click the **Transition Speed** drop-down list and choose **Medium**.
12. Click the **Transition Sound** drop-down list and choose **Chime**.
13. Click on **Slide 4**.
14. Click the **Slide Show tab** on the Ribbon.
15. Click the **From Current Slide** button on the Start Slide Show group on the Ribbon.
16. Press the space bar. twice
18. Press the **Esc** key to return to Normal view.
19. **Save** the active presentation.

6.5 Using Transition Triggers

Slide transition triggers allow you to specify when you want to advance to the next slide and provide you more control over your presentation. There are three basic triggers you can use:

- Advance to the next slide only when you click the mouse
- Advance to the next slide after a specific time interval
- Advance to the next slide after you click the mouse or after a specified time interval, whichever occurs first.

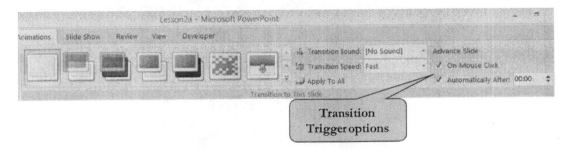

Transition Trigger options

Add Slide Transition Triggers

1. In the **Slides Sorter View pane**, select **Slide 8**.
2. Click the **Animations tab** on the Ribbon.
3. On the **Transition to This Slide** group on the Ribbon, click in the check-box next to **Automatically after**.
4. In the time interval box, type in: **:05** as shown.

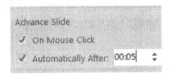

5. Display the **Slide Show** Ribbon.
6. Click the **From Current Slide** button on the Start Slide Show group on the Ribbon and wait 5 seconds. The slide automatically advances to Slide 9.
7. Switch back to **Normal View**.
8. **Save** the active presentation.
9. **Close** the presentation file.

6.6   Setting Up a Slide Show

O nce you are happy with the layout and content of your presentation, you can then set some additional Slide Show options. From the **Set up Show** dialog box, you can set the show type (speaker, individual or kiosk), set the presentation to loop continuously, choose which slides to display, how to advance the slides (manually or using timings) or whether to show them with or without animation or narration.

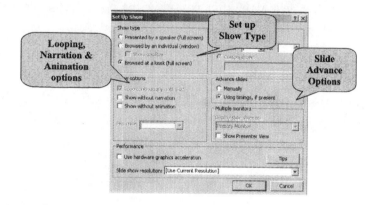

Set Up a Slide Show:

1.   Open **Lesson4** in the Lesson Files folder. *lab4?*
2.   Display the Slide Show Ribbon.
3.   Click the **Set Up Slide Show** button on the Set Up group of the Ribbon.

4.   Under **Show type**, click the **Presented by speaker** radio button as shown below.

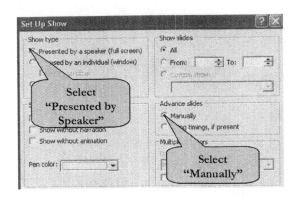

5. Under **Advance Slides**, select **Manually**. The slides will be advanced manually by the speaker and any slide timings will be ignored.
6. Click **OK.**
7. Click the **From Beginning button** on the Start Slide Show group.
8. Press the **Space Bar** to advance to the next slide.
9. Press the **Esc** key. This terminates the Slide show.
10. Click the **Animations tab** on the Ribbon. You are now going to add timing to the presentation.
11. In the **Advance Slide** area, click the **Automatically After** checkbox and type: 00:03 in the text box as shown.

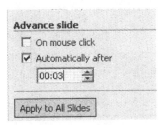

12. Click the **Apply to All** button on the Ribbon.
13. Click the **Slide Show tab** on the Ribbon.
14. Click the **Set Up Slide Show** button.
15. Under **Show type**, click the **Browsed at Kiosk** radio button. This sets up the slide show to run automatically and to loop continuously. This setting is best for an unattended presentation.
16. Under **Advance Slides**, click the **Use timings, if present** radio button. The slides will be advanced automatically using the timing settings we set in step 10.
17. Click **OK.**
18. Press the **F5** key and observe the slide show. After 3 seconds, the slides automatically advance.
19. Press the **Esc** key.
Terminates the slide show.
20. **Save** the changes.

6.7 Using Slide Show Navigation Tools

During a Slide Show presentation, use the **Slide Show Toolbar** located on the bottom left side of your screen to navigate to specific slides in your presentation. Move your mouse toward the left side of your screen to display the Slide Show Shortcut Toolbar. The toolbar provides easy access to slide show navigation while you are delivering a presentation.

In addition to jumping to a specific slide in your presentation, other options that you can access from the Slide Show Toolbar include:

- Jumping to a particular slide
- Moving to the Next or Previous Slide
- Setting Pointer Options (arrow, pen, etc.)
- Setting Pen Color
- Switching to another application
- Ending the Slide Show

Using the Pen feature allows you to annotate your slides during a presentation. You can highlight information on your slides by circling it, underling it or manually writing in additional information.

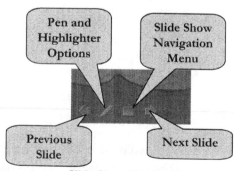

Slide Show Toolbar

You can also right-click anywhere on your slide during the presentation to display the Slide Show Navigation menu.

PowerPoint also provides keyboard shortcuts to quickly access slides in your presentation when in Slide Show View. The table below lists available slide show shortcuts.

Shortcut	Action
Click left mouse button	Advances to next slide
Click right mouse button	Displays the Slide Show Shortcut Menu
Pressing the Enter key	Advances to next slide
Typing in a slide number then pressing the Enter key	Moves to the slide number that you entered before pressing Enter
Pressing the Home key	Moves to first slide in the presentation
Pressing the End key	Moves to the last slide in the presentation
Pressing the Page Up key	Moves to previous slide
Pressing the Page Down key	Moves to next slide
Pressing the B key	Displays a black screen. Press again to redisplay the slide show.
Pressing the W key.	Displays a white screen. Press again to redisplay the slide show.

Use Slide Show Navigation Tools:

1. Click the **Set Up Slide Show button** on the Ribbon. You need to set up your slide show for a speaker presentation in order to access the Slide Show Shortcut Menu.
2. Under **Show type,** click the **Presented by speaker** radio button.
3. In the **Advance Slides** area, click the radio button next to **Manually**.
4. Click **OK.** This closes the Set Up Show dialog box.
5. Press the **F5 key** to display the presentation in Slide Show view.
6. Move your mouse pointer to the bottom left side of the screen until the **Slide Show Toolbar** appears as shown.

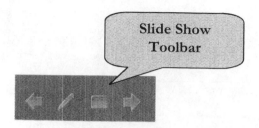

7. Click the **Slide Show menu button** and point to **Go to Slide** and then click **3 Learning Objectives** from the menu shown.
8. Click **Next Slide** button.
9. Click the **Pen and Highlighter Options** button and select **Ballpoint Pen** from the pop-up menu. This activates the Pen Tool. Notice that your mouse pointer has transformed into a small rounded pointer.
10. Click the **Pen and Highlighter Options** button, select **Ink Color** from the pop-up menu, and then choose **Yellow** under the Standard Colors area.

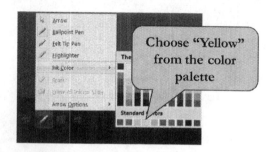

11. With the pen tool, **circle** the word "**structured**" and **underline** the word "**specific**" as shown.

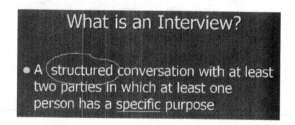

12. Click the **Pen and Highlighter Options** button and select **Eraser** from the pop-up menu
13. Click on the circle that you drew around the word "**structured**" to remove it.
14. Type the number **6** and then press **Enter**.
15. Press the **Home key** to move to the first slide.
16. Press the **B** key on your keyboard to blacken the screen.
17. Press the **B** key on your keyboard again. This redisplays the slide show.
18. Press the **Esc** key twice. A dialog box is displayed, asking you if you wish to keep or discard your ink annotations.
19. Click the **Discard** button.

6.8   Creating a Custom Slide Show

In this lesson, you will learn how create a slide show that is a subset of a larger slide show.

You can adapt a presentation that you have created to a wide range of audiences by creating **Custom Slide Shows**. A custom slide show is usually a subset of a larger presentation. For example, you might have a sizeable presentation about your company. The **Custom Shows** command allows you to build custom shows from your larger presentation tailored to a specific audience – one presentation for your financials, another for Human Resources information, etc.

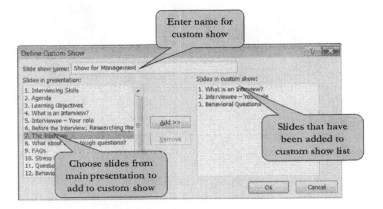

Create, Edit and Run a Custom Slide Show

1.   Display the **Slide Show** Ribbon.
2.   Click the **Custom Slide Show** button on the Start Slide Show group of the Ribbon and click **Custom Shows**.
3.   Click the **New** button.
4.   In the **Slide Show name** box, type: **My Slide Show**
5.   Click on **Slide 4** from the **Slides in presentation** list then click the **Add** button as shown below.

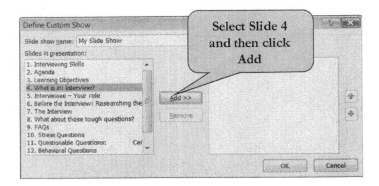

6. **Repeat** Step 5 for **Slides 7, 10, 12 and 14**.
7. Click **OK**.
8. Click **Close** to close the Custom Shows dialog box.
9. Click the **Custom Slide Show** button on the Start Slide Show group of the Ribbon and click **Custom Shows**.
10. Highlight **My Slide Show** and then click the **Show** button.

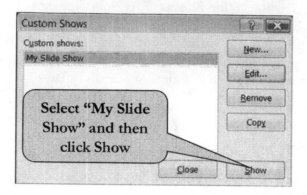

11. Move to the next slide.
12. Terminate the Slide Show and return to **Normal View**.
13. **Save and close** the active presentation.

PowerPoint Quiz

1. What are two ways to create a new presentation?

   Ctrl+N, office button-new

2. What are two ways that you can access the Microsoft PowerPoint Help System?

   F1 or question mark in top right corner

3. What is the name of the new PowerPoint object that consists of tabs, command sets and command buttons?

   Ribbon

4. Name three formatting effects to apply from the Font group on the Home Ribbon.

   text, color, size

5. You have seven text boxes on your slide. You want to be able to move them around together as one object. Describe the steps to group the text boxes so that you can work with them as a single unit.

   hold down the shift key while selecting the objects

6. How can you convert a text box to a SmartArt shape in PowerPoint?

   Select the text you wish to convert + select convert to smartart (home tab)

7. What is an Organization Chart? How do you add one to the active slide?

   Structures of businesses
   Insert-smartart-heirarchy

8. Name three options you can set in the Print Dialog box.

   Print what   print range (slides, All, current)
   number of copies

9. Outline the steps to print only your slide outlines.

   Print- print what- outline view-ok

Fundamentals of MS Office 2007

An Introduction to Access 2007

Table of Contents

Lesson 1 - Access Basics

1.1   Understanding Databases

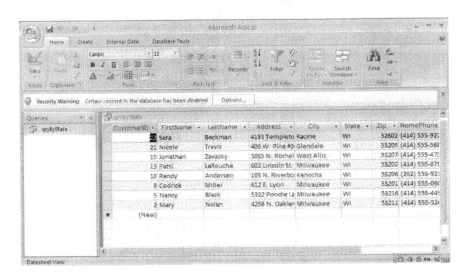

Databases are at the core of many business and organization operations. They permit centralized access to information in an efficient and consistent manner and reduce the inaccuracies of manual record keeping. A database can be thought of as an information repository pertaining to a specific topic that allows you to manage, store, retrieve and analyze information. Information in a database is stored in tables, which are the building blocks of a database. A table consists of rows (all of the information pertaining to one item) for each record and columns for each field.

Microsoft Access is a **relational database management system (RDBMS)**, the most commonly used type of database system in the world today. A relational database:

- Stores data in tables, which consist of columns and rows
- Enables you to retrieve subsets of data from tables
- Allows you to connect tables together for the purpose of retrieving related data stored in different tables

1.2   Using Database Templates

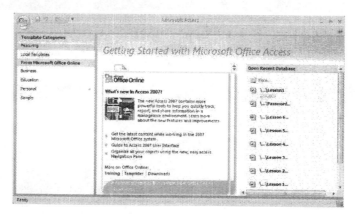

Access 2007 offers a new **Getting Started** feature that contains a wide range of templates – or fully-featured databases you can use to get started. Some of the available templates include:

- Asset Tracking
- Contact Management
- Customer Service
- Event Management
- Expenses
- Home Inventory
- Inventory Control

- Issues
- Ledger
- Marketing Projects
- Order Entry
- Resource Scheduling
- Service Call Management
- Time and Billing

To use a template, click the desired template category in the left pane. A selection of template styles for the template category will appear in the center pane. The **Local Templates** category will list templates stored on your computer. The **From Microsoft Office Online** section allows you to download templates from the Microsoft Web site.

If instead of using a template you prefer to create a blank database, click the **Blank Database** icon in the center pane.

Create a Database using a Template

1. Click on the Start button.
2. Select **All Programs** > **Microsoft Office** > **Microsoft Office Access** from the Start Menu. This launches the Microsoft Access Application and displays the Getting Started Task Pane.
3. Click **Local Templates** in the left pane.

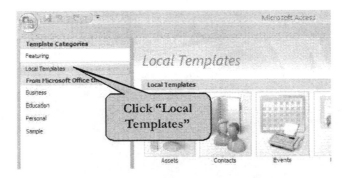

4. In the center pane, click **Contacts** under the **Templates** area. This displays template details in the third pane.

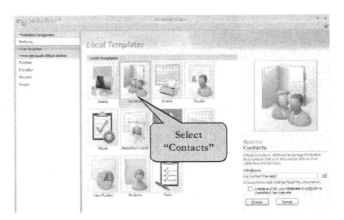

5. In the **File Name** box in the right pane type: **My Contact Manager**
6. Click the **Folder icon** in the right pane. This displays the File New Database dialog box that allows you to browse to the location where the database will be stored.

7. Locate your Course Docs folder and open it

8. **Double-click** the **Access Tutorials** folder. This is the folder where you will store your database. If you want to change the name of your database from here, enter the desired name in the File Name box.

10. Click **OK.** This closes the File New Database dialog box.

11. Click the **Create** button in the right pane. This creates a new database based on the template you selected and displays a table in Datasheet view.

1.3   Open an Existing Database

I f you've worked with previous versions of Access, you will notice that the **File > Open** command on the menu is no longer available. Instead of the word "File", the **Microsoft Office Button** indicates where the file menu commands are now located. To open an existing database, click the Microsoft Office button, click the **Open** icon, and navigate to the folder that contains that database file you wish to open. If you have recently opened a database, it may be listed in the right pane. Click on the database name in the recent files list to quickly open it.

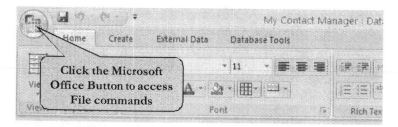

If you already have a database file open when you exectue the Open command, the database file you have open is automatically closed when the new database file is opened. Thus, you are allowed to have only one database file open per Access session.

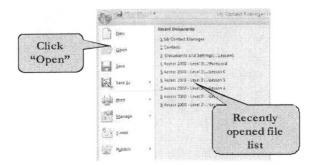

You can also display the **Open** dialog box by using the **Ctrl + O** keystroke combination. This command will bypass the Microsoft Office File Options menu and directly display the Open dialog box.

To open an existing database from the Getting Started dialog box when first launching Access, click the **More** icon in the right pane and navigate to the folder where your database is located.

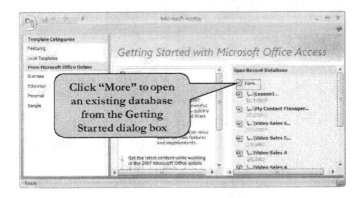

✓ Open an Existing Access Database

1. Click the **Microsoft Office Button** on the top left of your screen
2. Click the **Open** in the left pane to display the Open dialog box.
3. Locate your **Course Docs folder** and open it.
4. **Double-click** the **Access Tutorials** folder.
5. Click the **Lesson1.accdb** file.

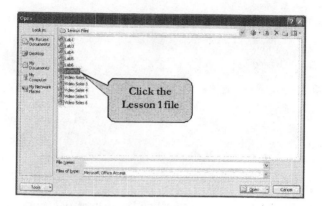

7.   Click the **Open** button.

> **Tip:** If there are macros in your database, you may receive a security message warning you of potential dangerous code. You can modify Macro warning messages from the Trust Center (click the Microsoft Office button, click Access Options, click Trust Center and then click Trust Center settings. The Macro Settings area allows you to decide which macros to disable.

1.4   The Access Environment

If you have worked with previous version of Access, you will immediately notice that the user interface has been completely redesigned. The menu and toolbar system have been replaced by the **Ribbon**. The Ribbon is designed to help you quickly find the commands you need in order to complete a task. On the Ribbon, the menu bar has been replaced by **Command Tabs** that relate to the tasks you wish to accomplish. The default Command Tabs in Access are: **Home, Create, External Data** and **Database Tools**.

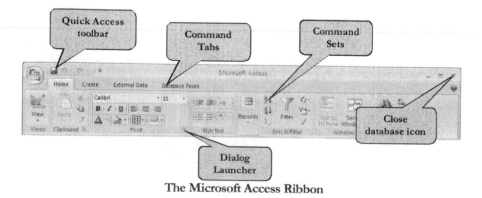

The Microsoft Access Ribbon

Different command icons, called **Command Sets** appear under each Command Tab. Each command set is grouped by its function. For example, the Tables, Forms, Reports and Other are all Command Sets for the Create tab in Access. **Contextual Commands** only appear when a specific object is selected.

On the bottom of many of the Command Sets is a **Dialog Launcher** that enables a dialog box for that set of commands.

To the right of the **Microsoft Office icon** is the **Quick Launch Toolbar.** This toolbar contains by default the Save, Undo, and Redo commands. In addition, clicking the drop-down arrow to the right allows you to customize the Quick Access Toolbar to add other tools that you use regularly. You can choose from the list which tools to display on the Quick Access Toolbar or select **More Commands** to add commands that are not in the list.

New in Access 2007 is the **Navigation Pane.** This replaces the Database Window in previous versions of Access. Like the Database Window, you can use the Navigation Pane to work with the various objects in your database (tables, forms, reports, etc.). Whenever you open a database, all of the objects in your dataset appear in the Navigation Pane. You can work on the design of your objects, enter data or run a report or query directly from the Navigation Pane.

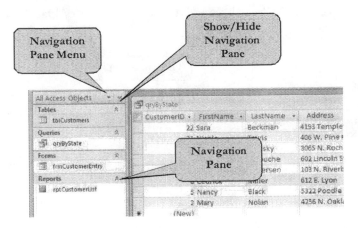

You will be working in detail with the various Access screens and database objects in subsequent lessons.

✔ Use the Navigation Pane

1. Make sure the **Lesson1.accdb** file is active. Click the **Create tab** on top of your screen
2. Click the **Database Tools tab** on top of your screen.
3. Click the **Home tab** on top of your screen..
4. Click the Navigation Pane Menu arrow and select **All Access Objects.**

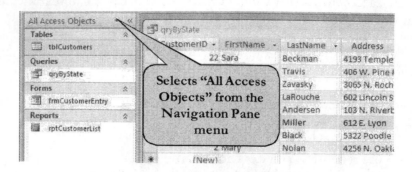

5.   Click the Navigation Pane Menu arrow again and choose **Tables**..

1.5   A Look at Tables

Tables are the building blocks of your database. They are where all of your data is stored. Tables are made up of columns and rows. Each column consists of a single field, such as First Name, Last Name, or Order Date. Each row of fields is called a record.

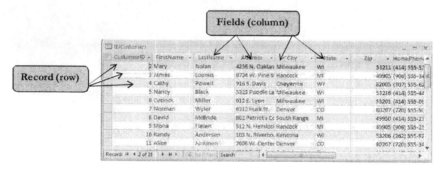

A database usually has more than one table. Each table should store different types of related information, such as a customer table that contains customer information and an orders table that contains order information.

To navigate records, click on the desired record navigation button on the navigation bar.

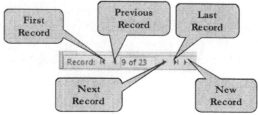

Click and drag the **vertical scroll bar** to move up and down in a table. Click and drag the **horizontal scroll bar** to move left and right in a table.

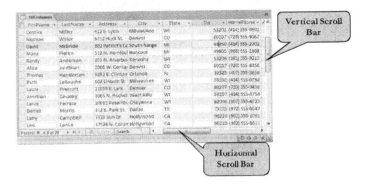

✓ Open a Table

1. Make sure the **Lesson1.accdb** file is active. Double-click **tblCustomers** in the Navigation Pane. Datasheet view is the mode where you can view, enter, update or delete data.

2. Click the **Next Record** button on the record navigation bar. The active record and the active field are color coded.

3. Click the Access window's **Restore down** button. This reduces the size of the window so that it does not fill the entire screen.

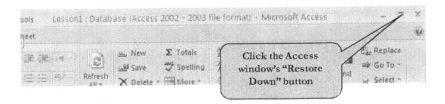

4. Click the **Last Record** button on the record navigation bar.

5. Click the **Previous Record** button on the record navigation bar.

6. Click the **New Record** button on the record navigation bar. This inserts a new record and moves to the first field of the new record.
7. Click the **Restore window** button **for the table widow**. This restores the window to its original position.

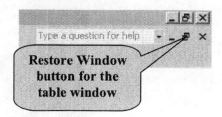

Restore Window button for the table window

8. Click the table window's **close button** (the lower "x").

1.6 A Look at Forms

Although you can enter, edit and review information in tables, many find using **Forms** to be much more user-friendly because it is more familiar. The form you use can be an on-screen representation of a paper form. This makes data entry much easier.

Forms contain labels and text boxes. Labels are informational — they tell you what to type in the text boxes. Data entered into text boxes is added directly to the table upon which the form is based. Forms can also include other objects such as checkboxes, list boxes, combo boxes, and radio buttons to make data entry even easier.

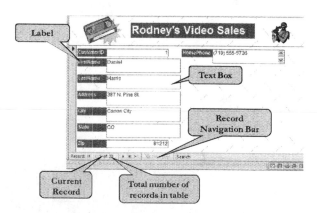

✓ Open a Form

1. Make sure the **Lesson1.accdb** file is active. Click the drop-down arrow on the **Navigation Bar** and select **Forms** from the menu. This displays all form objects.

2. Right-click the **frmCustomerEntry** form and then click the **Open** from the menu.

3. Click the **Next Record** button on the record navigation bar. The current record number and the total number of records in the table are displayed in the record navigational bar.

4. Using the Next Record button, move **to record 5**.

5. Click the **Last Record** button on the record navigation bar.

6. Click the **Previous Record** button on the record navigation bar.

7. Click the **New Record** button on the record navigation bar. This inserts a new record and moves to the first field of the new record.

8. Click in the **First Name** text box and type: **Daniel**.

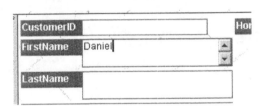

9. Press the **Tab key** and then type: **Siegler** in the **Last Name** field.

10. Type in the rest of the information. Remember to press **Tab** to move from one field to the next.

    Address: 423 W. Longview
    City: Indianapolis
    State: IN
    Zip: 42626
    Home Phone: 555-222-3555

11. **Close** the form.

> **Note:** When entering data into a table or form, you do not need to save your data manually – Access automatically saves your data when you move to a different record or when you close the table or form.

1.7   A Look at Queries

Queries are questions that you ask about your data. For example, you might want to ask: How many customers in Colorado spent more than $200 last year? To receive an answer to this question, you would use a **query**. Queries allow you to find all records that meet specific **criteria.**.

When the query is run, the results appear in a table. In addition to retrieving data, you can also enter data directly into the datasheet. Any data that is changed or added in the query datasheet is also changed or added in the underlying table.

Query Results

✓ Open a Query

1.   Make sure the **Lesson1.accdb** file is active. Click the drop-down arrow on the **Navigation Bar** and select **Queries** from the menu.
2.   **Double-click** the **qryByState** query. Notice the results only include customers from the state of Wisconsin.

3.   Click the **Next Record** button on the record navigation bar. The active record is represented by a black right arrow to the left of the row.
4.   Click the query's **Close button**.

1.8 A Look at Reports

Although you can print information from your tables, forms or queries, you have more options by using **reports**. Access allows you to display your data in a polished and professional manner. You can even add calculations to your reports for more complex data analysis.

Unlike the other objects you have seen so far, you cannot modify the data in a report. Reports are for displaying and printing data only.

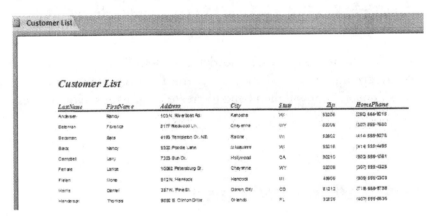

✓ To Open a Report

1. Make sure the **Lesson1.accdb** file is active. Click the drop-down arrow on the **Navigation Bar** and select **Reports** from the menu.
2. **Double-click** the **rptCustomerList** report. This displays the rptCustomerList report in Print Preview mode.

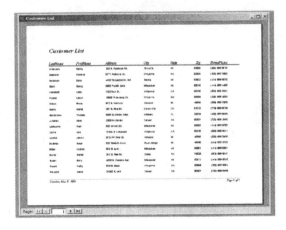

---

3. Click the **Next Page** button on the record navigation bar.

4. Move your 🔍 pointer over the report and then click with your left mouse button. This Enlarges the selected area allowing you to view a specific portion of the report.

5. Move your 🔍 pointer over the report and click with your left mouse button. Access Returns to full page view.

6. Click the report's **close button**

1.9   Creating a Blank Database

If you decide not to use any of the database templates, you can create a blank database by clicking **Blank Database** in the **Getting Started** pane. Once your database is created, you will then need to create all of your tables, queries, forms and reports.

✓ Create a Blank Database

1. Click the **Microsoft Office Button** and then click **New** from the menu. This displays the **Getting Started** pane.

2. In the **Center** Pane, click on **Blank Database** as shown.

3. In the **File name** text box, type: **Video Sales.accdb** .

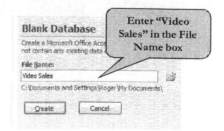

4. Click the **Folder icon** to the right of the File Name box. This displays the File New Database dialog box which allows you to browse to the desired location to save the database.
5. Locate your Course Docs folder and open it.
6. **Double-click** the **Access Tutorials** folder. This is the desired location for storing the blank database. If you want to specify the name of your database from here, enter the desired name in the File Name box.
7. Click **OK** to close the File New Database dialog box.
8. Click **Create**. A blank new table displays in Datasheet view.

1.10 Setting Access Options

In previous versions of Access, you could set preferences for specific program settings from the Options dialog box. The Options command has been moved to the **Access Options** button on the File Options menu which displays when you click the **Microsoft Office Button**. From the Access Options dialog box, you can specify such options as the default database format and database folder, open Navigation Pane items with a single-click instead of a double-click, have multiple opened objects appear in tabbed windows rather than overalpping windows, and much, much more.

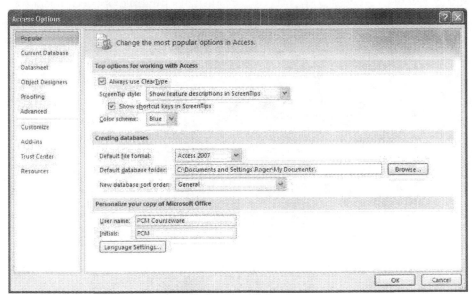

Access Options dialog box

✓ Set Access Options

1. Make sure the **Video Sales.accdb** file is active. Click the **Microsoft Office Button**.
2. Click the **Access Options** button.

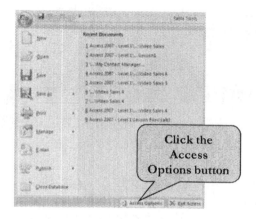

Click the Access Options button

3. Click the **Current Database** category in the left pane.
4. Under the Document Window Options, click the **Tabbed Documents** radio button. New in Access 2007, this options displays multiple opened object (tables, queries, forms, and reports) in a tabbed window instead of overlapping windows.

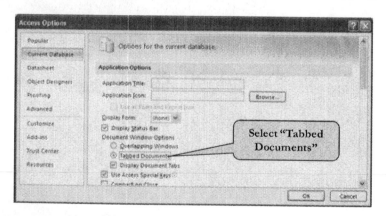

Select "Tabbed Documents"

5. Click **OK**. This closes the Access Options dialog box and applies the changes.
6. Click **OK**. This closes the message box that tells you that you must close and reopen the database for our changes to take effect.

1.11 Using Help

T he **Help system** is designed to provide **assistance** to users whether you are online or offline. To access the Help system, press **F1** or click the **Help icon** on the upper right-hand corner of the Access window.

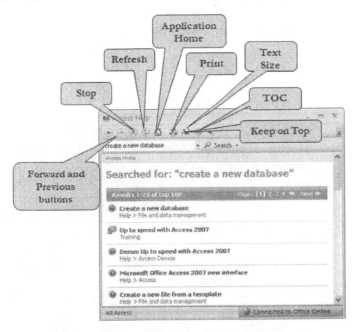

The Help system toolbar includes the familiar Back, Forward and Stop commands. Additionally, you will find the new **Refresh** tool, which allows you to update the content of the Help window. The **Application Home** tool brings you to the Access starting point, where you can browse through information related to the Microsoft Access application. The **TOC** tool displays a listing of available help topics through which you can browse. If you wish to increase or decrease the text size in the Help window, click the **Text Size** tool. Another nice feature on the Help toolbar is the **Keep on Top** tool, which allows you to keep the current Help page open while you work.

✓ Use the Help System

1. Make sure the **Video Sales.accdb** file is active. Click the **Microsoft Office Help icon** on the upper right-hand corner of the screen as shown. This displays the Access Help System window.

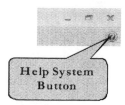

Help System
Button

2.   In the **Search box**, type: **Create a New Database**.

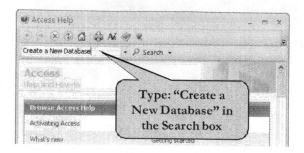

Type: "Create a
New Database" in
the Search box

3.   Press **Enter**. The results are displayed in the Search Results pane.
4.   Click the **Create a new database** link in the Search Results pane. This displays
the help topic for that link.

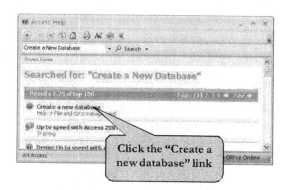

Click the "Create a
new database" link

5.   Click the **Table of Contents** button on the toolbar.

Table of
Contents
button

6.   Click the **Table of Contents** button again. This hides the Table of Contents.
7.   Click the Access Help **Close button** on the upper right-hand corner of the
screen to close the Help System window.
8.   Click the **Microsoft Office Button** to display the File Options menu.
9.   Click the **Exit Access** button on the bottom of the window.

Lesson 2 - Working with Tables

2.1 Using Table Templates

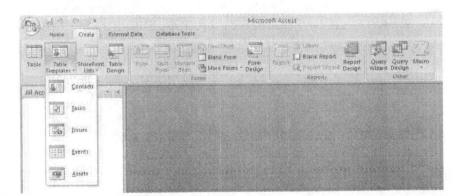

Table Templates allows you to build pre-designed tables that are commonly used in databases. Once your table is created, you can add or modify any of the fields later on. Table Templates included in Access 2007 are Contacts, Tasks, Issues, Events, and Assets.

If the tables you need to create are different than the available pre-designed tables, you may want to consider simply creating your table from scratch and save the time you would spend changing field names and data types. You may also wish to explore the collection of professionally designed database templates, which contain a usable set of data tables.

✔ **Create a Table using Table Templates**

1. With Access open, click the **Microsoft Office button** to open the **File Options** dialog box.
2. Click **Open**. This displays the **Open** dialog box.
3. Locate your copy of the Course Docs folder and open it
4. **Double-click** the **Access Tutorials folder**
5. Select the **Video Sales 2.accdb** file and then click **Open**.
7. Click the **Create** tab on the Ribbon.

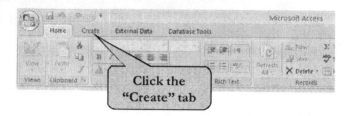

Click the "Create" tab

8. Click the **Table Templates** command icon. This displays a list of available table templates.
9. Click on **Contacts** in the template list. Access opens it in Datasheet view.
10. Click the **Close** button on the **table** window. This displays a message asking you if you wish to save the table.
11. Click **No** to close the table without saving.

2.2   Entering Data into a Table

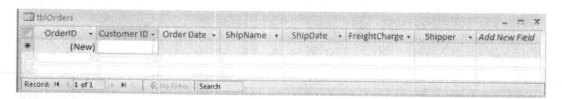

To enter data into a new table, click in the first field into which you wish to begin entering data and then type your information. Pressing the **Tab** key will move you to the next field. Note that you cannot enter data into an **AutoNumber** field.

To enter data into a table with existing data, click the **New Record** button on the Record Navigation Bar and then type your information into the new row.

✓ Enter Data into a Table

1.   Make sure the **Video Sales 2.accdb** file is active. Select **tblOrders** in the Navigation Pane and then press **Enter**.
2.   Click in the **Customer ID** field and then type: **32**
3.   Press **Tab** to move to the next column.
4.   Type: **05/02/02** in the Order Date field and then press **Tab**.
5.   Type: **UPS** in the Shipper field and then press **Tab**.
6.   Type: **05/07/2002** in the Ship Date field and then press **Tab**.
7.   Type: **5.95** and then press **Tab**. Note that you do not have to "save" your data – when you move off the row, the data is automatically saved.

The Completed Record

2.3   Adding New Fields to a Table

When you need to add new fields to your table, delete existing fields, or modify the formatting properties of your table, you will often want to work in **Design view**. In fact, as you become more comfortable working with Access, you may find yourself creating the majority of your tables in Design view, rather than using the table or database templates. Using Design view allows you to add fields, select a data type and enter a description for your fields. This gives you much more flexibility than using the Table Wizard.

In Design view, each field contains three properties:

- **Field Name** – the name of your field
- **Data Type** – allows you to specify what type of data can be entered in the field
- **Description**– allows you to add optional notes to describe the field in more detail

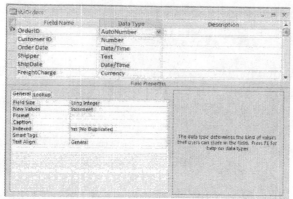

Table Design View

New in Access 2007 is the ability to add new fields while in Datasheet view. To add a new field in Datasheet view, double-click on the **column heading** that reads ***Add New Field*** and type in the name for your new field. You can then begin entering data in the new field. When you enter data in the new column, Access 2007 uses the information you type to recognize the appropriate data type. For instance, if you type: 5/17/2002, Access should recognize it as a date and set the data type for the field to Date/Time. If Access is unable to guess the data type, the default data type is set to Text.

Datasheet View   Design View

✓ **Add a New Field from Datasheet View**

1. Make sure the **Video Sales 2.accdb** file is active. Double-click on the column heading that reads **Add New Field**.

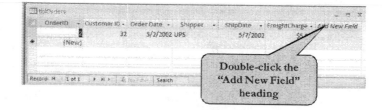

Double-click the "Add New Field" heading

2. Type: **Ship Via** and press **Enter**.
3. Click the **Design View button** on the lower right-hand corner of the Access screen.
4. Select the **ShipDate** field as shown.

25

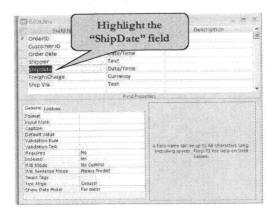

5. Type: **DateShipped**
6. Click the **Save** button on the **Quick Access toolbar**. Though you do not need to save changes to your data, you do need to save your design changes.
7. Click the table's **close button**.

2.4 Creating a Table from Scratch

A s you work more with Access, you will most likely want to create your tables from scratch rather than using Table Templates. Creating your tables from scratch allows you maximum flexibility.

When adding fields to a table, you will need to specify a field name and a **data type**. Data types tell Access what type of data to expect in that field. For example, you would be unable to calculate two numbers if their data type was set to Text. Thus, it's important to have a general understanding of data types.

Data Type	Description
Text	Stores text and/or numbers. Set for any field that will not be used for calculation. Entries can be up to 255 characters.
Memo	Allows you to store up to 64,000 characters.
Number	Stores numbers that will be used in calculations. For numbers beginning with 0, use the text data type as 0 will be dropped if data type is set for number.
Date/Time	Used for date and/or times.

Currency	Stores numbers with a fixed number of decimal places and a currency symbol.
AutoNumber	Sequentially numbers the records. AutoNumber is generally used for primary key fields for which unique values are required.
Yes/No	A Boolean value that represents a yes/no or true/false value.
OLE Object	Used for objects created in other applications such as Excel spreadsheets, graphics, and sound files.
Hyperlink	Used for clickable links for files on your computer or to sites on the World Wide Web.
Attachment	New in Access 2007, allows you to attach images, spreadsheet files, documents, and other supported files to records in your database. More flexible than OLE fields.
Lookup Wizard	Used to create a field that allows you to select a value from a list or from a field in another table or query.

Note: The **Attachment** data type is only available if your database is saved in Access 2007 format. Click the **Microsoft Office** icon, select **Save As** from the File Options menu and choose **Access 2007 Database** from the second pane. Note that databases saved in 2007 format are inaccessible by previous version of Access.

 Create a Table from Scratch

1. Make sure the **Video Sales 2.accdb** file is active. Click the **Create** command tab on the Ribbon. This displays commands related to the creation of database objects..
2. Click the **Table** command icon. This creates a new table and opens it in Datasheet view.
3. Click the **View** command icon on the Ribbon.
4. Type: **tblShippers** in the Table Name box.
5. Click **OK**. This saves the table and switches to Design view. Notice that Access automatically created our first field for us – the ID field.
6. Click on the **key** next to the ID field and then press the **Delete** key, as shown. Click **Yes** when asked if you want to delete the field. This deletes the default field that Access provided. You are going to create your own ID field.

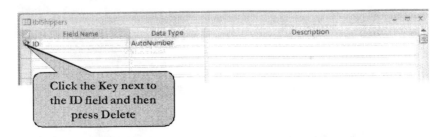

Click the Key next to
the ID field and then
press Delete

7. Click in the first blank **Field Name** box and type: **ShipperID**.
8. Press **Tab**. A default value of "Text" is displayed for the data type. Since the Shipper ID field will be used for a primary key field, you will want to change the data type to an AutoNumber field.

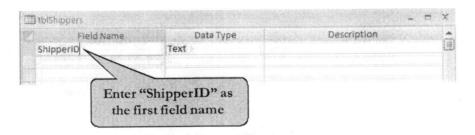

Enter "ShipperID" as
the first field name

9. Click on the **Data Type** arrow and then select **AutoNumber** from the list.

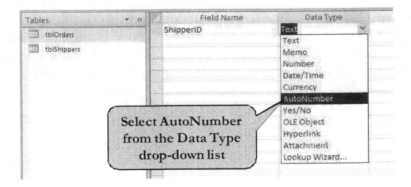

Select AutoNumber
from the Data Type
drop-down list

10. Press **Tab** to jump to the description field and then type: **This is the Shipper ID**

Enters a description for the first field.
11. Press **Tab**.
12. Type: **ShipperName**
13. Press **Tab**. Accept the default Text data type.
14. Press **Tab** and then type: **This is the Shipper Name**.
15. Press **Tab** and then type: **ShipperPhone**.
16. Press **Tab twice**. Access accepts the default Text data type and moves to the description field. As a telephone number contains non-numerical characters such as dashes and parentheses, you must set the data type as text, and not number.
17. Type: **This is the Shipper Phone Number**.

18. Click the **Save** the changes.

A Note about Naming Conventions

Most database developers use some sort of naming conventions to help them organize and quickly identify the database objects in their database. A popular naming convention uses the object type, in lowercase letters, as the first 3 letters of the object name. For example, a Customer's table would be named: *tblCustomers,* a customer's form would be named *frmCustomers,* a customer's query would be name **qryCustomers** and a Customer's report would be named *rptCustomers.*

Naming conventions are optional. However, it is considered good database programming practice to use some sort of naming convention for your objects.

2.5 Setting a Primary Key

When working with a relational database such as Microsoft Access, you will often need to **link** two or more tables to bring related information together. In order to do this, each table needs to include a field that uniquely identifies each record in the table. This means that the data in that field may not be duplicated in any other of the table records. This unique identifier field is called a **Primary Key**.

A primary key is typically a number, such as an order number, customer number, invoice number or social security number. The most important consideration when adding a primary key to a table is that it must be unique. Some additional rules to keep in mind when setting a primary key field:

- The primary key field can never be blank (or null)
- The primary key field can never be duplicated
- The primary key field should be as short as possible
- The primary key should describe the entity

Another purpose of the primary key is that it **indexes** the information in the record. Indexing helps Access find information quickly, especially when you have a large amount of data.

Designating an **AutoNumber** as the primary key for a table is often the easiest way to create a unique identifier. If you neglect to set a primary key, Microsoft Access will ask if

---

you want it to create a primary key for you. If you answer yes, Access will create an AutoNumber primary key. As you saw in a previous lesson, Access automatically creates an ID field with a primary key for all new tables.

✓ Add a Primary Key field to a table

1. Make sure the **Video Sales 2.accdb** file is active. Click in the **Field name** box (the blue box to the left of the field name) for **ShipperID**
2. Click the **Primary Key** command icon on the Ribbon. The key symbol to the left of the ShippperID field informs us that this field is set as a primary key field.

Primary
Key

3. **Save** the changes.

2.6 Changing Column Width and Row Height

After creating your tables, you may discover that your columns are not wide enough to accommodate your data. Since you have worked with Microsoft Excel, you already are familiar with the process of changing column widths and it works the same way in Access. The process is similar for changing the height of rows .

✓ Change the Width of a Column or the Height of a Row

1. Make sure the **Video Sales 2.accdb** file is active. Click the **View** command icon on the Ribbon. Access switches to Datasheet view.
2. Move your mouse pointer over the border between **ShipperName** and **ShipperPhone** until the pointer transforms into a black cross with a horizontal double arrow pointer. Click and drag to the right until the column is about **2 inches wide** as shown.

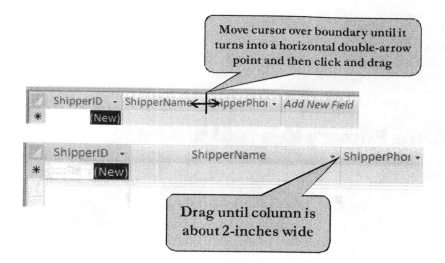

AutoFit

You can also use the **AutoFit** feature. This allows you to automatically change the width of a column to accommodate the widest entry.

✓ Change the Size of a Column using AutoFit:

1. Make sure the **Video Sales 2.accdb** file is active. Double-click on the **right border** of the column heading. The column width will adjust to accommodate the largest entry in that column.

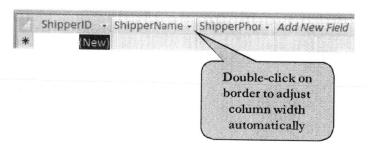

2.7 Rearranging Fields

A fter creating your tables, you may decide that some of the fields are not in the order that you would like. To move a field from one location to another, use the click-and-drag method (click the record selector for the field and drag it to the new location).

✓ Rearrange Fields in a Table

1. Make sure the **Video Sales 2.accdb** file is active. Click the **Close Button** for tblShippers. **Save** any changes.
2. **Right-click** on **tblOrders** and then choose **Design View** from the menu.
3. Select the DateShipped field.
4. Move your mouse pointer over the record selector for DateShipped, and then **click and drag** upwards until the DateShipped field is after the OrderDate field.

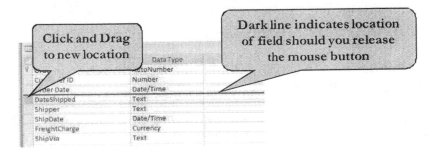

5. **Release** the mouse button to complete the move process.
6. **Save** the design changes.

2.8 Inserting and Deleting Fields

Y ou can insert new fields anywhere in your table in Design view. Select a field and then click the **Insert Rows** command button on the **Ribbon**. This inserts a new field below the selected one. You can also right-click a row and select Insert Rows from the menu.

To delete a field, select the field and then press the **Delete** key or click the **Delete Rows** command button on the Ribbon. But keep in mind that when you delete a field, all the data in this field is deleted along with it!

✔ Insert and Delete a Field in a Table

1. Make sure the **Video Sales 2.accdb** file is active. Click the record selector to the left of the **FreightCharge** field.
2. Click the **Insert Rows** command button on the Ribbon. This inserts a new field above the Freight Charge field.
3. Click in the **Field Name** box of the new field and then type: **TaxRate**
4. Press **Tab**. Accept the default value for the moment.
5. Press **Tab** again then type: **This is the customer's tax rate**.

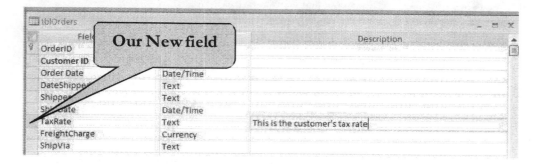

6. Click the **Save** button to save the design changes.
7. Click the table's **Close** button.
8. Select **tblShippers**, right-click and then choose **Design View** from the menu.
9. Select the **ShipperPhone** field.
10. Press the **Delete** key. This deletes the selected record. Since there is no data in the table, Access does not ask if you want to permanently delete the selected field along with its data.
11. **Save** the design changes.

2.9   Changing Field Properties

While data types tell Access what type of data to store in a field, the **field properties** govern how the data is displayed or stored. Each data type has its own set of field properties. For example, you can set the field size of the text data type to only allow 3 digits whereas the field size of the number data type is dependent on the size and type of number you choose (integer, long integer, single, double, decimal, etc.). In this lesson, you will look at a couple of the more common field properties.

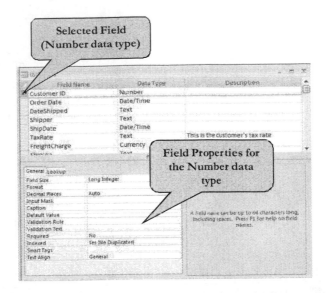

Selected Field (Number data type)

Field Properties for the Number data type

Common Field Properties

Field Property	Description
Field Size	Tells Access the maximum number of characters that can be stored in the field. For text, this is a number up to 255 characters. For numbers, this is a number type (long integer, double, decimal, integer, etc.)
Input Mask	A string of characters on the screen representing how data is to be entered by the user.
Format	How data entered is to be displayed. You can use a pre-defined format or use a custom format.
Decimal Places	The number of decimal places that will be displayed.
Caption	The text (or label) that should appear next to the text box control on a form. If no caption is entered, Access uses the field name.
Default Value	The value that Access automatically enters in the field for new records.
Validation Rule	An expression that controls the value that can be entered into a field.
Validation Text	The message the user receives when the validation rule is

	violated.
Required	A yes/no property that specifies whether a user must enter a value in the field.
Allow Zero Length	Specifies whether a string containing no characters (a zero-length string) is permissible. You enter a zero-length string by typing two quotation marks with no spaces between them ("").
Indexed	Specifies whether you want to Access to create a data index for the field that can speed up searches and sorts.

 Modify Field Properties

1. Make sure the **Video Sales 2.accdb** file is active. Click the **Close** button for tblShippers.
2. Right-click **tblOrders** and then choose **Design View** button from the menu.
3. Click in the **Data Type** box for the **TaxRate** field. This selects the TaxRate field and displays the drop-down data type arrow.
4. Click the drop-down arrow in the data type box and select **Number**.

5. Under the **Field Properties** area on the bottom of the window, click in the **Field Size** box .

6. Click the Field Size arrow and then select **Decimal.** A decimal field size will reserve 12 bytes of space.
7. Click in the box next to **Format.**
8. Click the drop-down arrow and then select **Percent** from the list.

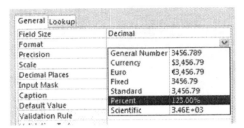

9. Click in the box next to **Scale** and then type: **3.** This sets the maximum number of places to the right of the decimal to 3.
10. Click in the **Default Value** box and then type: **.055**
11. Click in the **Field Name** box for the **Shipper** field.
12. Under the **Field Properties** area, click in the **Field Size** box and then type: **25.**
13. Click the **View** button on the ribbon. Click **Yes** when asked if you want to save the table. Click **Yes** when the "Data may be lost" information box appears. This saves the design changes and switches to datasheet view. Whenever you change the field size of a field to a smaller field size, the "Data may be lost" box will appear. If you had a Shipper name in our table that was more than 25 characters, the data would be truncated to match our new field size.

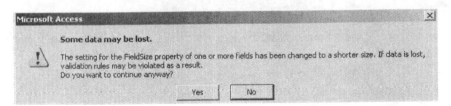

14. Click in the **Tax Rate** field for the first record and type: **.06.** Press **Tab.** Notice that a tax rate of 5.5% is automatically inserted for new records.

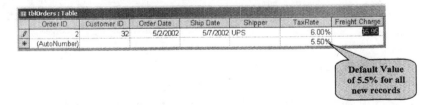

2.10 Designing in Datasheet View

I f you have worked with previous version of Access, you have no doubt done all of your design work in Design View. However, with the new user interface redesign, including many easy access Datasheet view design tools, you may find yourself doing much of your design work in Datasheet view.

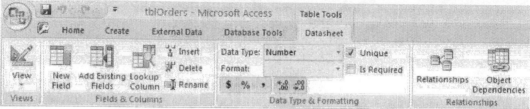

Command Sets under the Datasheet Tab

You have already seen that you can add new fields from Datasheet view. In addition, you can now specify Data Type and Data Format, insert new fields, delete and rename existing fields, set the Unique and Is Required property for fields and even add fields from other tables to the current field. With these new features right at your fingertips, you can spend less time switching back and forth from Design view to Datasheet view.

✓ Design from Datasheet View

1. Make sure the **Video Sales 2.accdb** file is active. Click the **Datasheet** command tab on the Ribbon.
2. Click in the **Ship Via** column and click the **Delete** command button on the Ribbon. Click **Yes** when asked if you want to delete the field.

Click the "Delete" button

Click in the ShipVia column

3. Click in the **Shipper** column and click the **Insert** command button on the Ribbon. This inserts a new field to the left of the Shipper column.
4. Click the **Rename** command button and then type: **DatePromised**. Press **Enter** when finished.

5. Click the **New Field** command button on the Ribbon as shown. This displays the Field Templates pane, from which, you can add one or more fields based on a specific template to your table.

6. Under the **Contacts** category of the Field Templates palette, double-click on **E-mail Address**. This adds a new field named "E-mail Address" to the table.

7. Scroll down and under the **Projects** category of the Field Templates palette, double-click on the **Notes** field template.
8. Click the **close button** on the Field Templates pane and observe the table.
9. Click the **Microsoft Office** button on the Ribbon and click **Close Database** from the File Options menu. Click **Yes** when asked to save the table layout.

Lesson 3 - Working with Data

3.1 Editing Data

I n the last lesson, you learned how to enter data into a table. Once your data is entered, you can modify it at any time by clicking in the field and then typing in your desired changes. When tabbing to a field, all of the data in the field is automatically highlighted so you do not even need to delete the data first - typing your changes will automatically overwrite the existing data.

✓ Edit Data in a Table

1. Open Microsoft Access.
2. Click the **More** button in the **Open Recent Databases** pane.
3. Locate your copy of the Course Docs folder and open it
4. **Double-click** the **Access Tutorials folder**
5. Select the **Video Sales 3.accdb** file and then click **Open**.
7. If necessary, click the **Navigator Pane** drop-down arrow and select **Tables** from the list.
8. Open **tblOrders** in Datasheet view.
9. In the **Shipper** field, select **UPS**.

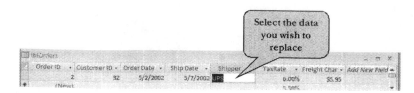

10. Type: **Federal Express**
11. In the Order Date field, click after the first **2** in 5/2.

12. Press the **Backspace** key and then type: **1** to change the date from 5/2/2002 to 5/1/2002.
13. Press **Tab**. Notice the calendar button that appears when you enter a date field. This is a new option in Access 2007 that allows you to select your date from a calendar.
14. Click the **Calendar button** that appears next to the Ship Date field. This opens the calendar allowing you to choose a date from the calendar.

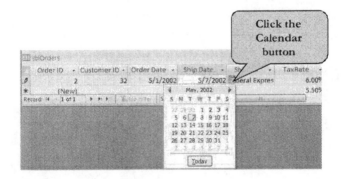

15. Click the **right-pointing blue arrow** on top of the calendar to move to the next month.
16. Click on the **3** in the calendar. This sets June 3rd as the Ship date.
17. **Save** the design changes.

3.2 Formatting Table Data

If you are unhappy with the size or font of the text in your tables, you can change the **Formatting** of your table text. For instance, you can change the font size, font type, font or fill color and text alignment. To apply formatting to a table, click the desired **Font command button** in the Font Command Set under the Home tab.

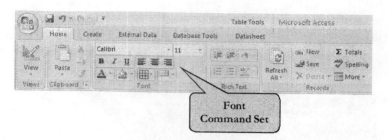

Font
Command Set

Any formatting changes will be applied to the entire table. However, Access 2007 now provides the ability to add **rich text formatting** to fields in your table that are set to the **Memo** data type. For instance, you can apply bold formatting or change the text color of individual words. To enable rich text formatting in Memo fields, you must switch to **Design view** and change the **Text Format Property** from Plain Text to **Rich Text**. Once you have changed the data type, the Rich Text command set is also enabled, allowing you to add additional formatting such as bullets and numbering, indenting and highlight color.

✓ Apply Formatting to Table Data

1. Make sure the **Video Sales 3.accdb** file is active. Click the **Home** tab.
2. Click the **Font Size** drop-down arrow and select **14** from the list.

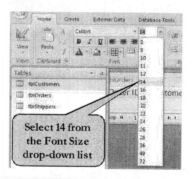

Select 14 from
the Font Size
drop-down list

3. Click the **Font Color** button and select **Red** from the color palette.

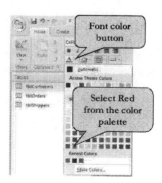

Font color
button

Select Red
from the color
palette

4.   Click the **Font Color** button again and select **Automatic** from the color palette.
5.   Click the **Close** button on tblOrders. Click **No** when asked to save your changes.

3.3   Importing Excel Data into an Existing Table

An extremely powerful feature of Access is its ability to **import data** from other applications. For instance, you can bring in data from an Excel spreadsheet or even from a plain text file into a new or existing table.   You can import data from a variety of formats such as: Lotus, dBase, Paradox, Text Files (delimited or fixed-width) and Outlook.

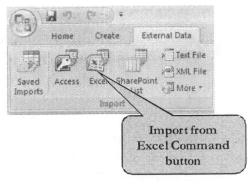

In this lesson, you are going to learn how to import data from Microsoft Excel into Access.

✓ Import Data fro0m Excel

1.   Make sure the **Video Sales 3.accdb** file is active. Double-click **tblCustomers**. Observe the table – it is empty.
2.   Click the **Close** button for **tblCustomers**.
3.   Click the **External Data** tab on the Ribbon.
4.   Click the **Excel** command button. This displays the 'Get External Data – Excel Spreadsheet' dialog box.
5.   Click the **Browse** button.
6.   Navigate to your **Course Docs** folder (if necessary) and select the **Customers** file.
7.   Click **Open**.

8. Click the radio button next to **Append a copy of the records to the table** and select **tblCustomers** from the drop-down list as shown.

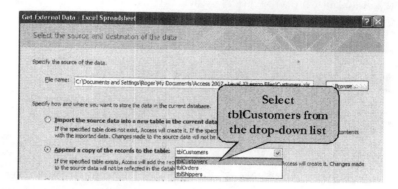

9. Click **OK.** This launches the Import Spreadsheet Wizard.
10. Click **Next.** Since there is only one worksheet in the file (Sheet 1), accept the default and move to the next step of the wizard.

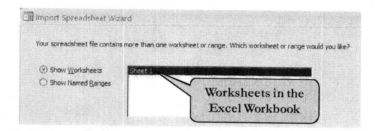

11. Ensure that the checkbox next to **First Row Contains Column Headings** is checked. Since the first row of the spreadsheet contains the headings or field names, ensure to check this box., otherwise the headings will be imported as regular data.
12. Click **Next.**
13. Click **Finish.** This completes the import process and imports the data.
14. Click **Close.** If you repeatedly import the same file into Access, you can now save your instructions so that you can quickly execute the same import without using the Wizard.
15. Double-click the **tblCustomers** table. There should be 23 records.
16. **Close** tblCustomers.

3.4   Importing a Text File into a New Table

If you want to import data into Access from an application that Access does not support, you can export the data as a text file and then import it into Access. Most applications support exporting data to **text files**.

There are two types of text files: **delimted** and **fixed-width**. In delimited text files, the fields are separated by a *delimiter* such as a comma or quotation marks. In a fixed width file, fields are separated by a tab stop of equal distance. The most common type of file is the comma delimited field.

Before importing a text file, you may have to "clean it up" a bit. For instance, if you are importing a comma delimted text file, there can be no commas within the data, as Access treats each comma as a new field.

✓ Import A Text File

1.   Make sure the **Video Sales 3.accdb** file is active. Click the **External Data** tab on the Ribbon.
2.   Click the **Text File** command button.
3.   Click the **Browse** button.
4.   Navigate to the **Course Docs** folder (if necessary) and then select the **Product_List** file in the Accesss Tutorials folder.
5.   Click **Open**.
6.   Click the radio button next to **Import the source data in a new table in the current database**. This time, you are going to import your data into a new Access table.
7.   Click **OK**. This launches the Import Text Wizard.

8.   Make sure that **Delimited** is selected and click **Next**.

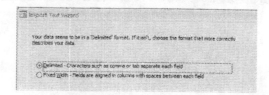

9.   Select Comma as the type of delimiter and then click the checkbox next to **First Row Contains Field Names** box as shown. This selects comma as the delimiter than separates the fields. Since the first row of our text file contains field names (or column headings), check the field names box.

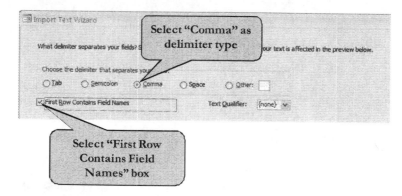

10. Click **Next**.
11. Scroll to the right until the **Price** field is visible.
12. Click the word **Price** to select the column and then choose **Currency** from the **Data Type** drop-down list.

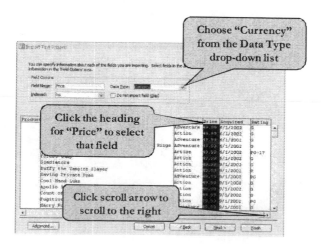

13. Click **Next**.
14. Click the **Choose my own primary key** radio button and then click **ProductID** field from the drop-down list.

15. Click **Next**.
16. Type: **tblProducts** in the **Import to Table** box.
17. Click **Finish**. This imports the data from the text file to a new table named tblProducts.
18. Click **Close**. to close the message box that informs us that our data was imported.
19. Double-click the **tblProducts** table and observe the data. There should be 128 records in the table.
20. **Close** tblProducts.

3.5 Selecting and Deleting Records

Deleting records from a table is straight-forward — click on the row selector to select the record and then press the **Delete** key or right-click and select **Delete Record** from the menu. You can select more than one record by clicking and dragging upwards or downwards over the records you wish to delete. Keep in mind though, that once you delete records, they are gone for good. There is no undo! The only way to get a deleted record back is to retype the information.

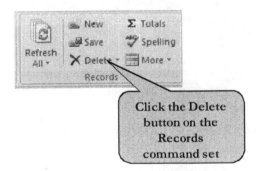

Click the Delete button on the Records command set

You can also delete records from the **Records** command set under the **Home** tab. Select the row selector and click the **Delete** button. Make sure that you click the Delete button under the Home tab and not the Datasheet tab as clicking the Delete button under the Datasheet tab will delete the entire field, not just an individual records.

✓ Select and Delete a Record

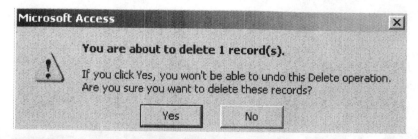

> **Note:** Clicking **No** will cancel the delete records action and the records will not be deleted from the table.

1. Make sure the **Video Sales 3.accdb** file is active. Double-click **tblProducts**
2. Click on the **Row Selector** for the **Matrix**, the 5th record in the table to select the record for the Matrix.

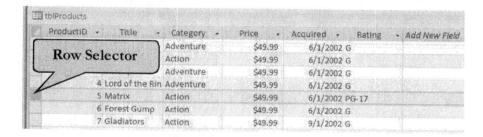

3. Press the **Delete** key. Access displays a message box warning you that you cannot undo the deletion and asking you if you really wish to delete the records.
4. Click **Yes**. This closes the message box and deletes the selected record.

3.6 Sorting Records

Records are automatically sorted alphabetically or numerically by the primary key field if there is one designated. If there is no primary key set, then the records appear in the order in which they were entered. To change the order of the records, you can use **sorting**. Sorting allows you arrange the records in a table in alphabetical or numerical order. You can sort your records in either **ascending** (A-Z) or **descending** (Z-A) order.

The easiest way to sort records is to click anywhere in the column of the field you wish to sort and then click either the **Sort Ascending button** or the **Sort Descending button** on the **Home** tab Ribbon. You can also right-click on the column you wish to sort and choose Sort **A to Z** or Sort **Z to A** from the menu. A new feature in Access 2007 is the ability to sort records by clicking on the drop-down arrow on the column heading and chose the desired sort order.

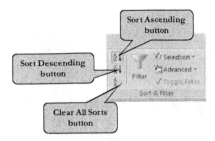

To remove a sort and return to the original order of the records, click the **Clear All Sorts** button under the Home tab.

✓ Sort Records in a Table

1. Make sure the **Video Sales 3.accdb** file is active. Click the **Home** tab on the Ribbon.
2. Click anywhere in the **Title** column to select the column to sort.

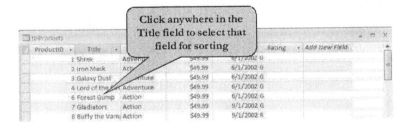

3. Click the **Sort Ascending** button in the Sort & Filter command set under the Home tab. This sorts the data in the Title field in ascending order.
4. Click the **Sort Descending** button in the Sort & Filter command set under the Home tab to sort the data in the Title field in descending order.
5. Select the **Column Heading** for the **Category** field.
6. Hold down the **Shift key** and click the Column Heading for the **Price** field. This selects both the Category and Price columns.
7. Click the **Sort Ascending** button on the Sort & Filter command set to sort the columns in ascending order by Category and then by Price.
8. Click the **Clear All Sorts** button on the Sort & Filter command set. This restores the records to their original sort order.

3.7   Finding and Replacing Data

There will be times when you need to find certain information in your table. It can become quite challenging to manually look for data, especially once your tables become large. The **Find** feature allows you to quickly search for information in tables, queries and forms.

If you know in which field the information resides, this will speed up your search. When searching, you can match either **Whole Field** (find data that is exactly the same as what you entered in the Find What box), **Any Part of Field** (find records that contain the data anywhere in the field), or **Start of Field** (locate records that contain the data at the beginning of the field).

To automatically change the data in a field to something else, click the replace tab and enter the new data in the **Replace With** box.

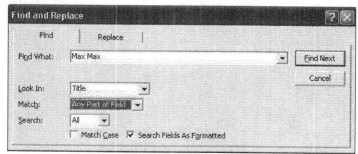

Find and Replace Dialog Box

✔ Find and Replace Data in a Table

1.   Make sure the **Video Sales 3.accdb** file is active. Click anywhere in the **Title** column.

2.   Click the **Find** button ![Find] on the Home tab.
3.   In the **Find What** box., type: **Mad Max.**
4.   Click the **Match** drop-down list and then select **Whole Field** as shown. The data must match exactly what you typed in the Find What box.

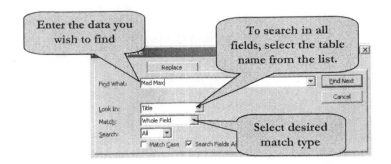

5. Click **Find Next**. This begins the search and stops when the first instance of Mad Max is found.
6. Click **Find Next** again to search for another instance of 'Mad Max'.
7. Click **OK**.

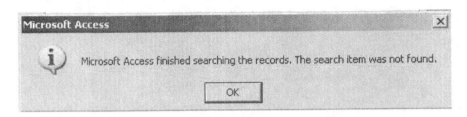

8. Click **Cancel**. This closes the Find dialog box.
9. Click anywhere in the **Price** column to select it.
10. Press the **Ctrl + F** keystroke combination to display the **Find and Replace** dialog box.
11. Click the **Replace** tab. Access displays the Find and Replace options.
12. Type: **$19.99** in the **Find What** box. Don't forget the currency symbol!
13. Type: **$22.95** in the **Replace with** box.
14. Click the **Replace All** button. This replaces all instances of $19.99 with $22.95.
15. Click **Yes**.
16. Click **Cancel**. This closes the Find and Replace dialog box.

3.8 Filtering Records by Selection

A **filter** is a tool that retrieves only a subset of the records in a table. For instance, if you only wanted to see customers in the state of Wisconsin, you could apply a filter that hides all the records except those with the state field value of Wisconsin. To apply such a filter, click in any field whose contents are "Wisconsin" and then click on the **Filter by Selection** button under the Home tab or right-click and choose the desired filter commands from the menu. The available filter commands will vary depending on the type of data selected. Once the filter is applied, all other records will be hidden from view.

To remove the filter and restore all records, click the **Toggle Filter** button under the Home tab or right-click and select **Clear filter from [Column Name]** from the menu.

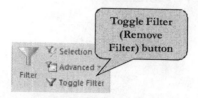

Toggle Filter (Remove Filter) button

✔ Filter Records by Selection

1. Make sure the **Video Sales 3.accdb** file is active. **Click** on any instance of the word **Comedy** in the **Category** column. This selects the data to filter.

Select the data for which to filter

2. Click the **Selection** button on the Sort & Filter command set and choose **"Equals Comedy"** from the command list. This hides all records except those whose category is "Comedy"

3.

Click the "Selection" button and choose "Equals Comedy"

3. **Click** on any instance of the number **$39.99** in the **Price** column.
4. Click the **Selection** button and choose **"Less than or Equal to $39.99"** from the command list. This hides all records except those whose category is "Comedy" and whose price is less than or equal to $39.99.
5. Click the **Toggle Filter** button to remove the filter and display all records.

3.9   Filtering Records by Form

Filtering by Form allows you to choose data from a drop-down list. Clicking the **Filter by Form button** displays a blank record row. Clicking in any of the blank fields displays a drop-down list of available data from which you can choose. This feature is especially helpful if you want to find a specific record or want to filter on several fields in a datasheet.

✓ Filter by Form

1. Make sure the **Video Sales 3.accdb** file is active. Click the **Advanced** button the Home tab and select **Filter by Form** from the menu. This opens a blank record row with the values automatically inserted from our previous filter.

2. Click the Category drop-down arrow and then select **Romance**.
3. Press **Tab**.
4. Click the Price drop-down arrow and then select **22.95** from the drop-down list.

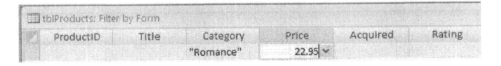

5. Click the **Toggle Filter** button. Only records with a Category of Romance AND a price of $22.95 are displayed
6. Click the **Toggle Filter** button again to restore the hidden records.

3.10 Using Common Filters

Common Filters allow you to quickly apply a filter to your data from a menu command. To access these command, click the **Filter** button on the Home tab or **right-click** the field you wish to filter by and then choose from the data type filter menu (the available commands will vary depending on the data type of the column). You can also click the drop-down arrow on the column heading to access common filters.

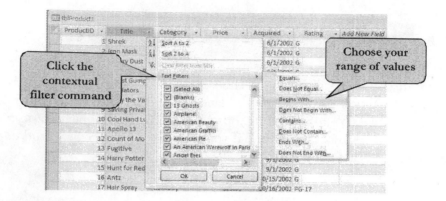

From the Common Filter box, you can either filter for specific values by using the check box list to include or exclude fields from the list. To filter for a range of values, choose the filter command (i.e. Date Filters, Text Filters, etc.), choose the range of values for which to filter and then enter your criteria.

✓ Use Common Filters

1. Make sure the **Video Sales 3.accdb** file is active. Click anywhere in the **Price** column and click the **Filter** button under the Home tab to display the Common Filter Menu.

2. Uncheck the boxes next to $29.99. $39.99, $49.99. This is the data to exclude.

3. Click **OK.** This hides all records except for those with a price of $22.95

4. Right-click on the **Price** column and choose **Clear Filter from Price** from the menu.

5. Click the drop-down arrow on the **Title** column header, click on **Text Filters** and then choose **Begins With** from the menu. This allows us to filter this column for a range of values. In this case, Access will only display records which begin with a specific letter.

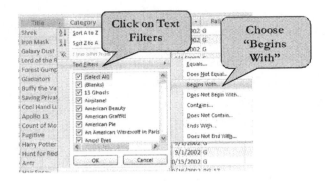

6.   Type **F** in the Custom Filter dialog box.

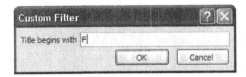

7.   Click **OK** to display records whose title begins with the letter "F"
8.   Click the **Toggle Filter** button on the Ribbon to remove the filter.

3.11 Hiding/Unhiding Columns

There may be instances when you wish to view only certain columns in a table Datasheet. Perhaps you need to print table data for only a few relevant columns. Or perhaps you want to hide sensitive columns from those entering data into the tables. To hide columns from view, click on the field name to select it, right-click and select **Hide Columns** from the menu or click the **More** button under the Home tab and select Hide Columns from the menu. Saving the design of your table will ensure that the columns will remain hidden the next time the table is opened.

✓ Hide / Unhide a Column

1.   Make sure the **Video Sales 3.accdb** file is active. Click the field name of the **ProductID** field. This selects the entire column.
2.   Right-click and select **Hide Columns** from the menu to hide the ProductID field.
3.   Click the **More** button on the Ribbon and choose **Unhide Columns.** This displays the Unhide Columns dialog box.
4.   Click the **ProductID** box to unhide the ProductID column

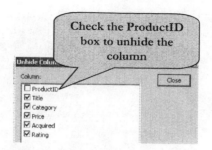

Check the ProductID box to unhide the column

5. Click **Close**.
6. Click the **Close** button for tblProducts. **Save** any changes.

3.12 Freezing Columns

I f you have a large table, you may wish to keep a particular column in view while you scroll to the right. To accomplish this, **freeze** your columns in place by using the **Freeze Columns** command. When scrolling to the right, the frozen column(s) is restrained to the left side of your screen.

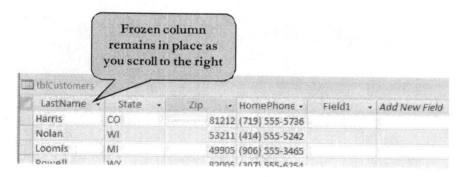

Frozen column remains in place as you scroll to the right

✓ Freeze / Unfreeze a Column in Place

1. Make sure the **Video Sales 3.accdb** file is active. Open **tblCustomers**.
2. Select the **LastName** column.
3. Click the **More** button under the Home tab on the Records command set and choose **Freeze** from the menu. This freezes the LastName column to the left side of the Datasheet.
4. Scroll to the right. Notice that the LastName column is now unscrollable.

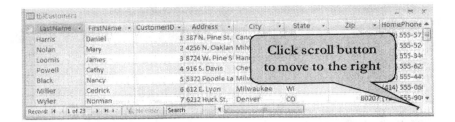

5. Right-click the Column Heading of the frozen column and select **Unfreeze All Columns** from the menu. This unfreezes all frozen columns.

3.13 Rearranging Columns

In Datasheet View, you can change the column order of your table by selecting the column you wish to move and then dragging it to its new location. Saving the table design will ensure that the column will be in the same position the next time the table is opened.

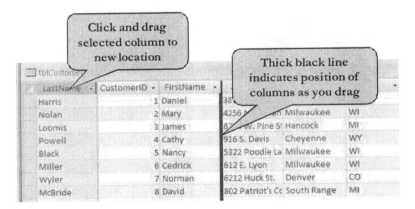

✓ Rearrange Columns

1. Make sure the **Video Sales 3.accdb** file is active. Select the column heading of the **LastName** field.
2. Click the **LastName** field name and hold down the mouse button. You are now ready to drag the column to its new location.
3. Drag to the right until the thick black line is to the right of the **FirstName** field.
4. Release the mouse button to complete the move process.
5. Click the **Close** button on the tblCustomers table. **Save** any changes.

3.14 Displaying Column Totals in a Datasheet

New in Access 2007 is the ability to display column totals in your datasheet. By clicking the **Totals** tool in the Records command set under the Home tab, you can quickly sum the values in a Datasheet column. In addition, you can also apply other aggregate function to the column. Available aggregate functions are: Sum, Average, Count, Minimum, Maximum, Standard Deviation and Variance.

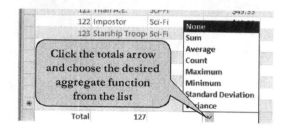

✔ Display Column Totals in a Datasheet

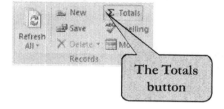

1. Make sure the **Video Sales 3.accdb** file is active. Double-click **tblProducts**.
2. Click the **Totals** button on the Ribbon. This adds a Totals row on the bottom of the datasheet.
3. Scroll down and click in the Totals row for the **Price** column.
4. Click the drop-down arrow and select **Sum** from the list.

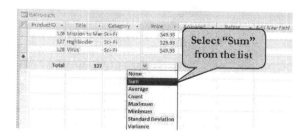

5. Click the **Totals** button on the Ribbon. This removes the Totals row.
6. Click the **Close** button on the tblProducts table. **Save** any changes.
7. Press the **Alt + F** keystroke combination and select **Close Database** from the File Options menu. Alt + F is the keyboard shortcut for displaying the File Options menu.

Lesson 4 - Working With Queries

4.1 Working in Query Design View

In the last lesson, you learned how to filter records in a table, using the *Filter by Selection* and *Filter by Form* tools. However, for more complex searches, it is often better to create a **query**. Queries are also the fastest and easiest way to retrieve information from a database.

A query allows you to **ask a question** of your data. For instance, you might want to know how many customers in the state of Illinois spent more than $250 in the year 2002. The result fields along with the search criteria are set in **Query Design View**.

The parts of a query in Design View are as follows:

Field Lists – the tables along with their fields that are part of the query. This section is the top part of the query.
Design grid – The lower part of the query broken down into rows and columns. This is where you add fields from the field lists that you want to be part of your query.

- **Field** – The table field whose data will be displayed when the query is run.
- **Table** – The table that contains the field.
- **Sort row** – designates how the results of the query are to be sorted.
- **Show row** – designates which fields will be displayed when the query is run.
- **Criteria row** – used to specify the limits placed on the records to be retrieved.

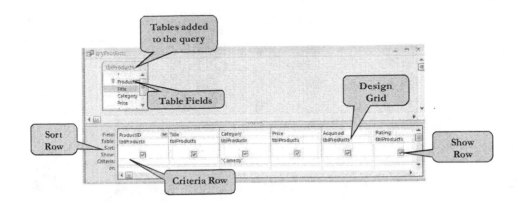

✓ To Open a Query in Design View

1. Click the **Microsoft Office** button to display the File Options menu.
2. Click **Open**.
3. Locate your Course Docs folder and open it.
4. **Double-click** the **Access Tutorial folder**
5. Select the **Video Sales 4.accdb** file and then click **Open**.
6. If necessary, select **Queries** from the Navigation Pane drop-down list.

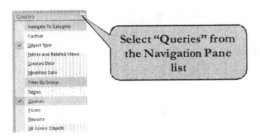

7. Right-click the **qryProducts** query.
8. Select **Design View**.
9. Observe the **criteria row** for the **Category** field. The results of the query are limited to those records whose category is **"Comedy"**

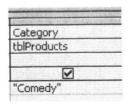

10. Observe the **sort row** for the **Title** field. The results of the query are sorted in ascending order by Title.

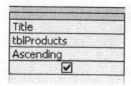

11. Click the query's **Close button**.

4.2   Creating a Query in Design View

There are two ways to create queries: using the query wizard or manually creating a query in Design View. In this lesson, you will create a query that returns data from a single table. This is accomplished by clicking the **Query Design** button under the Create tab and then choosing which table you wish to add to the query.

✓ Create a New Query in Design View

1.   Make sure the **Video Sales 4.accdb** file is active. Click the **Create** tab on the Ribbon.
2.   Click the **Query Design** command button. This lists all tables and queries in your database.

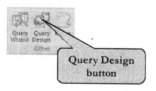

Query Design button

3.   Click **tblCustomers**.

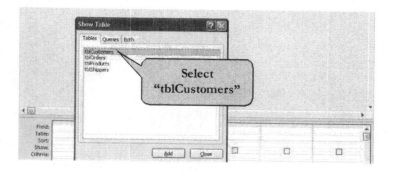

Select "tblCustomers"

4. Click **Add**. This adds **tblCustomers** to the Field Lists area (the top portion) of our query.

5. Click **Close**.

4.3 Adding Fields to a Query

O nce you have chosen the table, you will need to add the result **fields** to your query. There are several ways to add fields to your query:

- Click and drag the field from the Field Lists area to the design grid.
- Double-click the field in the table list.
- Click in the field row, click the arrow that appears, and then select the desired field.
- To add all fields, double-click the **title bar** of the field list box, click anywhere within the field list, and drag to the query grid.
- Click the **asterisk** in the field list box to add all fields to the query results (the individual fields in the query grid are not displayed).

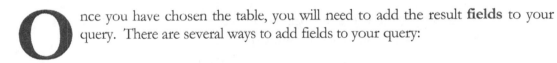

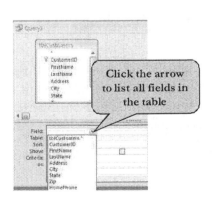
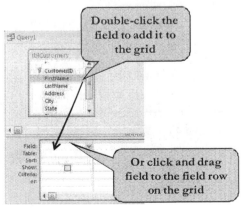

✓ Add Fields to a query

1. Make sure the **Video Sales 4.accdb** file is active. Double-click **FirstName** in the field list box. This adds the FirstName field to the first column of the query grid.

2. Click the **LastName** field in the field list box and drag it to the second column of the query grid.

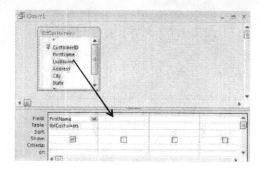

3. Press **Tab**.

4. Click the **arrow** and then choose **Address** from the drop-down list. This adds the address field to the third column of the query gird.

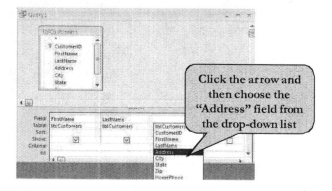

Click the arrow and then choose the "Address" field from the drop-down list

5. In the field list box (on the top section of the query), scroll downwards until the City, State, and Zip fields are visible.

6. Click the **City** field in the field list box.

7. Hold down the **Ctrl key** and click the **State** and **Zip** fields in the field list box.

8. With the Ctrl key still held down, click anywhere in the selected cells and then **drag** to the **fourth blank column** in the query grid as shown. **Release the mouse and Ctrl key** to add the City, State and Zip fields to the query.

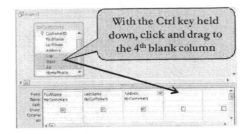

With the Ctrl key held down, click and drag to the 4th blank column

9. **Double-click** the **HomePhone** field.

4.4   Removing / Hiding Fields from a Query

After you have added fields to your query, you may decide that you do not want a particular field to be included in your query. To remove a field from the query grid, select the column by clicking the thin gray bar above the field row and then press the **Delete** key.

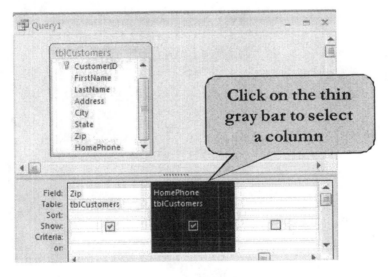

Click on the thin gray bar to select a column

You can also simply choose not to display a column in the query's results by clicking the checkbox in the **Show** row. The field will still be part of the query, but will not be displayed in the query's results.

✓ Remove / Hide a Field from a Query

1. Make sure the **Video Sales 4.accdb** file is active. Click the thin gray bar above the Field row for the **HomePhone** field. This selects the field to remove from the query grid.

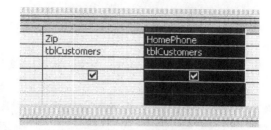

2. Press the **Delete** key. This removes the selected field from the query. Uncheck the checkbox in the **Show** row for the field whose results you wish to hide.

4.5   Saving a Query

If you need to generate the results for a query more than once, you may wish to **Save** the query rather than recreating it every time you need it. To save a query, click the **Save button** on the Quick Access Toolbar and then enter the name for your query in the Query Name box. Use accepted naming conventions!

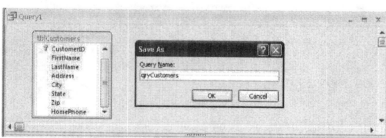

Saving a Query

✓ **Save a Query**

1. Make sure the **Video Sales 4.accdb** file is active. Click the **Save** button 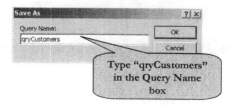 on the Quick Access toolbar. This displays the 'Save As' dialog box because the query is not yet saved.
2. Type: **qryCustomers** in the Query Name box:.

3.   Click **OK.**

4.6   Running a Query

We already know that a query is a question that you ask about the data in your database. To receive the answer to your question, you need to run your query. The answer to a query is called a **recordset** or a **result set**. It is also commonly referred to as a **dynaset.**.

The Query Result Set

To run a query if you are in Design View, click the **run icon** on the toolbar or click the **View** button on the Ribbon. To run a query that is not already open, double-click the query name in the Navigation Pane.

✓ **Run a Query**

1.   Make sure the **Video Sales 4.accdb** file is active. Click the **Run icon** on the toolbar. This runs the query and displays the result set.
2.   Click the **View** button on the Ribbon to switch back to Design View.
3.   Click the **View** icon on the Ribbon. This runs the query and displays the result set.
4.   Click the query's **close button.**
5.   Double-click **qryProducts.** This opens qryProducts in Datasheet View (in other words, you run the query).

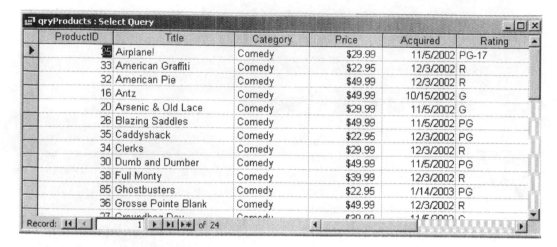

6. Click the query's **Close** button.

4.7 Adding Criteria to a Query

The **criteria row** of the query grid is where you enter the values to identify the specific records you wish to return. For example, instead of viewing all of your customers, you could enter **"CA"** in the criteria row for the State field. When you run the query, only customers from the state of California would be returned.

You can also use numerical expressions as your criteria. If you wanted to see all products whose cost was greater than $20, you would enter: **>20** in the criteria row. Notice that numerical expressions are not surrounded in quotes whereas string (text) expessions must be enclosed in quotation marks.

Specify Criteria for a Query

1. Make sure the **Video Sales 4.accdb** file is active. Right-click on the **qryCustomers** query.
2. Select **Design View** from the menu.
3. In the **Criteria** row for the **State** field, type: **"WI"**. In this case, you will see only those customers who reside in Wisconsin.

Field:	FirstName	LastName	Address	City	State
Table:	tblCustomers	tblCustomers	tblCustomers	tblCustomers	tblCustomers
Sort:					
Show:	☑	☑	☑	☑	☑
Criteria:					"WI"
or:					

4. Click the **Save** button on the Quick Access toolbar to save the design changes.
5. Click the **Run** button and observe the result set.

FirstName	LastName	Address	City	State	Zip
Mary	Nolan	4256 N. Oaklan	Milwaukee	WI	53211
Nancy	Black	5322 Poodle La	Milwaukee	WI	53216
Cedrick	Miller	612 E. Lyon	Milwaukee	WI	53201
Randy	Andersen	103 N. Riverboa	Kenosha	WI	53206
Patti	LaRouche	602 Lincoln St.	Milwaukee	WI	53202
Jonathan	Zavasky	3065 N. Rochell	West Allis	WI	53207
Nicole	Travis	406 W. Pine #2I	Glendale	WI	53209
Sara	Beckman	4193 Templeton	Racine	WI	52602

6. Click the query's **Close** button. Do **not** save the changes.

4.8 Specifying Multiple Criteria

As you work more with queries, you will inevitably want to add more than one limit to a query. For instance, you may wish to see a list of all customers who live in the state of Colorado **and** who rented Comedy or Adventure films.

To specify an **OR** condition for the **same field**, separate each item by the **Or** operator. In the example below, any films with the category of Comedy or Adventure will be returned.

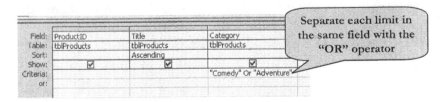

Field:	ProductID	Title	Category	Separate each limit in the same field with the "OR" operator
Table:	tblProducts	tblProducts	tblProducts	
Sort:		Ascending		
Show:	☑	☑	☑	
Criteria:			"Comedy" Or "Adventure"	
or:				

To specify an **OR** condition for **two different fields**, enter each value on a different row as in the example below.

Field:	ProductID	Title	Category	Price
Table:	tblProducts	tblProducts	tblProducts	tblProducts
Sort:		Ascending		
Show:	☑	☑	☑	☑
Criteria:			"Comedy"	
or:				>"$29.99"

To create a query where two or more conditions must be met, enter the criteria on the same row. For instance, you might wish to see all comedy films that cost more than $39.99. You would enter both values on the same criteria row. This is referred to as an **AND condition**.

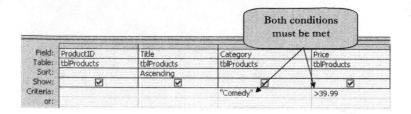

	Both conditions must be met	

Field:	ProductID	Title	Category	Price
Table:	tblProducts	tblProducts	tblProducts	tblProducts
Sort:		Ascending		
Show:	☑	☑	☑	☑
Criteria:			"Comedy"	>39.99
or:				

✓ Specify Multiple Criteria in a Query

1. Make sure the **Video Sales 4.accdb** file is active. Open **qryProducts** in **Design View**. Notice that you already have a limit of "Comedy" for the Category field.
2. Place your cursor after the word "Comedy" and then type: **Or "Drama"**. Films with either a category of Comedy or Drama will be returned in the results.

Field:	ProductID	Title	Category
Table:	tblProducts	tblProducts	tblProducts
Sort:		Ascending	
Show:	☑	☑	☑
Criteria:			"Comedy" Or "Drama"
or:			

3. Click the **Run** button. All films with a category of Comedy or Drama are returned.
4. Click the **View** button on the Ribbon to switch back to Design View.
5. Click in the Criteria row for the **Price** field and type: **> 29.99**. Now, only films with a Category of Comedy or Drama, and a price greater than $29.99 will be seen.

Field:	ProductID	Title	Category	Price
Table:	tblProducts	tblProducts	tblProducts	tblProducts
Sort:		Ascending		
Show:	☑	☑	☑	☑
Criteria:			"Comedy" Or "Drama"	>29.99
or:				

6. Press the **Run** icon on the Ribbon and observe the results.

7. Click the **View** icon on the Ribbon to switch back to Design View.
8. Select the criterion for the Price field, **right-click** and then choose **Cut** from the menu.
9. Press the **down arrow** key on your keyboard. **Right-click** and choose **Paste** from the menu. This pastes the limit one row below the original location.

Field:	ProductID	Title	Category	Price
Table:	tblProducts	tblProducts	tblProducts	tblProducts
Sort:		Ascending		
Show:	☑	☑	☑	☑
Criteria:			"Comedy" Or "Drama"	
or:				>29.99

10. Click the **Run** icon on the toolbar and observe the results. All films with either a category of Comedy or Drama or a price greater than $29.99 are shown.
11. Click the **View** button on the ribbon to switch back to Design View.
12. Click the query's **Close** button. Click **No** when asked to save your changes.

4.9   Sorting Data in a Query

To make the results of your query easier to work with, you will most likely wish to **sort** the query results. To sort a query by a particular field, click in the sort field and then choose either **Ascending** (A-Z) or **Descending** (Z-A) from the drop-down list.

You can sort by more than one query field. Access sorts from left to right. In the example below, the data would first be sorted by Category and then by price within each category.

Field:	ProductID	Title	Category	Price	Acquired
Table:	tblProducts	tblProducts	tblProducts	tblProducts	tblProducts
Sort:			Ascending	Ascending	
Show:	☑	☑	☑	☑	☑
Criteria:					
or:					

Access Sorts from Left to Right

✓ Sort the Results of a Query

1. Make sure the **Video Sales 4.accdb** file is active. Open **qryProducts** in **Design View**.
2. Click in the **Sort** cell for the **Category** field.

3. Click the arrow and then choose **Ascending** from the drop-down list.

Field:	ProductID	Title	Category	Price
Table:	tblProducts	tblProducts	tblProducts	tblProducts
Sort:			Ascending	
Show:	☑	☑	Ascending	☑
Criteria:			Descending	
or:			(not sorted)	

4. Click in the **Sort** cell for the **Price** field.
5. Set the sort order for the Price field to Ascending. The results will be sorted first by Category and then by Price.
6. **Save** the query design changes.
7. Click the **Run** button and observe the results. The data is sorted first by Category and then by Price.
8. Switch back to **Design View**.

4.10 Moving Columns in a Query

I n the last lesson, you learned that Access sorts from left to right. So what if the fields are not in the order in which you need them to be? In that case, you will have to rearrange the fields in your query.

To move a field in a query, click on the thin gray bar above the field name to select the field. Then, click the gray bar again holding down your mouse button and drag until the field is in the desired location. As you drag, a thin black line appears, letting you know the location of the field should you release the mouse button.

✓ Move a Column in a Query

1. Make sure the **Video Sales 4.accdb** file is active. Click in the **Sort** cell for the **Price** field to display the drop-down arrow for the Price field.
2. Click the arrow and choose **(not sorted)** from the drop-down list. To sort your results by Category and then by Title, you will have to move the Category field to the left of the Title field.
3. Click the thin gray bar above the **Category** field name and then release the mouse button.
4. Click on the thin gray bar, hold down the mouse button, and then drag to the left until the thick black line is to the left of the Title field. This is the new location of the Category field.

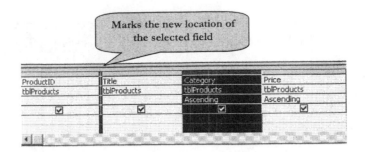

Marks the new location of the selected field

5.   Release the mouse button to complete the move process.
6.   Click in the **Sort** cell for the **Title** field to display the drop-down arrow for the Title field.
7.   Click the arrow and then choose **Ascending** from the drop-down list.
8.   Click the **Run** icon. Data is sorted first by Category then by Title.

4.11 Using the Query Wizard

R ather than create your queries manually, you can use the **Simple Query Wizard** to help you build your query. The Simple Query Wizard steps you through the process. You will be first prompted to choose the tables and fields upon which to base your query. Next, you select the desired view (Detail or Summary), and then provide a name for your query.

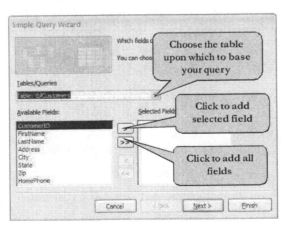

✓ Create a Query using the Query Wizard

Query Wizard button

1. Make sure the **Video Sales 4.accdb** file is active. Click the query's **Close** button. Click **Yes** when asked if you want to save changes. This saves and closes the qryProducts query.
2. Click the **Query Wizard** button on the Ribbon under the **Create** tab.
3. Ensure that **Simple Query Wizard** is selected and then click **OK**.
4. Click the arrow on the right of the **Tables/Queries** combo box and then select **tblProducts** from the drop-down list.

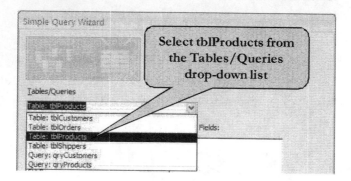

5. Select the **Title** field in the **Available Fields** window and then click the **>** button. This adds the Title field to the query.
6. Select the **Acquired** field in the **Available Fields** window and then click the **>** button.
7. Click **Next**.
9. In the **Title box**, type: **qryFilmList**.

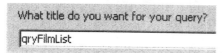

9. Click the **Open the query to view information** radio button and then click **Finish**.
10. **Close** the qryFilmList query.
11. Press **Alt + F** and select **Close Database** from the File Options menu.

Lesson 5 - Creating Forms

5.1 Using the Form Wizard

A **form** is an interface between the user and the data that is utilized primarily to enter, edit or display data in a database. The form window contains labels (descriptive text), text boxes, combo boxes, radio buttons, etc. that are linked to the data in your table and can help make your database more user-friendly. Entering or changing data in a form automatically enters or changes it in the underlying table.

Using the **Form Wizard** is the easiest way of creating a form. The Form Wizard is similar to the Query Wizard that you worked with in the last chapter – it will step you through the process of creating a form. While you create a form from scratch, using the Form Wizard makes it easy.

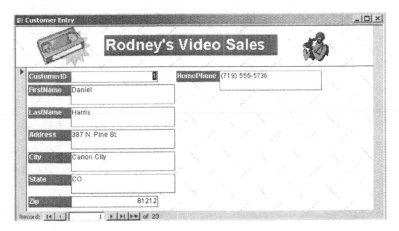

✓ Create a Form using the Form Wizard

1. Display the File Options menu.
2. Click **Open**.
3. Locate your copy of the Course Docs folder and open it
4. **Double-click** the **Access Tutorials folder**
5. Select the **Video Sales 5** file and then click **Open**.
6. Click the **Forms** button from the Navigation Pane drop-down menu. Currently, there are no forms created.
7. Click the **Create** tab.
8. Under the **Forms** command set, click the **More Forms button** and the click **Form Wizard**.

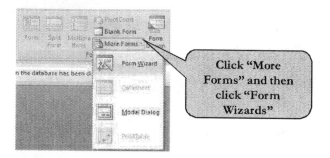

9. Click the arrow on the right of the **Tables/Queries** combo box and then select **qryProducts** from the drop-down list.
10. Select the **Title** field in the **Available Fields** window and then click the **>** button. This adds the Title field to the form.
11. Repeat Step 9 for the following fields:

   Category
   Price
   Acquired

12. Click **Next**.
13. Ensure that **Columnar** is selected as shown and click **Next**.

---

14. Select **Metro** for the **Form Style** and click **Next**.

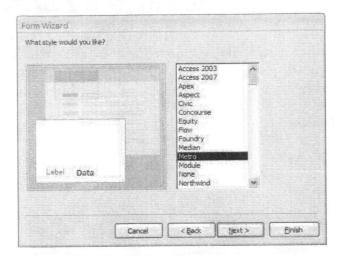

15. Type: **frmProducts** in the form title box.

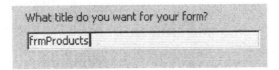

16. Ensure that **Open form to view or enter information** is selected, and then click **Finish**. This opens the form in Form View.

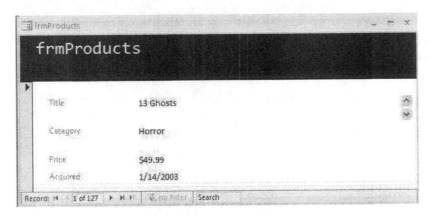

The Completed Form

5.2 Entering Data into a Form

Similar to tables, the navigation bar on the bottom of the form window allows you to move from one record to another. Clicking the **New Record** button creates a new blank record.

To enter data into a form, click in the first blank text box and begin typing. Pressing the **Tab** key moves you from one field on your form to another. When the cursor is in the last text box of the form, press the Tab key to insert a new blank record.

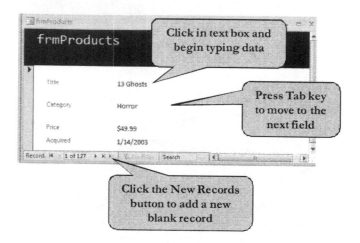

✓ Enter New Data into a Form

1. Make sure the **Video Sales 5.accdb** file is active. Click the **New Record** navigation button to insert a blank record.
2. Click in the **Title** text box and then type: **Shallow Hal**.

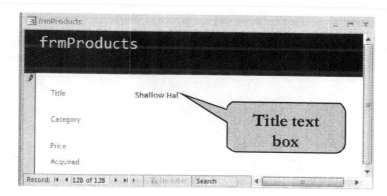

3. Press the **Tab** key.

---

4.   Type: **Comedy** and then press the **Tab** key.
5.   Type: **39.99** and then press the **Tab** key.
6.   Type: **2/15/2003**
7.   Press **Tab**. This inserts a new blank record.

5.3   Finding Records in a Form

T here will be times when you need to find a particular record in your form. The **Find** feature allows you to quickly search for information. To launch the Find and Replace dialog box, click the **Find button** on the Ribbon or use the **Ctrl + F** keystroke combination. If you know in which field the information resides, click in that field. When searching, you can match either **Whole Field, Any Part of Field**, or **Start of Field**..

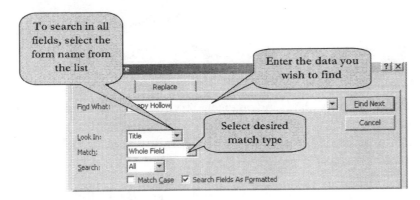

✓ To Find Data in a Form

1.   Make sure the **Video Sales 5.accdb** file is active. Click in the **Title** text box.
2.   Click the **Find** button on the Ribbon.
3.   In the **Find What** box, type: **Sleepy Hollow**.
4.   Click the **Match** drop-down list and then select **Whole Field**. Data must match exactly what was typed in the Find What box.
5.   Click **Find Next** to begin the search and find the first record matching the criteria.
6.   Click **Cancel** to close the Find and Replace dialog box.
7.   Click the form's **Close button**. **Save** any changes.
8.   Click the **Microsoft Office** button and select **Close Database** from the File Options menu.

Lesson 6 - Creating Reports

6.1 Creating a Basic Report

Access has wizards that help you create reports. Reports can be based upon either tables or queries, although basing your report upon a query allows you maximum flexibility. Reports, unlike Forms, Queries and Tables do not allow you to make any changes to the data.

The fastest and easiest way to create a report is using a **Basic Report.** A Basic Report creates a columnar report that is based on all fields in the selected table or query. You do not have the option of choosing which fields to include in your report. To only include specific fields in your Basic Report, you may wish to create a query with the fields you want included in your report, and then create a report based on that new query.

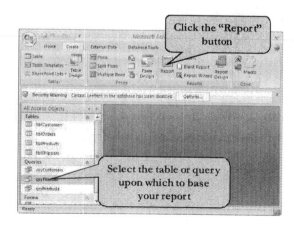

✓ Create an AutoReport

Report button

The Report Button

1. With Access open, click the **Microsoft Office** button.
2. Click **Open**.
3. Locate your copy of the Course Docs folder and open it
4. **Open** the **Access Tutorials folder**
5. Open the **Video Sales 6.accdb** database.
7. Click the **Title Bar** on the Navigation Pane and select **All Access Objects** from the list.

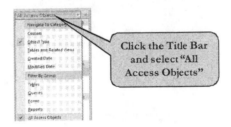

Click the Title Bar and select "All Access Objects"

8. Click on **qryProducts** in the Navigation Pane under the Queries category.
9. Click the **Create** tab.
10. Click the **Report** button on the ribbon on the Reports command set to create a basic report based upon qryProducts and display the Report in Layout view.
11. Click the **View** button on the leftmost side of the Ribbon and choose Print Preview from the list. This displays the Report in Print Preview view.

12. Click the **Close Print Preview** button on the Ribbon to display the report in Layout view.

6.2 AutoFormatting a Report

Once your report is created, the tab displays three sets of report tools: Format, Arrange and Page Setup. Under the Format tab is the **AutoFormat** command button, which allows you to apply quick formatting by choosing from a gallery of styles. The gallery of styles contains preset formats that you can quickly apply to your report. Hold your mouse pointer over a style to view the style name.

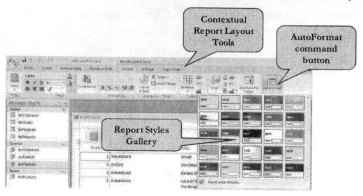

✓ Apply a Style to a Report

1. Make sure the **Video Sales 6.accdb** file is active. Click the **AutoFormat** button under the Format tab. This displays the Style Gallery.

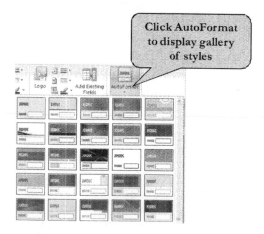

2. Click the **Equity** style in the 2nd row, 4th column.

3. Click the report's **Close button**. Click **No** when prompted to save your changes.

6.3   Using the Report Wizard

T he **Report Wizard** steps you through the process of creating an Access report. Unlike the AutoReport wizard, the Report Wizard allows much more control over the design of your reports. Like the Form Wizard, the Report Wizard allows you select the fields to be included in your report as well as choose various style options. Although you can create a report manually, it can be quite time consuming as reports can be difficult to design. Most people prefer to use the Report Wizard when designing reports.

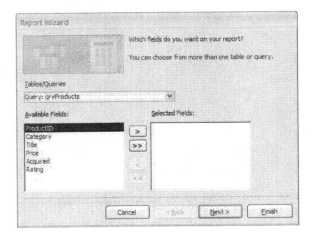

✓ Create a Report using the Report Wizard

1. Make sure the **Video Sales 6.accdb** file is active. Click the **Create** tab.
2. Under the **Reports** command set, click **Report Wizard** button.

Report Wizard button

3. Click the arrow on the right of the **Tables/Queries** combo box and select **qryCustomers** from the drop-down list.
4. Click the **>>** button. All fields in the query will be added to the report.
5. Click **Next.**
6. Click **Next**.
7. Click the first **combo** box and then choose **LastName**.

8. Click **Next**.
9. Click the **Tabular** radio button in the Layout section and choose **Landscape** in the **Orientation** section.

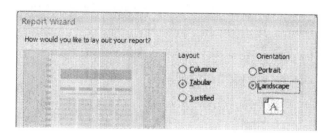

10. Click **Next**.
11. Click **Apex** in the **Style** window to preview the Apex Style.
12. Click **Tecnic** in the Style window.
13. Click **Next**.
14. Type: **rptCustomerList** in the report title box.

What title do you want for your report?

rptCustomerList

15. Ensure that **Preview the Report** is selected. Click **Finish.**

16. Click the **Next Page** navigation button on the bottom of the report window.
17. Click anywhere in the report window to zoom out.
18. Click again in the report window to zoom in.
19. Click the **Close Print Preview** button on the Ribbon to display the report in Design view.

6.4   Modifying Report Setup

Before printing your report, you may need to make some additional changes to the setup of your document, such as adjusting page margins, setting paper size, choosing a paper source, selecting a page orientation, choosing a printer and printing your report in columns. Display your report in **Print Preview** and chose your desired page setup options from the Page Layout command set on the Ribbon.

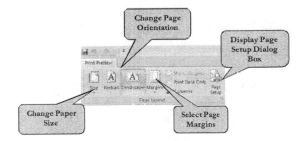

You can also enter custom settings in the **Page Setup dialog box** by clicking the Page Setup button on the Ribbon. From the Page Setup dialog box, click the **Margins** tab, the **Page** tab or the **Columns** tab, and then enter the desired settings.

To change page orientation, choose **Portrait or Landscape** in the Orientation section. To change paper size, select the desired size from the **Size** combo box in the Paper section. To change printer paper source, select the desired option from the **Source** combo box in the Paper section. To choose a different printer, click **Use Specific Printer,** click the **Printer** button and then choose the desired printer from the printer combo box

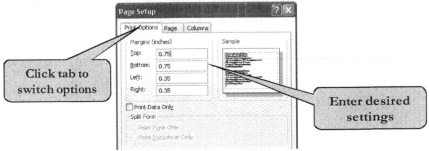

Note: You must have a printer driver installed to modify the page setup of a report.

Modify Page Setup

1. Make sure the **Video Sales 6.accdb** file is active. Click the **View** arrow and select **Print Preview** from the list.
2. Click the **Margins** button on the Ribbon and choose **Narrow** from the list.

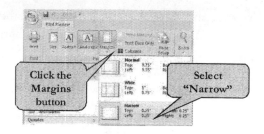

3. Click the **Page Setup** button on the Ribbon.
4. In the **Left Margin Box**, type: **.75**
5. In the **Right Margin Box**, type: **.75**
6. In the **Top Margin Box**, type: **1.5**.
7. Click the **Page tab.** Observe the settings.
8. Click **OK**.

Tip: You can also access Report Setup options from the Page Setup Tab on the Ribbon when in Layout View or Design View.

6.5   Printing Reports

Now that you've modifed the page setup, you are ready to generate a hard copy of your report. Click the **Print** button on the Ribbon when previewing a report to display the **Print Dialog Box** or press the **Ctrl + P** keyboard shortcut. The Print Dialog box allows you to:

*   Modify printer properties
*   Choose which printer to use
*   Set the page range
*   Set the number of copies to print

The print dialog box allows you to modify the final printer settings before generating a hard copy.

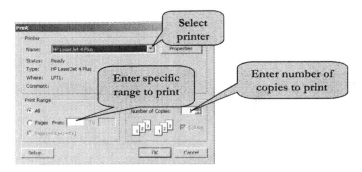

To send your document directly to the printer without displaying the Print Dialog Box, .click the Microsoft Office button, click Print from the menu and then choose Quick Print from the second pane. If you use the Quick Print feature often, you can add it to your Quick Access toolbar by clicking the arrow next to the **Quick Access Toolbar** and choosing **Quick Print** from the list. The Quick Print icon will now be displayed on the toolbar.

✓ Print a Report

1. Make sure the **Video Sales 6.accdb** file is active. Click the **Print** button on the Ribbon.
2. In the **Print Range** section, enter **3** in the **From** box and **4** in the **To** box.

3. In the **Copies** section, type **3**. This is the number of copies of the report to print.

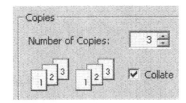

4. Click **Cancel**.
5. Click the **Close Print Preview** button on the Ribbon. Access returns to Report Design View.
6. Click the **Close** button on the Report window. If prompted, save your changes.

6.6 Using the Label Wizard

The **Label Wizard** allows you to create mailing labels in standard and custom sizes from the data in your tables. Like the Report Wizard, the Label Wizard steps you through the process of creating labels, allowing you to select various options as you go. Access supports most standard label sizes and manufacturers.

✓ Create Mailing Labels

1. Make sure the **Video Sales 6.accdb** file is active. Click on **qryCustomers** in the Navigation Pane under the Queries category.
2. Click the **Create** tab.
3. Click the **Labels** button on the ribbon on the Reports command set to launch the Label Wizard.
4. From the **Filter by Manufacturer** drop-down list, select **Avery**.

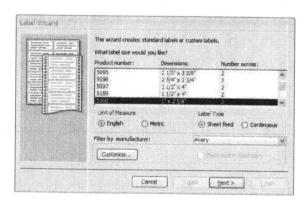

5. Choose product number **5160** from the label size window.
6. Click **Next**.
7. Click in the **Font name** drop-down list and type: **Tim** until **Times New Roman** appears.
8 Click **Next**.

9. Select **FirstName** from the **Available fields** list then click the **>** button. This adds the FirstName field to our Prototype label and then moves to the next field in the Available Fields window.
10. Press the **spacebar** to add a space after the First Name field.
11. Click the **>** button. This adds the LastName field to the Prototype label
12. Press **Enter** to start a new line in the Prototype label.
13. Double-click the **Address** field in the Available fields window.
14. Press **Enter**.
15. Click the **>** button to add the City field to the Prototype label.
16. Press **,** and then press the **spacebar**. This adds a comma and a space after the City field.
17. Click the **>** button.
18. Press the **spacebar** twice.
19. Double-click the **Zip** field. The prototype label should look like the example on the right.

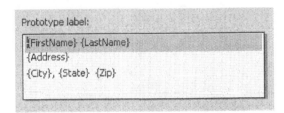

20. Click **Next**.
21. Double-click the **State** field in the Available Fields Window. This specifies that our labels will be sorted by the State field.
22. Click **Next**.
23. In the name box, type: **rptCustomerLabels**.

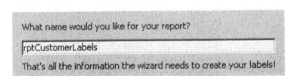

24. Click **Finish**. This displays our labels in Print Preview view.
25. Click anywhere on the report area to zoom in.
26. Click the **Close Print Preview** button on the Ribbon. This displays the Report in Design View.
27. Click the **Close button** on the Report window. **Save** any changes.
28. Click the **Microsoft Office** button and select **Close Database** from the File Options menu to close the Video Sales 6 database.

1. Where is information stored in an Access database?
    A. In queries
    B. In tables
    C. In forms
    D. In Reports

2. Tables consist of:
    A. Records and Fields
    B. Cells and Fields
    C. Columns and Command Sets
    D. Rows and Views

3. What is the unique identifier that specifies that data in that field may not be duplicated in any other of the table records called?

4. From Design view, how can you rearrange fields in your table?

5. What is a delimited text file?

6. What are three ways that you can add fields to the query grid?

7. What are two ways to execute (run) a query?

8. From Design view, you want to display the properties for a text box. Name two ways you can accomplish this.

9. Which view allows you to view your actual data while being able to rearrange the fields on your form?

10. Which views allows you to view your actual data while being able to rearrange the fields on your report (select all that apply):

    A. Report View; B. Layout View; C. Print Preview; D. Design View

11. You want to browse your live data while being able to apply filters to view only specific records. What report view would best accomplish this?

    A. Layout View; B. Browse View; C. Design View; D. Report View